RECLAIMING EVOLUTION

In this unique book, Howard J. Sherman and William M. Dugger engage in a dialogue on social evolution from institutionalist and Marxist perspectives, each representing one side. It is their intention to explore the way society develops using the equally radical, but very different approaches of Thorstein Veblen and Karl Marx.

The dialogue proceeds with a series of questions – each answered from the two perspectives. Beginning with an intellectual history and definition, *Reclaiming Evolution* examines social evolution in terms of causal elements (economic relations, technology, enabling myth and political relations) and then in terms of social processes (structural change, social tension and social conflict). It thus provides an invaluable guide on how different economic theories can be used as a tool to view society – and the way different standpoints can both complement and contradict each other.

The result is an extremely accessible study of economic evolution that will be essential reading for students of political economy.

William M. Dugger is Professor of Economics at the University of Tulsa, USA. **Howard J. Sherman** is Professor Emeritus at the University of California, USA.

ADVANCES IN SOCIAL ECONOMICS

Edited by John B. Davis
Marquette University

This series presents new advances and developments in social economics thinking on a variety of subjects that concern the link between social values and economics. Need, justice and equity, gender, cooperation, work poverty, the environment, class, institutions, public policy and methodology are some of the most important themes. Among the orientations of the authors are social economist, institutionalist, humanist, solidarist, cooperatist, radical and Marxist, feminist, post-Keynesian, behaviouralist, and environmentalist. The series offers new contributions from today's foremost thinkers on the social character of the economy.

Published in conjunction with the Association of Social Economics.

Books published in the series include:

SOCIAL ECONOMICS
Premises, findings and policies
Edited by Edward J. O'Boyle

THE ENVIRONMENTAL CONSEQUENCES OF GROWTH
Steady-state economics as an alternative to ecological decline
Douglas Booth

THE HUMAN FIRM
A socio-economic analysis of its behaviour and potential in a new economic age
John Tomer

ECONOMICS FOR THE COMMON GOOD
Two centuries of economic thought in the humanist tradition
Mark A. Lutz

WORKING TIME
International Trends, Theory and Policy Perspectives
Edited by Lonnie Golden & Deborah M. Figart

RECLAIMING EVOLUTION
A dialogue between Marxism and institutionalism on social change
William M. Dugger & Howard J. Sherman

RECLAIMING
EVOLUTION

A dialogue between Marxism and
institutionalism on social change

William M. Dugger
&
Howard J. Sherman

London and New York

First published 2000
by Routledge
11 New Fetter Lane, London EC4P 4EE

Simultaneously published in the USA and Canada
by Routledge
29 West 35th Street, New York, NY 10001

Routledge is an imprint of the Taylor & Francis Group

© 2000 William M. Dugger & Howard J. Sherman

Typeset in Garamond by
HWA Text and Data Management, Tunbridge Wells
Printed and bound in Great Britain by
Clays Ltd, St Ives plc

British Library Cataloguing in Publication Data
A catalogue record for this book is available from the British Library

Library of Congress Cataloging in Publication Data
Dugger, William M.
Reclaiming evolution: a dialogue between Marxism and institutionalism on
social change / William M. Dugger & Howard J. Sherman
p. cm. — (Advances in social economics)
Includes bibliographical references and index.
1. Communism and culture. 2. Communism and society. 3. Social change.
4. Social evolution. 5. Marxian economics.
I. Sherman, Howard J. II. Title. III. Series
HX 523.D813 2000
335.4—dc21   00–036892

ISBN 0-415-23263-5 (hbk)
ISBN 0-415-23264-3 (pbk)

DEDICATED WITH LOVE
TO
PAULINE J. DUGGER
AND
BARBARA SINCLAIR

CONTENTS

CONTENTS

ACKNOWLEDGEMENTS

Some of the material came – with permissions – from the following articles:

William M. Dugger, "Class and Evolution – an Institutionalist View" in Baiman, R., Boushey, H., and Saunders, D. (eds) *Political Economy and Contemporary Capitalism*, Armonk, New York: Union for Radical Political Economics, M.E. Sharpe, forthcoming.

Howard J. Sherman, "Class and Evolution – A Marxist View," in Baiman, R., Boushey, H., and Saunders, D. (eds) *Political Economy and Contemporary Capitalism*, Armonk, New York: Union for Radical Political Economics, M.E. Sharpe, forthcoming.

William M. Dugger, "Enabling Myths," in Pollin, R. (Ed.) Festschrift in Honor of Howard Sherman. Brookfield, Vermont: Edward Elgar, forthcoming.

Some materials from the following two articles are reprinted from the *Journal of Economic Issues* by special permission of the copyright holder, the Association for Evolutionary Economics:

William M. Dugger and Howard J. Sherman, "Comparison of Institutionalism and Marxism," Vol. 28 (March 1994): 101–128.

William M. Dugger and Howard J. Sherman "Institutionalist and Marxist Theories of Evolution," Vol. 31 (December 1997): 991–1010.

John B. Davis, the series editor, gave us his enthusiastic support and was very helpful in getting this project into print. We also wish to thank those who have read parts or all of our manuscript and have given extremely valuable constructive criticisms, namely: Paul Burkett, John Henry, and Philip O'Hara. We also wish to express our appreciation for the profoundly useful comments of the two anonymous reviewers for Routledge Publishers. Their extraordinary efforts went way beyond the call of duty.

Part I

PRELIMINARIES

1

WHAT IS EVOLUTION?

We begin with the evolution of evolutionary thought to find where it went astray and how it may be reclaimed for its original path.

Reclaiming evolution

For centuries in the medieval period and beyond, the dominant view was that nothing important ever really changes. Loren Eiseley expresses that dominant view as follows:

> Throughout eternity the same waters hurry to the sea, the same animal forms expand or contract their habitat. All things pass and come again. The Newtonian world view, the eternal and balanced machine of the heavens, is repeated upon earth.
>
> (Eiseley 1961: 329)

As late as the nineteenth century that was still the dominant view, but it was being challenged. Some geologists began to talk about gradual changes leading to major changes of the Earth over millions of years. Some astronomers began to talk about the evolution of the solar system and other star systems (Eiseley 1961: 332–34).

Some biologists, such as Darwin, talked about the evolution of biological species. In the introduction to his book, *The Origin of Species*, Darwin changed our thinking forever when he said the following:

> I am fully convinced that species are not immutable; but that those belonging to what are called the same genera are lineal descendants of some other and generally extinct species, in the same manner as the acknowledged varieties of any one species are the descendants of that species.
>
> (Darwin 1859: 14)

Marx and Veblen

A few social scientists also began to talk about social evolution – the evolution of society. The first major social scientist in the nineteenth century to present a theory of evolution was Karl Marx. Marx was very impressed by Darwin's theory of biological evolution and stated that it was one of the three greatest discoveries of the nineteenth century (see quote of Marx and discussion of context in John Henry 1990: 49). Marx's contribution to the theory of social evolution was called historical materialism. His view of evolution includes both gradual change and revolution, and will be discussed in later chapters. Marx's collaborator, Frederick Engels, wrote his famous book on the family and evolution in the 1880s (Engels, 1886, 1942). He emphasized that the family is a major institution of society, that it had evolved, and that it varied greatly in different societies. He also traced the history of government and found that its form and content – like that of the family – had evolved in relation to changes in class and property relations. Years later in 1946, following up on Engels, the Marxist economist, Maurice Dobb, wrote the classic book on the transition from feudalism to capitalism. After a long tradition of Marxist literature on evolution, the well-known anthropologist and archeologist, V. Gordon Childe, published a careful book on social evolution from a Marxist view in 1951. For the next half century Marxist historians and anthropologists filled in the details and argued about theoretical issues of evolution in a large number of books (see discussion of the literature in Ollman 1987, Sherman 1995, Chapter 4, and Sitton 1996).

Other evolutionary thinkers were also hard at work. At the turn of the twentieth century, the great US social scientist, Thorstein Veblen, criticized orthodox economics for not being an evolutionary science. In his famous 1898 essay, "Why is Economics not an Evolutionary Science," Veblen clearly differentiated between evolutionary and pre-evolutionary views. Veblen emphasized that it was not so much what scientists have gained through adopting the evolutionary view; rather, it is the biases they have lost that really matters. In the pre-evolutionary view, explanations of facts and social relations are grounded in the belief in a "guiding hand of a spiritual agency or a propensity in events" (Veblen 1898: 63). Veblen critiqued the pre-evolutionary view and presented his own theory of social evolution. Veblen's critique and his theory will be presented at length in later chapters. His followers would become known as institutional economists and have maintained a rich literature expanding Veblen's theory of evolution (a useful survey of Veblen's thought on evolution appears in the institutionalist work on evolutionary theory by Hodgson 1996).

The theory of social evolution, as both Veblen and Marx originally used it, was quite subversive. What made it subversive was the belief that society can change radically, that society is not bound into a single iron mold by something unchanging called human nature. Charlotte Perkins Gilman's poem in the Appendix to this chapter provides a delightfully subversive illustration. Gilman was a leading American feminist working around the same time as Veblen.

It should be stressed that because of its subversive nature, the evolutionary theory of Marx and the evolutionary theory of Veblen were both rejected by orthodox social scientists – so all orthodox economists (and most orthodox political scientists) still state eternal, ahistorical laws based on psychological axioms.

Marx's ideas spawned various competing theories. The prevalent theory among the dominant socialist party in the late nineteenth century and early twentieth century – the German Social Democrats – declared it was inevitable that capitalism followed feudalism and it was inevitable that socialism would follow capitalism. The German Social Democrats found unalterable laws of historical evolution that predetermined historical events and inevitably led to progress. They traced all social change back to economic causes. Soviet Marxists from 1917 to 1990 followed the German Social Democrats on these key points, even though they feuded violently over everything else. The Communist parties were uncritical of inherited dogma and they were uncritical of the practices of the Soviet Union and the other countries of its bloc.

Contemporary Marxists have criticized these official party views unmercifully and have developed a completely different viewpoint, which they also trace back to Marx. Thus the old uncritical Marxism has been replaced with a new critical Marxism. In this book it is the new critical Marxism that readers will find as one side of a dialogue on social evolution. (Further discussion of the history of Marxist thought on these subjects is in Sherman 1995.)

Veblen (see, e.g. Veblen 1919), the founder of institutional economics, also gave rise to competing views. For forty years after Veblen's death in 1929, many of Veblen's evolutionary insights were submerged. Influenced by the more conservative institutionalism of John R. Commons (see e.g. Commons 1934), swayed by Joseph Dorfman's conservative biography of Veblen, (see Dorfman 1934, 1972) and dazzled by the brilliant theorizing of Clarence Ayres (see e.g. Ayres 1978), institutionalists submerged Veblen's radical institutionalism under a more moderate (liberal) institutionalism. The baleful effects of the Cold War also kept Veblen's radical insights in the underground of American economics for years. The red thread was nearly lost. (But see Dugger 1992.)

The moderate institutionalists believed that there was evolutionary change in society, but that it was mostly smooth, virtually irresistible, involved little class conflict and led to progress. The moderates also believed that such progress seldom, if ever, took place through revolution. Nevertheless,

Veblen's radical institutionalism re-surfaced in the 1970s and, with the end of the Cold War, has become widely recognized as an important tradition. In this book it is that re-surfaced radical institutionalism of Veblen that readers will find as the other side of our dialogue on social evolution. We discuss mainly the new Veblenian radical institutionalism. (Further discussion of institutionalist thought is in Dugger 1989b.)

Evolution gone astray

Immediately after Darwin, many conservative religious writers completely rejected evolutionary theory – and at this time it is still vehemently rejected by some of the people who control schools in Kansas! Some, however, put forth a version of evolution that was a conservative weapon – and was the dominant view of evolution for some time. Nineteenth-century Social Darwinists, led by Herbert Spencer, argued that western "races" and societies had evolved and spread because they were superior to all others (see discussion in Hofstadter 1944). Twentieth-century Sociobiologists, led by Edward O. Wilson, argue that human behavior is genetically determined to be selfish and competitive (see discussion in Dugger 1981). This type of thinking was dominant in the nineteenth century and some of it came back during the period of the Cold War from 1950 to 1990. In biology, it has been attacked and superseded by a whole new generation of biologists who believe very differently. A leading figure in the revival and renaissance of biological evolution freed from reactionary notions from the nineteenth century and freed from absolutist belief in inevitable progress is Stephen Jay Gould (see e.g. Gould 1996).

The biologists have put the theory of biological evolution on a scientific, Darwinian track. But the social scientists and their theory of social evolution have lagged far behind. We want to close the gap between the advanced state of the theory of biological evolution and the retarded state of the theory of social evolution. However, while we can get some inspiration from the progress made in the theory of biological evolution, there is a great difference between biology and society – and our interest in this book is social evolution. So, we do not just apply the concepts of biological theory directly to social theory. We are social scientists, not biologists. We study the evolution of societies, not the evolution of species.

In addition to modern Sociobiologists, we also take issue (as discussed above) with the uncritical Marxist view of the Cold War that there is inevitable progress to a socialism in which there is harmonious progress forever. We also disagree with the Cold War view of some institutionalists (discussed above) that sees automatic progress from technology and a constantly improving capitalist society.

Instead of using the concept of social evolution as an ideological weapon in the Cold War, we reconstruct or reclaim the idea of evolution as a crucial part of all critical social thought. We do not believe that our world or any subset of it is the best of all possible worlds. The mountains of corpses we humans stacked up in the twentieth century have bloodied us, forced us to our very knees, humbled us profoundly, vaporized our arrogance. Therefore, we cannot possibly believe in Social Darwinism. Nor can we possibly believe in its later manifestation – Sociobiology. We cannot believe that all of time has been moving towards our selfish and competitive society as its crowning achievement. Instead, we believe that through all of time there has been only one ultimate or constant – change, itself. We believe change can be understood and that such understanding is inherently radical. We also believe that understanding change can reclaim the concept of evolution from the Cold War Warriors of both sides, and from the Social Darwinists and the Sociobiologists. The concept of evolution, reclaimed from those who misused it, is for the use of critical thinkers everywhere.

What is social evolution?

Having explained some of the evolution of evolutionary theories and what evolution is not, we must begin the task of saying what it is. This task will require the whole book. To start, a four-fold definition is offered here. First of all, evolution means not only incremental change in all aspects of society, but also structural change in the basic institutions and relationships of society. Second, evolution means change caused by the internal dynamics of society (called endogenous change), rather than change caused by external causes from outside of society. Third, evolutionary change cannot be reduced to the affects of a single factor, but is due to the operation of the relationships of the whole of society (holistic or relational change). Fourth, evolution in all stratified or class divided societies involves conflict between groups.

Structural change

Evolution includes both gradual, incremental change and revolutionary structural change. Structural change means that social structures – basic institutions – actually change in fundamental ways. Institutions have a beginning and an ending. They do not have an infinite future. Nor do they have an infinite past. Slavery, for example, has not always existed. It had a beginning and an ending in particular times and places. Feudalism has not always existed. It too, had a beginning and an ending in particular times and places. Contrary to some dogmatic Marxists who saw all societies evolving the same way, some societies have never even been feudal and some have never even practiced slavery. Contrary to many orthodox economists, economies have not always been capitalistic, either. Nor will they necessarily always be capitalistic. Because it involves basic structural change, evolutionary change is profoundly subversive. Evolution tells us a very radical story about human institutions. It tells us that what is, was not. Furthermore, it tells us that what is, will not be forever. So for those in stratified societies, evolution alerts us to Edmund Burke's great fear that society could be turned upside down so that the aristocracy ended up on the bottom and the common people the top. Evolution informs us that in the future, the first in line for privilege and power could become the last and the top of society could become the bottom. Evolution also tells us that in the future, there may be no top and bottom of society, but equality, instead.

Internal dynamics

Evolution happens because of the internal dynamics of society, not because of forces altogether outside of society – this is called endogenous change. Evolutionary change does not drop from the sky. And it is not directed from the sky. It is not the unfolding of a predetermined plan, divine or otherwise. Furthermore, this last point means that evolution is not necessarily progress. It is not necessarily the moving of humanity toward some level of existence deemed in some way to be better than or higher than any previous level. Evolution does not preclude progress. But evolution itself is not necessarily progress; it is simply change caused by internal dynamics. The two may or may not coincide. Nevertheless, since evolution is real, the possibility of changing a society from one state to another is also quite real. Such a change in social states could be progress, but progress is not assured and not predetermined. We, the authors of this book, hope that the direction of social evolution is away from stratified societies and toward egalitarian societies. We believe that evolution makes such a direction possible, but how probable, we do not know.

Holistic, relational change

Evolutionary change is more than just structural and endogenous. Evolutionary change is not based on a single factor, but must be understood in terms of the whole society (holism), as the entire set of relationships within that society (relational). It occurs in and through the relations between stratification and inequality, technology, politics, economics, cultural institutions (such as education and religion) and beliefs. No aspects of society are isolated from the whole. Drug addiction, for example, cannot be understood in terms of single individual's preferences, but must be understood in terms of the situation of such individuals in the entire matrix of our evolving society and the social forces that lead to drug addiction.

Conflict and change

Evolutionary change is not only understood in structural, endogenous, and relational terms. In divided and unequally stratified societies, evolutionary change occurs through conflict. Inequality involves many different kinds of divisions. Class, nation, race, gender, religion, ethnicity, and sexual orientation are all important ways of dividing people into groups and then treating the groups unequally. These divisions result in the formation of a small group of privileged people at the top of society and a large group of underprivileged people at the bottom. The elite try to claim for themselves most of the power, privilege, status, income, property, and related good things and then try to foist all the bad things off on the common people.

The divisions between the elite and the common people can build on a number of characteristics. Economists emphasize class, but the importance of race, gender, nation, sexual orientation, religious tradition, and ethnic background cannot be ignored. Conflict arises over the division into groups because the groups have competing interests.

A new class, such as the merchants and manufacturers of the late feudal period may challenge the power of the old elite (such as the feudal lords) and may – in alliance with the common people – change the basic institutions by revolutionary means. A new institution, such as the nation-state, can create a whole new kind of division between people. The nation-state in Europe created a new division between its own nationals and foreigners – the nationals of other nation-states. The national rulers taught the nationals of each nation-state that they were superior to the foreigners. Wars between shifting groups of allegedly superior nationals and the allegedly inferior foreigners went on for centuries and transformed many of the basic institutions of Europe.

Institutionalists speak of the power of the vested interests, while Marxists speak of the power of opposing classes. In our conversation, vested interests and class relations are important evolutionary elements because they are used to explain why some institutions and groups resist change while others promote it. But we avoid reducing everything down to class relations and economics. Any unequal division between people – not just class divisions – can cause serious conflict between the divisions.

The framework of analysis

Social evolution can be studied in a variety of ways. We start our study in chapter 1 with an intellectual history and a definition of social evolution.

Then, we have found it useful to look at social evolution in terms of causal elements and social processes. First we study four causal elements: Economic relations are studied in Chapter 2, technology in Chapter 3, enabling myth in Chapter 4, and political relations in Chapter 5. Next we study three social processes: Structural change is studied in Chapter 6, social tension in Chapter 7, and social conflict in Chapter 8. We draw conclusions and explore implications in Chapter 9. In an afterword, we study some difficult issues – technological determinism, progress, and related questions.

Technology warrants a cautionary note. Chapter 3 investigates the role of technology in social evolution. Technology is a powerfully dynamic factor in the evolution of societies. But we shall see that technology affects events only in the context of the rest of society – and technology itself does not drop from the sky. It is important to ask: how do economic relations, ideology and myths, and political and social institutions affect technological change?

A dialogue

In this book we will attempt to reclaim the theory of social evolution for the radical institutionalism of Thorstein Veblen and the critical Marxism of Karl Marx. In doing so, we have two objectives. First, we want to explore the evolution of society, for social evolution is itself an inherently radical concept. Second, we want to do so through the two radical paradigms founded by Veblen, on the one hand and by Marx on the other.

We pursue our quest through a dialogue between us. We proceed in our dialogue by asking a series of questions. Each question is answered by one author within the institutionalist paradigm – William M. Dugger – and also by the other author within the Marxist paradigm – Howard J. Sherman. We believe that this dialogue procedure is not only interesting, but gives the reader more to think about than two monologues, each given separately. In order to keep the dialogue within brief limits, we stick to the main elements of our respective paradigms and do not indulge in internecine warfare within each of our traditions, except to make those distinctions that are necessary to clarify where we stand.

We begin the dialogue in Chapter 2. But before you start reading it, take a look at the wonderful poem in the Appendix to this chapter.

Appendix: a feminist's poem on evolution

As a feminist economist, Charlotte Perkins Gilman stressed that things really can change in revolutionary ways in economic relations and in relations between women and men. She argued that it was really possible to have a very different economic system. She wrote in the last half of the nineteenth century, when women could not vote, when men still owned all of women's wages and property in some states, and when women were always paid lower wages than men. She argued in many books, that women need not be inferior to men but that women were perfectly qualified to vote and to have equal rights to wages and property with men and that such a system of gender equality was not a utopian dream but could actually be institution-alized. This notion was so revolutionary – and so contrary to all the myths that people took for granted – that her opponents did not even argue with her, but usually just laughed at her. It was to counter this emotional, unreasoning prejudice about the impossibility of basic change in the economy and in social relations of women to men that, over a century ago, Gilman wrote the following wonderful poem:

Similar cases

There was once a little animal,
No bigger than a fox,
And on five toes he scampered
Over Tertiary rocks.
They called him Eohippus,
And they called him very small,
And they thought him of no value–
When they thought of him at all;
For the lumpish old Dinoceras
And Coryphodon so slow
Were the heavy aristocracy
In days of long ago.

Said the little Eohippus,
"I am going to be a horse!
And on my middle finger-nails
To run my earthly course!
I'm going to have a flowing tail!
I'm going to stand fourteen hands high
On the psychozoic plain!"

The Coryphodon was horrified,
The Dinoceras was shocked;
And they chased young Eohippus,
But he skipped away and mocked.
Then they laughed enormous laughter,
And they groaned enormous groans,
And they bade young Eohippus
Go view his father's bones.

Said they, "You always were as small
And mean as now we see,
And that's conclusive evidence
That you're always going to be.
What! Be a great, tall, handsome beast,
With hoofs to gallop on?
Why! You'd have to change your nature!"
Said the Loxolophodon.
They considered him disposed of,
And retired with gait serene;
That was the way they argued
In "the early Eocene."

There was once an Anthropoidal Ape,
Far smarter than the rest,
And everything that they could do
He always did the best;
So they naturally disliked him,
And they gave him shoulders cool,
And when they had to mention him
They said he was a fool.

Cried this pretentious Ape one day,
"I'm going to be a Man!
And stand upright, and hunt, and fight,
And conquer all I can!
I'm going to cut down forest trees,
To make my houses higher!
I'm going to kill the Mastodon!
I'm going to make a fire!"

Loud screamed the Anthropoidal Apes
With laughter wild and gay;
They tried to catch that boastful one,
But he always got away.
So they yelled at him in chorus,
Which he minded not a whit;
And they pelted him with coconuts,
Which didn't seem to hit.
And then they gave him reasons
Which they thought of much avail,
To prove how his preposterous
Attempt was sure to fail.
Said the sages, "In the first place,

The thing cannot be done!
And, second, if it could be,
It would not be any fun!
And third, and most conclusive,
And admitting no reply,
You would have to change your nature!
We should like to see you try!"
They chuckled then triumphantly,
These lean and hairy shapes,
For these things passed as arguments
With the Anthropoidal Apes.

There was once a Neolithic Man,
An enterprising wight,
Who made his chopping implements
Unusually bright.
Unusually clever he,
Unusually brave,
And he drew delightful Mammoths
On the borders of his cave.
To his Neolithic neighbors,
Who were startled and surprised,
Said he, "My friends, in course of time,
We shall be civilized!
We are going to live in cities!
We are going to fight in wars!
We are going to eat three times a day
Without the natural cause!
We are going to turn life upside down
About a thing called gold!
We are going to want the earth, and take
As much as we can hold!
We are going to wear great piles of stuff
Outside our proper skins!
We are going to have Diseases!
And Accomplishments! And Sins!!!"

Then they all rose up in fury
Against their boastful friend,
For prehistoric patience
Cometh quickly to an end.
Said one, "This is chimerical
Utopian! Absurd!"

Said another, "What a stupid life!
Too dull, upon my word!"
Cried all, "Before such things can come,
You idiotic child,
You must alter Human Nature!"
And they all sat back and smiled.
Thought they, "An answer to that last
It will be hard to find!"
It was a clinching argument
To the Neolithic Mind!

Charlotte Perkins Gilman (1893)

Part II

ELEMENTS

2

ECONOMIC RELATIONS

This chapter is a dialogue on how economic relations – meaning basic economic institutions, vested interests, and class relations – shape technological change and social evolution.

Economic relations and social evolution – an institutionalist view

Inequality is a key starting point.

Inequality

The most important relations in stratified societies – nation, class, gender, race, ethnicity/religion, and sexual orientation – are all modes of inequality. At different times and in different places, one mode of inequality and then another may be more influential in affecting the direction and rate of evolution in stratified societies. The following will focus on the class mode of inequality.

To understand social evolution, class inequality cannot be a mere statistical category. It cannot refer to a statistical interval such as all families with incomes in, say, the $50,000 to $75,000 range. From the point of view of evolution, class inequality means much more than that. The number or proportion of families receiving an income within a particular range can rise or fall without evolution taking place. Such rises and falls are important, and may even correspond to dramatic structural change – to evolutionary change. Alternatively, they may represent mere mechanical movement – mere rises and falls in the positions of families within a stable economic structure. So to understand evolutionary change, class inequality must be thought of as a social relation, not as a statistical interval (see Dugger 1996a, b).

Class should be understood in terms of four different social relationships: (1) Relationship to income, (2) Relationship to work, (3) Relationship to wealth, (4) Relationship to technology. Each form of class relationship will be discussed in turn.

Relationship to income

When a person is able to establish a differentially advantageous relationship to a particular source of income through whatever keeps the money going to them rather than someone else, they establish a vested interest. Vested interest is the pecuniary aspect of class and is emphasized by institutionalists. Vested interest under modern conditions is some kind of protected or strategic position in the commercial flow of traffic. It is a product of power (see Tool and Samuels 1989). A vested interest is legalized as a property right or a contract right (see Commons 1968, and Dugger 1980a, b). In textbook economics, if it is discussed at all, vested interest is defined in the form of individual rent-seeking behavior. But individual rent seeking is too narrow a concept to include the class conflict that can form around issues involving vested interests.

Vested interest is frequently related to capital. A vested right in a flow of income frequently can be capitalized and sold for some multiple of the actual flow itself. Forming a corporation and issuing shares of stock to investors usually does this. For such corporate stock, the ratio of capitalized value to income flow is the price-earnings ratio. The price-earnings ratio for different stocks can vary widely without altering the fundamental fact that corporate stock represents ownership of capital. For example, a ratio of 40 for the annual earnings of a growth company is not unusual, while the ratio for a utility company is usually closer to 20.

Rent seeking, vested interest, class conflict, and power can all be illustrated by the economic relations institutionalized in professional sports. Each popular sport has been organized into a league made up of competing teams. Football, basketball, and baseball leagues are the most prominent. Each team is owned, but not by the players. Instead, each team is a commercial concern, owned by an outside interest that pays the players a contracted amount. The team owners, not the players, control the league. The owners have the right to charge a fee to anyone who wants to see their team play. They have acquired a vested interest in the pecuniary flow of traffic in tickets and in broadcast rights. Whatever money is left after paying the players and the other team expenses goes to the owners. They get the residual.

The owners use their league (association of team owners) to help them defend and enlarge their rights as owners. In addition, the court system will come to their defense in disputes over their right to collect for tickets and for broadcast rights. The court system also decides disputes when players seek the right to play wherever they wish or when players seek to dip into the flow of ticket and broadcast revenues. The players have formed unions to defend and enlarge their rights as players.

Nowadays, all big cities have city boosters – local business persons who want their cities to grow faster. So city boosters all try to get the publicity that a professional team brings to their home city. The boosters form political coalitions with city politicians and compete for the publicity by offering to build stadiums and roads for teams and to give tax breaks to the team owners. The owners usually move their teams to the highest bidder, getting enormous subsidies so that their flow of ticket and broadcast revenues is not reduced by stadium costs or taxes. Once their costs have been shifted off to the city's taxpayers, the owners can then sell part or all of their engrossed vested interest at a high price-earnings ratio in a public offering of their sports team corporation. The owners make the players move to the new city and play in the new stadium – probably paying some of them quite nicely to do so. The team owners get a huge pay-off in the higher capitalized value of their residual and the taxpayers get the bill for the new stadium, roads, and tax breaks.

The owners were "rent-seekers" when they moved their team to the highest bidding city. But they were also power-users when they formed political coalitions which used the bidding city's power to tax to pay for their stadiums or coliseums. The owners were also capitalists who told their workers (players) to move to the new city and who told their investment bankers to sell capital (vested interest) in a public offering of their corporate stock. So capital is an especially important kind of vested interest.

Regardless of their size or business, those who benefit from the same kind of vested interests share a class interest as a group. Furthermore, those who are harmed by the same kind of vested interests share a different class interest as a group. One capitalist may own stock in Coca Cola, and another in Montana Power, while a third owns stock in a sports team. Nevertheless they all share many interests. All would benefit by a reduction in the capital gains tax and an exclusion of dividends from taxable income. All would be harmed by an increase in taxes on corporate profits. All would be helped by laws that restricted the power of labor unions. (Most professional athletes and most utilities workers are represented by strong unions; so too are many employees of Coca Cola.) Their vested interest in a particular relationship to income is an important element of their shared class position.

Relationship to work

A second element of class is the relationship to work. Veblen emphasized this element in his *Theory of the Leisure Class*. In this book, Veblen explained that the leisure class was a class because of its particular relationship to work. Members of this class received income but did not have to work for it and they flaunted their exemption in front of everyone. Their conspicuous leisure and their conspicuous consumption were all symbols of their privileged relationship to work. Others, who were beneath them in class position, had to work for their money. Members of the leisure class were superior, and did not. So, relationship to work is another element of class. Those exempt from work are dominant creatures of power and prestige. Those who must work to obtain income are subservient creatures of weakness and contempt. Furthermore, those exempt from work have the time to cultivate their own status and power while those who must work, do not.

Of course, complications exist. Most have had to work for money most of their lives. But if they can finally retire on a government pension they are exempt from work. Nevertheless, they are not leisure class. Although receiving a flow of income, they are not receiving it because they are in possession of substantial wealth. Therefore, they are not receiving their income under normal capitalist institutions, but as a special decision of government. They can neither capitalize their flow of income, nor call it a return on capital. They are not owners, but government pensioners. The true leisure class does not respect pensioners. Pensioners have not spent a lifetime refining their abilities to flaunt their wealth and power. They have spent a lifetime working for a living.

Owners do not share a major interest with pensioners. Owners do not want to protect the pensioner's exemption from work. On the contrary, they wish to cancel out the pensioner's income so the pensioner is pushed back into the work force. If income comes from an inheritance, then the lucky recipient can devote their life to cultivating their own prestige and power instead of to earning a living working for someone else. Only then are they truly leisure class.

Their relationship to work strongly impacts the texture of a working person's daily life. The largest piece of waking time must be devoted to working for money – to paying the bills. Care of the children, preparation of food, maintenance of the home, maintenance of personal health, recreation and relaxation – all these aspects of daily life must be fit into the day around the over-riding requirements of work. Little time is available to develop themselves. Such is not the case with people in the leisure class. Instead, the texture of their daily life is strongly impacted by the fact that their leisure gives them the opportunities to cultivate themselves and to show off their cultivation.

Relationship to wealth

A third element of class, clearly related to the first two, is the relationship to wealth. To be in the leisure class, one must own substantial wealth. Veblen stressed the contemporary fact of the growing absentee ownership of wealth.

Most important in this regard has been the rise of collective structures that enable the owners of wealth to enjoy the benefits of wealth ownership without the burdens of wealth management. The operating corporation and the conglomerate, the holding company and the mutual fund have all facilitated the concentration of ownership in a class of people who are absent from its management. This relationship to wealth in the form of absentee ownership is another important element of class. It helps institutionalize the exemption from work for members of the leisure class in a way that gives them more leisure time while maintaining their power over wealth. Pensions for retired workers cannot do the same thing. Pensions cannot institutionalize retirees into the top roles that exercise power and that yield prestige, even though pensions do institutionalize the retiree's exemption from work. Furthermore, a pension cannot be passed on to one's heirs. Wealth can. Herein lies the importance of laws regulating inheritance and laws establishing trusts that are designed to avoid the taxation of wealth at the time of death. (At one time, trusts were used in place of corporations to facilitate the management of absentee ownership of concentrated wealth and also to form wealth into monopoly. Such trusts as the Standard Oil Trust gave rise to the Sherman Antitrust Act. Trusts proved to be far less flexible and adaptable collectives for concentration and monopolization purposes than corporations. Now trusts and their variants are the collectives used by the leisure class to pass wealth in tact to the future generation, while corporations and their variants are used to manage absentee wealth for the current generation.)

Absentee ownership of wealth through operating corporations, conglomerates, holding companies and mutual funds have given rise to a new relationship to wealth that is a kind of hybrid, or maybe even a mutant class. This mutant is the "manager." Numerous layers of managers in both large and small business bureaucracies now have a new kind of relationship to wealth. They do not own it and enjoy its usufruct as an absentee. So they are not, strictly speaking, leisure class. They do not work with it in actually making a product or performing a service. So they are not, strictly speaking, working class either. Instead, they manage the working class as it uses the wealth of the leisure class in the making of goods and performing of services.

Managers are a kept class. Seldom do they pursue their own interests in conflict with the leisure class, but instead are usually content to be kept in the good graces and good pay of that class. One reason for the lack of conflict is that the higher levels of managers usually own large blocks of stock, so to that extent they have the same pecuniary relationship as the leisure class.

In special circumstances, however, managers may come to form a true class and pursue their class interests against the interests of other classes. John Kenneth Galbraith, a close student of Thorstein Veblen, argued that in the 1950s and 1960s special circumstances in the United States gave rise to what he called the technostructure – a true managerial class (Galbraith 1967). The special circumstances of the 1950s and 1960s included the wide separation of ownership from control of the corporation, with ownership losing some of its power over management (control). As long as management earned sufficient profits to keep the diffused, absentee stockowners content, management was the more powerful of the two. This created a kind of gap between ownership and management. But the gap was soon closed by the creation of a "market" for corporate control. By the 1970s and 1980s corporate ownership (the leisure class stockowners) had regained the more powerful position relative to management (Dugger 1992).

Class relationship to work can still be summed up as fairly straightforward. If you have to work most of your life for someone else, you are working class. You have no time to cultivate yourself. On the other hand, if you do not have to work, you are leisure class. You have the opportunity – the leisure – to spend most of your life cultivating yourself. But you can do so only because someone else cannot.

Relationship to technology

The relationship to technology is a fourth element of class. In his *Engineers and the Price System* Veblen examined this crucial relationship. It involves working with the highest state of the industrial arts "on the due allocation of resources and a consequent full and reasonably proportioned employment of the available equipment and man power; on the avoidance of waste and duplication of work; and on an equitable and sufficient supply of goods and services to consumers" (Veblen 1921 (1965 reprint): 142). Engineers, Veblen argued, are interested in this technological relationship. Absentee owners, the leisure class, and those with vested interests in the existing business system are more interested in making money than in applying technology. Relationship to technology, then, is the last important element of class to Veblen and to institutionalists who have built on his original formulations. Members of the leisure class do not have to relate directly to work through technology. Members of the working class do.

How many classes are there?

In one sense, very many classes exist. In this sense, the nature and position of each class is determined by the myriad of relationships to income, work, wealth, and technology. In this sense, college students would be a class; school teachers a class, pensioners a class, corporate managers a class, owners of football teams a class, and many other such groups would be a class because they share particular relationships, either to income, work, wealth, and/or technology. In this sense, classes are quite fragmented sets of people sharing very specific interests. Shifting coalitions and loose alliances continually form and break up amongst these classes as special interest group politics pull them this way and that. The winners and losers change places, but the system does not necessarily undergo evolutionary change.

In another sense, however, just two classes exist – the leisure class and the underlying population. In this sense, classes are not fragmented sets, but more unified and larger sets of collectivities. Members of the leisure class have acquired a vested interest in the continued receipt of income without working for it. Most have acquired this vested interest through absentee ownership of securities. Members of the underlying population, on the other hand, have not acquired such vested interests in income and do not enjoy such exemption from work. Instead, they have to earn their bread through the sweat of their brow. And, since the leisure class does not work, part of the work done by the underlying population must, by necessity, go to support the leisure class. Only if members of the underlying population come to fully understand their subordinate position and the interests they share with their fellows, only then would they become a working class instead of just an underlying population. If the underlying population coalesces into a working class, class conflict between the working class and the leisure class may begin to move the whole system into evolutionary change. This, however, seldom happens. (See also Galbraith 1992 and Strobel and Peterson 1997.)

Although they are a class, when their class situation is unclear to them, the lower strata are an underlying population rather than a class formation. An underlying population does not act together as a class. Often, members of the underlying population do not connect their lack of income, wealth, status, and power to their class situation. They may attribute their plight to low-class lazy people or people of another color getting an unfair share or to women or foreigners doing the same. Such confusion protects leisure class interests from popular discontent. Instead of thinking in terms of the leisure class versus the working class, people of the lower strata often think in terms of industrious people versus lazy welfare cheats, humble white folks versus arrogant black ones, hardy men versus frail women, and true Americans versus shifty foreigners. Furthermore, homophobia makes it difficult for working people to connect how hard they must work to how much their work hurts their families. It is easier to blame gay people for a decline in "family values."

An important issue in the analysis of class is the condition of the middle class. Most members of the middle class work in what John Kenneth Galbraith identified as the "technostructure." The technostructure is composed of those lower to middle layers of management essential to the actual workings of the concern and includes those technical workers whose knowledge is crucial to the efficiency of the modern corporation. Galbraith explained how, in the 1950s and 1960s, the technostructure had obtained a significant degree of autonomy from the capitalist owners.

But as mentioned above, the autonomy of the technostructure was curtailed, beginning in the 1970s. The fate of the technostructure is a fascinating illustration of the interplay between new technology and economic institutions. Rapid improvement in computer and communications technology made centralization of control more effective. As automation had earlier decimated the ranks of industrial workers, the new computerization and related high-tech developments decimated the managerial and technical ranks. Furthermore, the creation of a new market in buying and selling whole corporations – the takeover market – made it financially feasible for ownership to buy up control of any corporation whose technostructure dared to be independent. The resulting merger waves and downsizing squeezed the "excess" numbers and the independence out of the technostructure, significantly weakening America's fabled middle class. (Galbraith 1967, Peterson 1994. Further discussion of class is in Veblen, 1964. Hunt, 1994 contains an introduction to the institutionalist literature on economic relations.)

Economic relations and evolution – a Marxist view

The earliest socioeconomic institutions, which lasted for millions of years, were very simple. Society consisted of a small group, which was an extended family of several generations. All of the women collected fruit and vegetables, while all of the men hunted. All of the food thus obtained was consumed collectively by everyone – more or less egalitarian societies with almost no property to fight over.

About five to ten thousand years ago in a few places, there were larger societies based on agriculture with stratification and division between economic classes. There have been many societies based on the institution of slavery, such as ancient Egypt or the old South of the United States. In slave societies, the master owns the slave, buys and sells slaves, gives the slave a tiny amount of the most basic necessities, and owns the product as well as the slave. Marx called this exploitation.

In feudal Europe and many other places, serfs were ruled by feudal lords. The serf did not belong to the lord, but was legally tied to the land, and owed a couple hundred days a year of labor to whoever held the land. Marx called this exploitation.

Capitalism is an economic institution existing in a given historical period. It is a system in which capital (plant and equipment in its physical form and money in its financial form) is owned by a small class of people called capitalists. Labor – skilled and unskilled, manual and technical, professional and untrained – is done by a very large class of people. The capitalist employers own the means of production. The employees (called workers by Marx) are paid a wage (which may be an hourly wage or a monthly salary or a bonus or commission). The employers (usually in the form of corporations owned by capitalists) own the product of the labor of their employees. Employees who work for an employer are free to quit their job. They are then free to starve if there is unemployment (or get a government hand out if there is unemployment compensation) or move to another job if there is a job offered by another corporation. All this is very different than earlier class societies, but the end result is that the corporation still profits from the labor of its employees, so Marx still calls it exploitation. Marxists define each economic institution, such as capitalism, by its specific class relationships.

Social scientists using an individualist approach to class – and almost all popular references to class – define class in terms of the attributes of an individual. How much wealth does the individual own? What is the individual's income? What is the individual's status and prestige? The attributes exist along a continuous spectrum and there is harmony between classes because each individual gets income according to his/her productivity.

Marxists always insist that class is a relationship, not an individual attribute. Marxists ask which group works and which group profits? Which group exploits other groups – and which group is exploited by other groups? What is the relationship between the worker and the capitalist in the productive process? Capitalists, that is, businesses employing people, are defined as a group of people who own the means of production and appropriate profit from workers. Workers or employees are defined as people who own little or none of the means of production and work for capitalist employers to earn their wage.

In the Marxist view, in which classes are defined by their relation to other classes, there is a discontinuity: capitalists do not simply have a little more money than workers do; they own capital and exploit workers. Thus, in the individualist view there is no room for conflict between classes, while the Marxist view focuses on the relationship of conflict or harmony between classes.

Of course, only in abstract models do we find pure classes, such that every individual exactly meets the definition. In reality, some worker-employees own tiny amounts of stock, while some capitalist employers also do managerial work. Therefore, members of classes must be defined by the source of most of their income, not all of their income.

Marx's enemies always assume that he thinks there are only two classes in every society – a ruling, exploiting class and a ruled, exploited class.

Although Marx used a simple two-class model in some parts of his basic economic model, where many classes were an unnecessary complication to his argument, Marx was perfectly clear that this was a simplification of reality: "... the actual composition of society ... by no means consists of only two classes, workers and industrial capitalists" (Marx 1867, 1967: 493). In his actual historical discussions of class, Marx tells us that in England there are three main classes: the landlords, the capitalists and the workers – but he also refers to the small business people, craftspeople, and small farmers.

Is there a middle class? There are obviously many people with incomes in the middle of the spectrum, but that does not fit the Marxist definition of a class. More seriously, there are strata of the working class, such as managerial workers and professional workers, who are like other workers in some respects, but unlike other workers in some other respects. The capitalist firm pays managerial and professional workers for their work in the same way that other workers get paid. But they are different as they have far more independence, they often issue commands to other workers, and they get many types of benefits that ordinary workers do not get. So their relationships are complex and often ambiguous – and they might be called a new middle class. In US history, at one time the middle class consisted of independent farmers and small craftspeople. Now the bulk of the new middle class can probably be described as lower level managers and professionals.

Some dogmatic Marxists used to see class conflict only at the economic level in such things as strikes for higher wages or less hours. On the contrary, most contemporary Marxists – who are critical of the simple dogmas of the past – have focused not only on economic conflict, but also on class conflict at the political level and on class conflict at the ideological level (see e.g. Wright 1985, Chapter 1, Wolff and Resnick 1987, Sherman 1995, Chapter 6). What exactly does class conflict mean at these three levels?

At the economic level of strife in production many Marxists have explained how employees are exploited by capitalists and how employees fight back (see, e.g. Marx 1867, Sweezy 1942, Sherman 1995, Chapter 7). Exploitation comes about because individual employees (and even employees in unions) have less power than corporations. Workers must have a job in order to eat. And there is always some unemployment in capitalism so that workers are under coercive pressure to accept a job. Therefore, they accept a wage that generally covers their average consumption needs; employees are forced by need to spend almost all of their income on consumer goods and save little as a group – since many are always going into debt and are forced to use their little plastic credit cards for much spending. But workers produce on the average a much larger product than their own consumption goods in our society, so the employer makes a profit from each worker – a worker who produces no profit is fired. The amount that workers produce above their wage is the source of profit – and is called exploitation by Marxists.

It must be emphasized that the term exploitation does not apply only to an illegal migrant worker coerced to work under miserable conditions for a dollar an hour. All workers are exploited regardless of the height of their wages. For example, suppose an employee gets ten dollars an hour and works an eight hour day, so she receives $80 dollars – but if she produces $130 worth of goods a day, then the corporation makes a profit of $50 a day. If a computer engineer for a giant computer company is paid ten thousand dollars a month, but produces new products worth twenty thousand a month, then a giant computer company makes a profit of ten thousand a month. Suppose a basketball player makes a million dollars a year, but brings in an additional two million dollars a year for the team owner, then the owner makes a million dollars profit a year on this player. All of these are exploitation.

Still at the economic level, there have been numerous hard fought battles between employees' unions and corporations in the United States, some becoming violent. For a very careful description of the amazingly violent labor history of the United States, see Foner, 1947, 1955, 1964, 1965.

Marxists have analyzed class conflict at the political level (see e.g. Miliband, 1973, 1991; Sherman, 1995; and all of Chapter 5 in this book). For example, the air traffic controllers in the United States felt that they were being overworked and that this could lead to airplane accidents. When they went on strike in the early 1980s, President Reagan fired all of those on strike, relying on a law that had been passed by Congress. So every time there is a labor law passed by Congress, there is a clear class conflict over which class is benefited by it and which class is hurt by it.

Similarly, when Congress passed the National Labor Relations Act, farm workers were left out, so it took a protracted political struggle in California to get them covered by an act in California. Perhaps most importantly, every item in the federal budget – and in state budgets – helps some class and hurts another. For example, whose taxes are to be cut, who gets tax breaks, who pays more taxes? Should there be universal health care, which would mean that rich tax payers must pay towards care of the poor? Who gets lucrative military contracts?

There is also class conflict at the level of ideology. For example, there are those who push the myth that all inequality is due to differences in intelligence (the infamous bell curve). This argument implies that the working class is stupider than the capitalist class and therefore deserves less income. This is a prime example of a social myth that helps support the privileges of the elite (see Fischer, Hout, Jankowski, Lucas, Swidler, and Voss 1996). The origins of such social myths are discussed in detail in Chapter

4. We shall also see in Chapter 4 that Marxists have long argued over the exact importance of ideological class conflict versus economic and political conflict, but most modern critical Marxists now emphasize that all three levels are important.

There is nothing in contemporary Marxism that says that class conflict is the only conflict or even that it is always the most important conflict at any given time. Class relations, however, are considered the best beginning point to understand the structure of any class-divided society (see the interesting discussion of class as an entry point in Wolff and Resnick 1987). Without understanding the social and economic processes of a society, one cannot understand race, gender or nationality within it. Having found and examined class conflicts, however, one must then also study in depth racial, gender, and nationality conflicts. Of course, one must examine how each of these conflicts is affected by class conflict – but one must also examine how class conflict is affected by race, gender, and nationality conflicts. Race, class, gender and nationality conflicts are all part of one unified social matrix (see Sherman 1996, on the holistic or relational view of the relationship of these different conflicts).

In the United States, Marxists have protested the rape of the land from native Americans; a very high percentage of native Americans are unemployed and continue to live in poverty. Mexican Americans had their land taken from them by force in the Mexican American War; then have been subject to oppression and exploitation ever since as the largest minority of the Southwest. Latinos of all types in the United States are still subject to very strong discrimination in jobs and housing – they are fighting back by every possible political means; and since they are mostly poor workers, it is not only a racial conflict but also a class conflict.

Jews suffered from intense discrimination for much of US history, but that has largely disappeared – except for occasional acts of violence by US fascist groups. Japanese Americans suffered from extreme, irrational prejudice in the Second World War, when most were illegally imprisoned in concentration camps. But after a long struggle, they – like the Jews after their long struggle – are now over-represented in higher education and higher income groups. All Asian Americans still face some discrimination at times, but it has not stopped their amazing progress.

Race and class: the example of African Americans

In US history from the Revolutionary War (for the inalienable rights of all people) to the Civil War, African Americans remained in the chains of slavery. They often revolted and often escaped, but it took a long bloody war to break the resistance of the slave owners and end slavery. The evolution of

US slavery to its end is discussed in Chapter 8. After the Civil War most African Americans became sharecroppers, which is better than slavery, but still a very exploitive system – it is discussed later in this chapter.

During the Second World War most African American workers changed from sharecropping on isolated farms to industrial work concentrated in parts of urban areas. There was still racist prejudice and institutionalized, legal, racial discrimination and segregation in housing, schools, and every other facet of life. But since they were now concentrated in the cities, African Americans were able to lead a heroic and often dangerous Civil Rights movement to end all legalized discrimination. After a difficult struggle, they succeeded completely in changing all the laws, so that discrimination was no longer legal, but rather was an illegal act. This did not end racial prejudice or discrimination, however, though it greatly reduced it. The reasons for the persistence of racism under capitalism are discussed in Chapter 4.

Gender and class

All good Marxists are feminists. Marxists dispute the sexist myth that women have always been inferior to men and that the family has always remained the same. There have been many drastic changes in the relations of men and women – each associated with different class relations in which they existed. In very primitive societies, there were no classes and women and men lived in a rough degree of equality. Women gathered fruits and vegetables, while men hunted. The hunting was never dependable, so the clan depended more on the production of the women, giving them at least equal respect. Of course, this situation of equality was not idyllic because – according to our standards – there was extreme poverty. When women invented a crude form of agriculture in some areas, their respect and authority grew.

The situation under Greek and Roman slavery was entirely different. Men captured slaves and put them to work in heavy agriculture as well as mining. Male masters owned the slaves, male masters owned the wealth produced by the slaves, and male masters virtually owned all women as property. The male owners exploited all slave women economically, but they also exploited them sexually whenever they wished. Slave women had no rights. On the other hand, private property in slaves and land was inherited by the legitimate heir, so the legitimate wife of the master was treated as very valuable because she alone could have a legitimate heir. So women of the master class were first totally obedient to their fathers, then their fathers gave them to their husbands. Their husbands kept them isolated from all other men. The penalty for illicit sex by a woman of the master class with a slave was death for the slave and could be death for the woman. Thus, there was a complete double standard in which men of the master

29

class had sex as they pleased, while the women of the master class were kept isolated from casual sex, but also isolated from worldly conversation, from politics, and from power. So while women of the slave class were doubly exploited, women of the master class were totally subservient to their husbands with the narrowest possible life.

There was not much change in the position of women from slavery to the Feudal System. In that system, a feudal lord had complete political and economic power over everyone on the feudal manor, from the serf to his wife. The lord sometimes claimed the right of the first night, the right to sex with a serf woman on the night of her marriage! So the lord had sex with as many serf women as he pleased. The wife of the lord was strictly prohibited from being alone with any other man. She was completely subservient to the lord of the manor and could also be put to death for sex with any other man. Women of the serf class labored as hard and long as any man, in addition to being sexually exploited by the feudal lords. Thus women remained completely inferior and the double standard was taken for granted in sexual matters by the feudal ruling class.

In the United States in the first half of the nineteenth century, there were several types of socio-economic systems and women fared differently in each of them. In the South there were slave class relationships. Under US slavery the pattern of ancient Rome and Greece with respect to women was repeated to a large degree. Slave women were exploited economically and sexually. In the master class the double standard was the norm in which men had as much sex as they wished with slave women, while women were severely punished for any sex except with their husbands. Women of the master class had no property rights, while men owned all of the slaves and all of the other property. Men controlled politics and women had no business in politics. Thus both slave and master class women were in a subordinate position to men in the economic, political, and sexual spheres. The dominant role of the male master class was challenged only during slave revolts (see Chapter 8).

In the early nineteenth century western US lands, there was family farming without employees as the norm, so capitalism did not exist. Women worked just as hard as men, though at different tasks, so they were roughly equals in day to day life. Many of the farms were practically self-sufficient with little market exchange. Only much later when some farmers hired farm workers, became part of the capitalist market, did men acquire property and control. Then women slowly fell to the usual subservient role in early capitalism, where they were considered the man's property. Women had no right to their own property, and women could not even keep their own wages.

Throughout the United States in most of the nineteenth century where capitalism was the dominant system, men controlled all property, men controlled women's wages, men had the right to keep the children in a separation or divorce, women could not testify in court nor be on juries, and women were excluded from most professions. Most women did spend long hours working, not just on farms, but also in factories in bad conditions for very low pay. In the 1870s and 1880s a women's movement fought for control of their own wages and property brought to the marriage. They won in some states after more than a decade of struggle, though other states resisted for several more decades.

To gain some political power, women fought for the right to vote from 1848 till 1920, meeting ridicule, scorn, and relentless opposition. The right wing claimed that the right to vote would hurt the family, while business worried that they might have to pay equal wages if women had political power. After winning the vote, women made very slow progress with other reforms. Slowly, the number of women working for pay increased, but it was not until the 1960s that so many women were at work in the paid economy the myth that women did not work for pay became ridiculous. Only then, on the basis of their emerging new positions in class relations – from manual workers to professionals – were women able to organize around issues of equality in the work place and the professions. Equal pay for women was not put into law until 1963 – and in practice discrimination continues in wages, segregated occupations, and lack of promotions. The causes and effects of sexist prejudice and sexist discrimination are discussed in Chapter 4. All of these issues, both historical and theoretical, are discussed in an excellent and very readable book by Barbara Sinclair Deckard (1983).

Health care and class

As one example of the importance of a class analysis, Vincente Navarro (1993) has shown in great detail exactly how class interests have shaped health care and how health care reform has been held back by the interests of the capitalist class. As a result of class relations, the United States spends the highest proportion of gross domestic product of any country in the world on health care, 14 per cent in the latest data. Yet the United States does not provide good health care to its citizens, since 17 per cent of the population have no health care benefits (Navarro, p. 15).

Why is the health care system so bad for most people? The problem is that most people have very little political power, while those with power have very little interest in extending health care to everyone. The people without health care are poorly paid workers and the unemployed. But poorly paid workers and unemployed workers have little economic power and little political power. The poor and the unemployed mostly do not even vote; only half the eligible voters do vote even in presidential elections, whereas turnout is pitiful in other elections. Those who have immense economic power do not need public health care and resent paying taxes to maintain it. The capitalist class not only has vast economic power, but this economic power is used to control political outcomes (see Chapter 5). Rather than universal public health care, much of the health care industry is directly controlled by giant corporations, including the insurance companies, who make enormous profits and want to keep it that way (Navarro, p. 26).

Change of class relations

These class relations do not change rapidly. The average person born into the working class never has much savings. Therefore, he or she can never become a capitalist with significant ownership of corporate stock. Sixty per cent of the American people have little or no savings. So the average employee (including the median income receiver in the United States) must remain an employee because he/she has no opportunity to become a capitalist. This view, of course, is exactly contrary to the individualist, rational choice view that one always has a choice.

The average capitalist inherits a significant amount of ownership of capital. Moreover, the average capitalist family can afford to help its children get the best university education they can use, regardless of cost. Therefore, with a significant initial capital and a good training, she/he can remain a capitalist by getting an average profit on capital plus an average managerial salary. Class structure is also reproduced through the working of the political structure, which is heavily influenced by the economic structure (discussed in Chapter 5). Class structure is also supported by the dominant ideology and dominant set of social myths (discussed in Chapter 4). Probably the most systematic and empirically comprehensive treatment of class by a contemporary Marxist is by Eric Olin Wright (1985 and 1989); also see Sherman (1995 Chapters 5 and 6). A very readable, comprehensive and inspiring history of the US labor movement is in Foner, 1947, 1955, 1964, 1965.

How do economic institutions and vested interests affect technology? – an institutionalist view

New technology involves doing things in a new way or doing new things. Technology involves knowledge about all the things that we do and all the ways that we do them. The things we do use tools and the ways we do them require skills. Technology is an accumulated stock of knowledge about tools and skills. The stock of knowledge has accumulated over many generations and has been passed down to each succeeding generation by the community. Changes in technology add to the communal stock and are passed on too.

Although particular changes in technology are often invented and implemented by particular individuals or groups, such invention and implementation are mere additions to the already immense accumulated stock. Inventors invent new technology. Their new ways of doing things or new things to be done may appear to be the product of great individualistic genius but are more the product of generations of communal learning and nurturing. None of the great inventors would have amounted to much of anything if generations of technological improvements had not resided in the community's repertoire of tools and skills, ready for the inventor to draw upon and to implement, ready for them to turn to account.

Edison could not have invented the light bulb in medieval Paris. At that time, few of the things a light bulb required were a part of the community's repertoire of tools and skills (the required things included advanced abilities to work metal, glass, and other materials, and advanced abilities to generate and control a flow of electrical current). However, once all the needed knowledge had finally become a part of the community's repertoire, it was only a matter of time before someone put them together into a light bulb. Edison, the individual man, was not even necessary. If he had not done it, someone else would have done.

In fact, many scientific discoveries and inventions are made at the same time by two or more people working independently. Discoveries and inventions are made because their time is ripe, not because a genius is born. The community's repertoire of tools and skills becomes so bursting with everything needed for the new discovery, that two or more people discover it at about the same time.

The broad communal nature of technology must be emphasized. New technology is the result of the interrelationship between how the communal stock of knowledge is preserved and passed on and how the additions to that common stock are made and put into use. Anything that restricts access to or growth in the common stock will retard the process of generating and using new technology. Anything that promotes access or growth will expand the process. Public policy regarding education, research, patents, and free inquiry all affect the rate and direction of technological change. Furthermore, government policies that create exclusionary property rights in the community's stock of knowledge can retard its application. Technology is largely a product of the community (see Veblen 1919). The more open the community, the faster the rate of technological change, both through local invention and through borrowing new technology from outside.

Going concerns, vested interests, and sabotage

John R. Commons, a pioneer in institutional economics, explained that communities are made up of sets of going concerns – business corporations, labor unions, regulatory agencies, courts, governments, churches, political parties and schools (Commons 1961). Such going concerns are made up of a created harmony of interests with regard to the technologies they use. In textbook economics, a concern is called a firm. However, almost everything is lost in the translation. A firm is assumed to be a simple, profit-maximizing owner. It makes no difference if the firm is the General Electric Corporation or Bill's Burger Shop. Each is assumed to behave in the same way when presented with the same circumstances. A firm is a kind of behavioral black box. It does not matter what is inside the box – ten thousand stockholders and six thousand employees or Bill and his dog. The behavior that comes out of the box is the same. A going concern, however, is not a black box. It matters what is inside the concern – what interests are found there. So the real concerns found operating in the world are more complicated than the firms of text book theory.

All going concerns have both mutual interests and conflicting interests. In the case of the business corporation, the suppliers, customers, workers and the owners all have mutual interests in keeping the concern going to protect jobs and profits. None of them want the concern to fail because they would be hurt by its failure. They are mutually interested in its continuation. But they also have conflicting interests in the going concern. The suppliers want higher prices for what they supply and easier quality control standards that they have to meet. The concern itself wants lower material costs and higher standards. The customers want lower prices for the good or service they buy from the concern and they want higher quality. The concern wants higher prices and fewer complaints from their customers. The workers want higher wages and better working conditions. The owners want lower wages and more flexible workers. Out of the conflict and mutuality that make up each enterprise, come working rules that keep the enterprise going by creating, for the time being, a harmony of interests in which the mutual benefit of the participating interests overcomes their conflict of interest. The created harmony of interests is always fragile and temporary. It is not an equilibrium.

The going concern must work new technology into the delicately-tuned and tediously-created harmony of interests, or the going concern breaks down, to the mutual loss of all interests in the concern.

Within the going concern, new technologies are constantly disrupting the workplace by changing the working conditions or the procedures, leading to grievance hearings, complaints, wildcat strikes, rapid turnover, terminations, even mass murders.

Within the going concern, new technologies are constantly changing the relations between suppliers and the going concern by introducing new materials and new standards. The change frequently benefits one interest far more than another, or benefits one interest at the expense of the others, disrupting the delicate harmony of interests they had created between themselves.

A going concern is a harmony of interests. Otherwise, it could not keep going. Commons emphasized that there was nothing natural or automatic or spontaneous about harmony of interest. Any harmony of interest had to be created by long and arduous processes of devising working rules out of the conflict and mutuality inherently included in all going concerns. New technology upsets the fragile compromises and agreements that went into the working rules that kept the concerns agoing. New technology alters both the specific terms of the conflict of interest and the specific terms of the mutuality of interest, to the benefit of one or more of the participating interests and to the detriment of one or more of the other interests. The alteration may be so extreme that the participants cannot recreate a new harmony of interests through implementing new working rules. Then, either the going concern stops agoing or an outside force steps into the dispute. That outside force is sovereignty. Sovereignty, ultimately, resides in one or more agencies of the state. Sovereign adjudication of disputes is by the courts. When necessary or expedient, a security apparatus uses physical force to support the judicial decision.

When a going concern introduces a new technology into the community, some individuals and groups promote it because they think they stand to gain by doing so while others oppose it because they think they stand to lose if it is adopted. The community's going concerns are all, to greater or lesser extent, drawn into a protracted conflict over implementing the new technology. The conflict may split evenly across class lines, with the owners squared off against the workers. Such is frequently the case with various forms of automation that cost many workers their jobs. The workers oppose automation. The owners support it.

The conflict could split across gender lines, if the new technology involves human reproduction. The family is also a going concern, with vested interests, conflict of interests, and mutuality of interests in how it keeps agoing. Women support the morning after pill, patriarchs oppose it. Women have always had an interest in expanding their control over the reproduction done by their own bodies. Patriarchal men have always had an interest in denying their women such control. The struggle rolls on. On one hand, women in the United States and Europe have managed to gain access to birth control pills and other reproductive health care against the resistance of many men. On the other hand, the women of Afghanistan have lost almost all their rights to men who call themselves the Taliban.

Conflicts also cut across national borders instead of class or gender borders. French and other European lovers of fine cuisine strongly object to the foods produced by US genetic engineering and by chemical and hormone additives. Not everybody loves Ronald McDonald. Surely the French sheep producer, who tried to tear down a McDonald's that was under construction, was not too fond of the clown.

How such conflicts turn out is not predictable. But clearly, a whole series of different vested interests frequently resist new technologies. Workers might be able to successfully resist a particular new technology, or might not. Women might be able to get legal access to abortion pills in the United States, or they might not. Afghan women may win out over the Taliban, or they might not. The US might get its high-tech food accepted more widely, or it might not. We do not know. But we do know that economic institutions, class relations, gender relations, international relations, perhaps race relations also, all affect new technology. They affect it through the concrete way in which specific new technologies affect a community's going concerns and by the concrete way in which the interests that make up those going concerns react to the new technology. Within going concerns, some interests introduce new technology – owners introduce automation. Other interests resist new technology – workers resist automation. Medical researchers introduce new ways for women to control their reproduction. Within the family, women support it. Patriarchs resist it. One interest tries to promote and the opposing tries to sabotage new technology. Each case is different, but who wins out and how they win out strongly affect the rate and direction of technological change.

How do economic institutions and class relations affect technology? – a Marxist view

Where does technology fit into the framework of analysis? First, society is divided by our definition into economic processes and social processes. The social processes are of two types, processes focusing on ideas and processes focusing on institutions.

In the economic sphere, it is equally important to understand that there are two types of relationships affecting the process of evolution. Marx called them the forces of production and the relations of production. The relations of production refer to the relations of groups of people in the production process. In every primitive society, there is only one group constituting the entire society. In all stratified societies there are many groups called classes related to one another, such as the slaves and masters in slavery, or the employers and employees in capitalism.

The forces of production are constituted of nature, labor, capital, and technology. Technology is defined very broadly to include the ways humans change nature, the training and education of labor, and the quality or improvements in capital. Nevertheless, the quantity of natural resources, the number of workers, and the total amount of capital are equally vital parts of the evolutionary process. Often, technology is the most rapidly changing force of production, but it sometimes happens in a war or a plague that the number of workers diminishes rapidly or the stock of capital is destroyed – so it is a mistake to think that only technology changes among the forces of production.

Leaving aside the other forces of production for the moment, why does technological change occur? Technological change is not God given nor is it external to a society. There have been many societies in which, because of the socio-economic structure, stagnation has been the rule for centuries – while the social structure causes rapid change in other cases.

For hundreds of thousands of years in primitive societies, in which the extended family was the economic unit and hunting and gathering was the technology (with a few stone tools and no specialists), there was little or no economic progress. In some of the early stratified, class-divided societies, such as Mesopotamia, Egypt, Greece, and Rome, there were vast accomplishments in the sciences reflected, for example, in enormous monuments that still make us marvel. What was the secret of their accomplishments? One important part of it was the division of labor. On the basis of an agricultural surplus, they were able to support full-time specialists. There were specialists in tool-making, weapons, and pottery. The priests included specialists in astronomy, writing, and arithmetic. The noble's entourage included engineers, doctors, artists and architects. So on the basis of division of labor, embedded in class division, productivity improved rapidly for a while.

Yet there were periods in the mature Roman society where there were centuries without technological progress, but only progress in government procedures, how to run an empire, and how to optimize military operations. What held back technological advance in ancient Rome has much in common with what held back technological advance in the US South before the Civil War. In Chapter 8, it will be shown that the institution of slavery, which was very productive relative to the most primitive societies, impeded further progress in the later Roman empire and in the pre-Civil War South. Why? The basic economic unit in the Roman empire as well as the old South, was the plantation or the latifundia, on which a large number of slaves produced agricultural goods. But Chapter 8 will show in detail that slavery limits the use of complex equipment and the use of scientific crop rotation, so productivity remains low and the land is exhausted. We shall also see in Chapter 8 that the myth of the low worth of work, due to slavery, prevented the elite from paying much attention to technological progress. Finally, we shall note in Chapter 8 the large number of slave revolts in both

Rome and the old South, so armed class conflict played a vital role in determining the evolution of these societies.

Technological change was extremely slow in feudal Europe. Chapter 8 will show in some detail that one major reason was that feudal society was built on serfdom, which meant that the serfs had to work a certain number of days a year on the lord's land, but also had their own small plot (working perhaps 200 days a year on the lord's land and the rest on their own). In Chapter 8 we shall see that the feudal lords lacked both the incentives and the work experience to affect any major technological innovations – while the serfs lacked both the time and the resources. We shall also see that the training, myths, and social conditioning of the feudal lords inclined them away from technological innovation and toward merely exploiting their serfs more if they wanted more wealth. In fact, so little change had occurred in feudal society over hundreds of years that myth said any change was impossible in technology or in institutions – a view supported by the most powerful myth-maker in feudal Europe, the church. When exploitation grew too great, we shall also see in Chapter 8 that the serfs revolted, so class conflict played a vital role in feudal evolution.

Still the system of feudalism, as it evolved in Western Europe but not in some other places, did provide more incentives and possibilities than slavery, so slowly over many centuries better technology was used that led to more agricultural productivity and to more crafts and more trade – all discussed briefly in the next chapter and more fully in Chapter 8.

Example: sharecropping relations

After the Civil War the US South switched from slavery to sharecropping. The former slave masters had lots of land but no slaves. The former slaves had freedom, but no money and no land. Thus the former slaves leased land from the landowners for a part – usually half – of the future crop. The sharecroppers also had to borrow money from the landlords to live till the crop came in and to get or borrow farm equipment. Since they had only a share of the crop, they went deeper in debt each year ("one day older and deeper in debt" as the song says).

There was an all-pervasive ideology of racism, which had originated as an apologia for slavery, but continued as a justification for the exploitation of African-American sharecroppers. Based on the class relations, the political institutions were rigged against the African-American by the Hayes-Tilden compromise of 1876. By that compromise, the Northern industrialists and their Republican party kept control of the federal government, but the Southern landowners and their Democratic party were given the Southern state governments. The federal army withdrew and the Ku Klux Klan rode over the countryside, and Jim Crow segregation laws replaced the slave code.

In this context, sharecropping was a convenient relationship, better than slavery, but far from freedom. The class relations of sharecropping, however, held back technological progress. On the one side, the sharecropping tenant had only a one-year lease, so he or she could be forced to pay a higher amount – or be pushed off the land entirely – if it were improved. According to two economic historians: "Not surprisingly, the tenant insisted on maximizing the value of the current crop (to half of which he was entitled) and showed little interest in long-run investment prospects from which he would be unable to benefit unless he were allowed to continue to work the farm" (Ransom and Sutch 1977: 101).

On the other side, the landlord would continue to own the land, so one would think the landlord might be willing to pay for improvements. "Yet, since the landlord would receive only half of the benefits of investments in the quality of his farm, his incentive to make such outlays would be reduced. Only if the return expected was worth twice what it cost would the landlord find a particular investment to his advantage" (Ransom and Sutch 1977: 102). To these dis-incentives must be added the debt peonage process, whereby the sharecropper was almost always in debt to the local merchant or landowner, so was required to plant only the safest cash crop, namely cotton. The combined effect of these two relations of production – share-cropper-landlord relations and debtor-creditor relations – held back the forces of production in the South for many miserable decades (see further details in Ransom and Sutch 1977).

Capitalism and the forces of production

Capitalist economic institutions put heavy pressure on the capitalist entrepreneurs – the heads of businesses and corporations, whom Marx called the bourgeoisie – to expand or go bankrupt, which makes for rapid advance. According to Marx and Engels:

> The bourgeoisie ... has accomplished wonders far surpassing Egyptian pyramids, Roman aqueducts, and Gothic cathedrals .... The bourgeoisie cannot exist without constantly revolutionizing the instruments of production .... The need of a constantly expanding market for its products chases the bourgeoisie all over the globe .... The bourgeoisie, by the rapid improvement of all instruments of production, by the immensely facilitated means of communication, draws all nations, even the most barbaric, into civilization.
>
> (Marx and Engels 1848: 11–13)

Thus capitalism became a world economic system with vast accumulation of capital, billions of workers, and rapid technological progress. What could be nicer?

Unfortunately, capitalist institutions and class relations also distort the direction of economic progress, make it very rapid sometimes, but also hold it back at other times. Capitalism distorts technological change, for example, by producing and strenuously advertising unhealthy cigarettes. It produces fast cars that add vast pollution to the air.

As was shown above, capitalism also distorts the potential use of technology in health care to the extent that one might say that capitalism is bad for your health. The analysis of health care by Navarro given above is confirmed by a grim newspaper report headlined: "Cost now a key Factor in the Health Care Equation: Doctors find that the long-held ideal of separating finances, treatment is no longer realistic" (Anonymous reporter, *Los Angeles Times*, November 15, 1999, p. 1).

Capitalism has economic crises at irregular intervals, during which production moves rapidly backward to lower levels, investment in new technology is postponed, millions of workers are unemployed and thousands of factories are idle or at partial capacity when they could be expanding the social product. In the Great Depression it was admitted that 26 per cent of US workers were unemployed – and many dug in the garbage to eat or went without food. Contractions have continued as a fact of US capitalist life and about ten per cent of workers were unemployed in California for some years in the early 1990s. In the 25 years from 1973 to 1998 the average growth of the US gross domestic product was slow, and almost all of the growth went to profits (plus rent and interest), so the real wage in 1998 was no higher than in 1973. Such depressions and stagnation due to lack of demand are not found in any society with other economic institutions, but are rather caused by the economic institutions and class relations of capitalism. (For a detailed discussion of this thesis, see Chapter 7 of this book; for a book-long exposition and empirical proof of this thesis, see Sherman 1991.)

In a class-divided society, technological change requires not only a stable and appropriate class structure, but also a supportive ideology and psychology, and a stable and supportive political structure. Ideology and politics are discussed in Chapters 4 and 5, but one example here will help the reader know what to expect. How did the United States get a private nuclear industry? During the Second World War, the US government built a nuclear industry and dropped the atomic bomb. This nuclear development was caused by a powerful US government, by the support of the US ruling class, and by an ideology of winning the war unconditionally at all costs. After the war, the entire nuclear industry was given away to private enterprise. This was done because of the free market ideology, because of the economic power of the corporations who gained from the giveaway, and because of the political power the corporations could exert through money in politics. Development of nuclear power could not be stopped by the environmental movement because nuclear power was thought to be highly profitable to the ruling class.

How technology is shaped by the social-economic environment of capitalism in nineteenth and twentieth century United States is spelled out in fascinating detail in two books by David Noble, 1979 and 1984. With special emphasis on the evolution of the electrical, chemical, and machine industries, as well as the role of engineers and engineering schools in universities, Noble proves that technology does not evolve in some straight-line, natural fashion, but according to the bottom line of profit in capitalism, which is not necessarily the same as the good of all citizens. However, the social-economic environment of capitalism does cause extremely rapid technological change to meet competition, far more rapid than the slow creep of technology in slavery or feudalism, for reasons discussed below. The problem in capitalism is not the rapidity of technological change during periods of expansion – though there are often severe cyclical downturns in which production actually declines – but rather the profit-distorted direction of change.

In a striking article, Noble shows how universities today are being bent out of shape by the commercialization of new research as well as new teaching technology within the framework of corporate influence (see Noble 1998). With UCLA (University of California at Los Angeles) a leading example, he examines two trends toward making research and teaching commodities for sale in the corporate market. First, in the last twenty years, he finds that universities have increasingly formed profit-making companies in partnership with industry to exploit new research. He also shows the increasing trend toward corporate grants to university researchers in return for complete proprietary control over the research. The resulting knowledge is kept secret to protect its capitalized value. Such proprietary research does not directly help further progress nor does it further the freedom of expression so vital to university life. Second, at UCLA and many others, education is being made a commodity to be sold on the net. Each course at UCLA must have a web page. Many virtual universities are now selling degrees that can be obtained over the net without ever seeing a professor. Major universities such as UCLA have also taken a few steps in this direction because every course that is on a disk and can be sold independently of the faculty is seen as reducing labor costs as well as costs of building classrooms. So in the beautiful future faculty will work for many years to research, build and record a perfect course, after which they will receive a new assignment. In the beautiful future students will stare at computer terminals, but will not have to meet live faculty face to face.

The manner in which class relations condition new technology has been evident in many other ways in the information revolution. Each revolution in information technology also causes a legal crisis because it causes situations not previously foreseen by the laws of capitalist states. As one small example of law and technology, high resolution television will soon be available. But this means the necessity of an entirely new set of television channels to generate the new type of signal. Yet ownership of the old channels is a fabulously expensive resource. Do all the old owners have to pay for new channels? Instead of paying the public for new channels, it has been decided in the United States that each of the old owners of television stations will simply be given a new channel as charity. Yet, the average worker is not only deprived of the revenue that would have gone to government to reduce taxation, but must also pay for a new, more expensive television set when the new technology becomes the sole mode of transmission. Thus, existing class relations determined how the new technology will go into effect, but the new technology will shift wealth from all workers and from some capitalists to those new owners of the transmission rights. The legal compromise in the United States on acquiring the new technology also sought to balance the interests of computer production giants with the telecommunications industry – everyone's interests were considered except ordinary workers.

Conclusion

Institutionalists look at economic relations and evolution in terms of economic institutions, vested interests, conflicts of interest and mutuality of interests, also in terms of going concerns. Radical institutionalists look at class as a very important type of inequality. But they also look at race, gender, nation, ethnicity/religion, and sexual orientation. Institutionalists believe that economic institutions affect the direction of technology and whether technology advances rapidly or stagnates.

Marxists have a quite different concept of economic relations and social evolution which focuses on class relations. Class conflict is the motor of history and class relations determine the direction of technology as well as whether it advances rapidly or stagnates.

The two treatments are different, but are not incompatible. In fact, we believe the two views complement each other as two radical perceptions of reality from different angles. Having discussed our views of how economic relations affect technology in this chapter, we discuss in the next chapter how technology affects economic relations.

3

TECHNOLOGY

Both Marxists and institutionalists emphasize the importance of new technology in social evolution. But to properly understand the role of technology, one must avoid the mistake of technological reductionism, sometimes called technological determinism. Technological reductionism means that technology is the prime mover. It means that technology determines the rest of society and explains all social phenomena. Technological reductionism also means that technology develops independently, so the rest of society does not determine it. Technological reductionism is false because the relationship between technology and the rest of society is not a one-way street. We replace technological reductionism with the interdependence of technology and society.

Interdependence of technology and society –
an institutionalist view

The question of how society and technology are interrelated can be answered in three interrelated ways. The ways are not mutually exclusive. First is the "primary" way in which technology is the chief cause of change. Second is the "autonomous" view in which technology is independent of society. Third is the "interdependent" way in which society and technology are interdependent in every respect. Although combining the first two leads to technological reductionism, with proper care, each way helps understand the relationships between technology and society.

If technology is primary, the old adage that "necessity is the mother of invention" is wrong. Instead, as Thorstein Veblen would restate it, "invention is the mother of necessity." The phenomenal spread of the Internet is an illustration in which necessity was not the mother of invention, but instead, invention was the mother of necessity. At first, only a handful of computer scientists and related specialists needed the Internet at all. Hardly anyone else needed it or even knew about it, at first. But now that it has spread, virtually no middle-class home or college student can be without it. The

Internet has become a necessity for most of us, but only after it was invented. Its invention created the necessity.

If technology is primary, people and their culture do not create new technology simply because they want it or need it. People do not force technology to adapt to them and their needs. The reverse is closer to the truth. When change comes, it starts with new technology. When technology changes, humankind changes to adapt to the new technology. When technology is primary, it is not society that changes technology but technology that changes society. Technology is the senior partner, society the junior. The primacy of technology was particularly true of modern society, with its emphasis on the scientific point of view, argued Veblen, in his inimitable style.

> In the modern culture, industry, industrial processes, and industrial products have progressively gained upon humanity, until these creations of man's ingenuity have latterly come to take the dominant place in the cultural scheme; and it is not too much to say that they have become the chief force in shaping men's daily life, and therefore the chief factor in shaping men's habits of thought. Hence men have learned to think in the terms in which the technological processes act. This is particularly true of those men who by virtue of a peculiarly strong susceptibility in this direction become addicted to that habit of matter-of-fact inquiry that constitutes scientific research.
>
> (Veblen 1919: 17)

If technology is autonomous, it is independent in the sense of being self-generating. A new technology is the result of a combination or hybridization or cross-fertilization of other technologies that already exist. So the evolution of new technology is strongly affected by previously existing technology. Clarence Ayres called this the "tool-combination principle," knowing full well that technology requires far more than tools and mechanical gadgets. Nevertheless, Ayres argued that the frequently observed accelerating proliferation of new technology is due to the tool-combination principle. The more tools available, the faster they will be combined; and the faster they are combined, the more tools become available for further recombination. The general level of technology, then, becomes the result of an accelerating and self-generating process. The process is one of exponential growth. That process is autonomous because not only is the speed of the process self-generated, but the direction of the process is as well. (Further discussion, with appropriate qualification, is in Ayres, 1978, pp. 11–124.) In this autonomous view of technology, society does not affect technology, except, possibly, to slow it down.

When technology is viewed as both primary and autonomous, the unqualified result is technological reductionism. If the Internet evolves completely on its own and if its evolution leaves family members, corporate owners, government officials, and workers no choice but to adjust to it, then the Internet would be an example of primary and autonomous technology. It would be a case of technological reductionism.

Few contemporary theorists espouse technological reductionism. Few argue that technology is an independent force in history that determines the broad outline of historical evolution, both its speed and its direction, but is not itself determined by society. Few hold that technology is the Aristotelian prime mover, the one big cause. In some places in their writings both Veblen and Ayres came close to technological reductionism, but both quickly drew back from the position with numerous qualifications and caveats.

If technology and society are interdependent, then neither dominates the other in social evolution. Those with this view reject technology as the single cause and society as the single effect of evolution. We reject technology as the single cause and society as the single effect because such a view is incomplete at best. It leaves out how society affects technology and does not explain technology itself. It is a linear rather than a cumulative and circular way of understanding cause and effect. We believe that in society, the relation between cause and effect is seldom linear – just from cause to effect, from A to B. Instead, the relation between cause and effect in social relations is usually circular and cumulative – from A to B and then back from B to A, round and round in a cumulative circle. So in one round of causation, A is cause and B is effect. But then in another round, B is cause and A is effect. Cause and effect can change places. Technology causes society but society also causes technology, in a constant causal process. Technology is not the Aristotelian prime mover, the one big cause. Instead, there are many interrelated causes. Social processes affect technology and technology affects social processes. In the Internet example, the evolution of the Internet certainly has affected family members, corporate owners, government officials, and workers. However, the choices and collective actions taken by all of us strongly affect the continued evolution of the Internet in a cumulative and circular way. The reactions of families, corporations, governments, and unions all change the Internet. Then, changes in the Internet react back again on our families, corporations, governments, and unions.

Those with this interdependent view could find common theoretical ground with the anti-essentialism of Stephen A. Resnick and Richard D Wolff. Resnick and Wolff reject the traditional social scientist's search for essential causes of "apparent" complexities.

[E]ssentialism is the presumption that among the influences apparently producing any outcome, some can be shown to be inessential to its occurrence while others will be shown to be essential causes. Amid the multifaceted complexity of influences apparently surrounding, say, some historical event of interest to an essentialist, one or a subset of these influences is presumed to be the essential cause of the event. The goal of analysis for such an essentialist theory is then to find and express this essential cause and its mechanism of producing what is theorized as its effect.

(Resnick and Wolff, 1987, pp. 2–3)

In this interdependent view, technology is not the essential cause of social change, but technology is itself caught up in a whole series of interdependent relationships that constitute social change. Resnick and Wolff use the phrase "overdetermination" to describe their particular version of the interdependent view (Resnick and Wolf, 1987, p. 2). Although they would probably identify themselves as critical Marxists, Resnick and Wolf's overdetermination concept is quite descriptive of the way most institutionalists try to view the interdependence of technology and society in the evolutionary process.

Interdependence of society and technology – a Marxist view

If we dissect the technological reductionist view, it says two things:

1. Technology is the sole cause of everything else in society;
2. Technology progresses regardless of the rest of society.

The first proposition has a grain of truth in that technology does have some affect on everything else. Every day we see new revolutions in technology that change our lives – that is pretty close to a truism today, though in the middle ages when change was very slow most people would have laughed at such a strange idea.

But technology is not the only thing that affects the rest of society. It would be absurd to try to explain a political change solely in terms of technology, though new technology does play a role in political change. For example, the new information technology has changed the way politicians campaign. But other things also play a big role in explaining political events. For example, the way that politicians campaign is also greatly affected by huge financial contributions. This is partly a function of the laws on what contributions are allowable. But more important is the fact that our society has class relations in which some people have control of immense fortunes and others have nothing but debts – so some can afford huge contributions and some can afford no contribution. Moreover, the allowing of large contributions in politics is supported by the myth that this is important for the free speech of those with money – so ideology plays a role. The clear conclusion is that technology is important in explaining social phenomena, but it is not the only factor.

The second proposition – that technology progresses independently of society – is dead wrong. It seems to rely on a notion of inherent human nature to want to improve things, mixed with the idea that great men produce inventions regardless of their social environment. But it was shown at great length in Chapter 2 that the rest of society creates the conditions for technological advance, sets its direction, and determines its pace. One cannot imagine creating computers in a primitive society. Even if the idea of a computer dropped from heaven into some one's mind, nobody could take the time away from survival activities to do such a thing. The parts of computers are built in many countries, then assembled in one – so they presume, not only previous technology, but also international trade, governments to enforce agreements, and economies with some incentive to produce computers. And only in a complex society does one need a computer in the first place. Moreover, our ideology must have progressed from witchcraft to science. And so forth. Thus the rest of society determines technology, while technology is one major influence on the rest of society.

How the rest of society affects technology

We divide this vital question into three different processes: how myths affect technology, how political and social institutions affect technology, and how economic relations affect technology.

- *How myth affects technology* – this question is discussed in Chapter 4.
- *How political and social relations affect technology* – this question is discussed in Chapter 5.
- *How economic relations affect technology* – this question was discussed at length in Chapter 2.

How technology affects the rest of society

We divide this question into three different processes: how technology affects economic relations, how it affects myths and other ideology, and how it affects political democracy and other social institutions (such as education and religion).

- *How technology affects myths* – this question is discussed in Chapter 4.
- *How technology affects political and social institutions* – this question is discussed in Chapter 5.

How technology affects economic relations
– an institutionalist view

What is technology?

Technology means the way we do things. (For the classic text on technology from the institutionalist literature see Ayres 1978.) If you follow textbook economics and think of land, labor, and capital as the factors of production, then technology is not itself one of the factors of production, but is instead, the way we combine and use them. Technology uses tool-skill pairs. We do things with tools, all sorts of tools. Even ideas are used as tools. But we can only use tools if we have learned the corresponding skills required to make them work. Technology is far more than a collection of gadgets displayed in a museum or a set of patents held by an inventor. Technology is the most wonderful inheritance received by each generation of the human species. It is the community's joint stock of know-how that one generation passes on to the next through all forms of teaching and learning (Ayres 1978).

New technology, learning, and conflict

Technological progress occurs when the community's joint stock of know-how grows, when we learn how to do more things and how to do things better. The most important human relations involved in technology are learning and teaching, and so the school and laboratory are important institutions. More than just the school and laboratory, however, are involved in teaching and learning. All human institutions include substantial amounts of learning and teaching.

A culture's non-technological ideas and values may hold back or encourage technology, so they are a vital part of the process of technological creation. The leading institutions and dominant groups shape the dominant ideas and values, and these in turn may help or hinder technological improvement.

Not all learning and teaching promotes new technology. In fact, much institutionalized learning and teaching draw upon ideology and superstition rather than tools and skills. Two conflicting kinds of social learning are involved here: the learning of ideology and superstition about why things are done in the established ways versus the learning of how to do new things or how to do the old things in new ways. In times of rapid technological change and of social turmoil, the learning that goes on in different institutions can conflict. For example, the learning in the family as to why things are done in the old ways can conflict with the learning in the school of new ways. At the close of the twentieth century, ideas of hierarchy, patriarchy and purdah learned within the family can be contradicted by the equal status of students and by mixed gender classes in state-sponsored schools. Some families resist the mixing of the races or the mixing of the sexes. No stratified society is exempt from this conflict between the two kinds of learning. C. E. Ayres lamented that the family could have a very negative impact: "[I]t is the sacred right of parents to malnourish and mis-educate their children" (Ayres 1978: 181).

In school we learn (at least, we should) that all people are basically equal, men and women, different races, different religions, different ethnic groups, different classes, different sexual orientations. This kind of learning helps us work effectively with other people. As an institutional economist, I call it technological learning because it involves how to do new things and how to do things better. But in the family or the church or the media or the workplace, we are often socially conditioned into believing in elaborate systems of inequality. As an institutional economist, I call such social conditioning ceremonial learning because it teaches us that certain people deserve the credit for good things while certain other people deserve the blame for bad things. The first group is to be emulated. It is ceremonially pure and good. The second group is to be scapegoated. It is ceremonially impure and bad. Ceremonial learning runs counter to technological learning, but is required to shore up the power of the patriarch in the family, the hierarchy in the church, the political elite in the nation, and the owner in the workplace (Bowles and Gintis 1976, Dewey 1961, R. Dugger 1974, Veblen 1965).

Frontier America provides a vivid illustration of ceremonial learning. After the Revolutionary War and up until the late nineteenth century, European Americans conquered indigenous tribes, seized from European claimants and purchased the contiguous 48 states, and then Alaska and Hawaii. The Iroquois Confederation and the Creek Federation were crushed. President Andrew Jackson forced The Five Civilized Tribes to move to Oklahoma. The plains tribes and others were hunted, starved, and more or less subdued – Sitting Bull and others were forced to pay with their lives for defeating Custer at the Little Bighorn – the last great battle of the conquest. During the centuries of conquest European Americans taught themselves that it was their "Manifest Destiny" to control the continent, to subdue the savages occupying it, and civilize them if possible or kill and incarcerate them if not. The conquerors claimed ceremonial purity and goodness for themselves and assigned ceremonial impurity and badness to the conquered. So, it came to be that in ceremonial teaching, we – their offspring – learned that the Native Americans were inferior. They were "savages" who massacred, tortured and raped. But the Europeans were superior. They were pilgrims who tamed the wilderness, settled the land, made it fruitful, and gave civilization to those former savages who were able to accept it. To the victor went the spoils, including the power to whitewash what really happened. That whitewashing is ceremonial learning. (Further reading on these issues is in Bird 1996; Dunbar-Ortiz 1998, Foreman 1934 and Jahoda 1995.)

Technological learning is different from ceremonial. It is not about who is superior and who inferior. It is about how to do things better and how to do new things. You could say that technological learning teaches us how to get a job done while ceremonial learning teaches us who to credit for doing the job. Technological learning touches everything we do, stretching far beyond the workplace and the method of production. Technology is important in all human activities and affects all social relations. It can generate conflict and meet resistance in any of them.

Social instability and technology

On one hand, a given level of technology is maintained, institutionalists believe, when a society is stable. Then, people keep learning and doing the same things in the same ways, generation after generation. The community does not change. On the other hand, when new technology finds its way into society, stability is disrupted. Then people begin learning and doing different things or learning how to do the old things in different ways. The community changes as a result. New technology can cause social change, but particularly in stratified societies, it almost never comes without conflict.

New technology (new learning) changes virtually any kind of society, even very static ones. It disrupts old routines and discredits old conventions. In textbook economics, routines and conventions are viewed as external interference with the rational consumer or the rational producer as she maximizes her utility or maximizes her profit in the natural harmony of interests assumed to exist in the free market system. But routines and conventions do not interfere with the pursuit of economic interests. Instead, routines and conventions make that pursuit possible. Without them, there is chaos. Economic interests cannot be pursued in a natural harmony of interests because in the real world outside the textbooks, interests do not naturally harmonize themselves.

There is a big difference between the natural harmony assumed in the textbooks and the created harmony found in the world. The first is a product of smoke and mirrors. The second is a product of social evolution. In the world around us, humans have both conflict of interests and mutuality of interests. That is, one person's interests conflict with another, but each person also shares with others a mutuality of interests along with their conflict of interests. For example, in a corporation, the workers want higher wages at the expense of lower profits for the owners – conflict of interests. But, both the company's workers and its owners have a mutuality of interests in keeping the company going so it will pay one of them wages and the other one profits. If the company collapses, they both lose.

To hold their societies together, humans must create a harmony of interests out of their conflict and mutuality of interests. They do so through creating working rules of behavior. Routines and conventions are such working rules of behavior which make it possible for all of us to pursue our conflicting interests within a mutually-accepted structure. Examples are everywhere. Any set of human beings that groups itself together is made up of individuals with their own conflicting interests. But as a group, they also share a mutual interest in continuing the group. Here is a very simple group: Members of a college chess club, for example, will want the club to continue, but each member will want something at least slightly different from the club. Conflict will arise out of when the club should meet, who should lead the club, how individual matches and tournaments should be organized, how members should be recruited, what dues should be paid? These conflicts will either destroy the club to the mutual detriment of all its members or will be worked out through the evolution of club rules, routines, conventions.

Rules, routines, conventions, working rules and laws – all make up the structure of the social world. The market itself is such a structure (Dugger 1992: 87–115). New technology can disrupt that structure. New technology can cause structural change.

To capture what is going on with new technology, new learning, and conflict over them, institutionalists paint their pictures of social evolution with very fine strokes. They usually find that using class interest as a paint brush results in too broad a stroke to capture the details they seek. Following John R. Commons on this point, they seek the details found in the conflict of interests and mutuality of interests that go into a created harmony of interests. You could even say that institutionalism is a micro-economics while Marxism is a macro-economics of technological change.

Vested interests and institutionalized resistance

What new technology does is disrupt and discredit old ways of doing things, and doing so leads to changes in social roles and status. In the days before the internal combustion engine was used to make powerful tractors and automobiles, the village blacksmith occupied a position of status. His ability to shoe horses and repair wagons and carriages yielded him a decent income in most villages and towns across the country. His shop was an important gathering place and his opinion on many practical matters was influential. But new technology changed all that. The automobile and the tractor destroyed the village blacksmith and his shop. People began doing things differently. The job, status, and income of the blacksmith went elsewhere. In fact, a whole new industrial complex grew up in his place. By creating new things to do and new roles for new people to perform, new technology lowers the status and the income attached to old roles and old ways of doing things. Old socially conditioned beliefs, values, and meanings give way to new ones as the new people and their new roles come to believe in what they are doing, come to value what they are doing, and come to give meaning to what they are doing. Such changes articulate the new order – fit it into and express it in terms of and/or in place of the old order. (The best discussion is still Veblen 1919: 1–55.)

Such changes in roles and status benefit some people and harm others. So, if they understand how they are affected by new technology, those who are benefited promote it while those who are harmed resist it. For example, during the Industrial Revolution in England, the landed aristocracy frequently resisted the advance of the new industrial capitalists. The landed aristocrats knew full well that the rising industrialists were a threat, not just to the income of the aristocrats, but also to their social role and status – to their very way of life.

However, it is seldom easy to predict exactly how a specific new technology will be used, let alone how it will affect the incomes, status, and roles of different groups. A simple new aid to writing, introduced at the turn of the nineteenth century in Europe, illustrates the unpredictable nature of specific technologies. People who were blind had trouble telling when their quill pens ran out of ink (no ball points back then). So they could labor hard and long, only to find that they produced blank pages. In a case of necessity being the mother of invention, someone invented carbon paper and a hard writing stylus so that blank pages would no longer be a problem for blind writers. However, invention then became the mother of necessity, when carbon paper became essential for all kinds of uses, including business communications and other applications. It would have been difficult to predict the spread of carbon paper far beyond the use of the blind. Now, of course, carbon paper has become outmoded because of copying machines and blind people can use voice recognition systems to write with.

Technology and unpredictability

Its unpredictability means that new technology may sneak change into a society, behind the backs of its powerful groups. The automobile is an important example. Automobiles came into use for a variety of reasons, most of which were far removed from the social changes actually wrought by the automobile. For one thing, the automobile transformed relations within the family. When women and younger members of the family learned to drive, the power of the family patriarch was reduced. Perhaps Amish patriarchs, most of whom refuse to own autos, have been aware all along of the auto's effect on their power and status as patriarchs? Be that as it may, most folks did not predict the family changes caused by the car. The same is frequently true of other kinds of new technologies. Seldom can technology be counted on to affect society in a predictable manner. Instead, technology can usually be counted on to change, and to change the surrounding society in hard to predict ways. Furthermore, those who feel threatened by it can be counted on to resist new technology. But it is hard for folks to determine whether they are threatened by a specific new technology or not. And, of course, those who feel benefited by new technology can be counted on to promote it. But again, it is not always so clear that those who think they will be benefited actually are.

Technology not only has an immediate effect on production processes and workers, but it also has powerful effects on consumption and consumers. Technology enters the social system not only through the sphere of production, but also through all forms of human activities. Automobile technology not only affected society through its transformation of the factory, but also through its transformation of the family, city, and nation. Technology becomes embodied in all kinds of skills and tools, that much is clear. However, technology also becomes embodied in all kinds of social relationships and just how it does so is not at all clear to those who implement the new technology.

Specific groups of workers in specific industries can figure out how specific new machines and new processes will affect their immediate jobs. Blacksmiths quickly recognized the automobile and the tractor as their enemies. Specific groups of owners in specific industries can figure out how specific new technology will affect their profits. Both groups will act in terms of their interests, and either resist or promote the new technology (see Landes 1969, and Braverman 1974). Nonetheless, the general question of how new technology will affect the broader reaches of society is an extraordinarily difficult one to answer. So how different groups will respond to the new technology – resist or promote it – is hard to tell beforehand.

New technologies involve far more than worker resistance to automation and capitalist promotion of it. The new technologies of the 1940s and the 1950s, along with the new roles performed in the wars (WWII and Korean) profoundly altered what it meant to be a person of color in the United States. The mechanical cotton pickers and the war production assembly lines were particularly important in the great migration from the agrarian south to the industrial north. A material/technological foundation composed of newly intertwined roles and tool-skill combinations was laid out by these new technologies. These new intertwining influences affected the great civil rights movement because it changed many people of color from being isolated sharecroppers into being urban industrial workers. Furthermore, these new intertwining issues also made the women's movement possible and ready to begin action because they changed many women from isolated housewife to urban worker.

Nonetheless, while technology giveth; it also taketh away. New technology does not necessarily have liberating effects on members of oppressed groups. As the new technologies of the freeway system and the suburb altered forever what it means to be an urban family in a large northern city, those new technologies also facilitated the massive white flight from the increasingly black core of the city. Good jobs, good housing, good schools, good doctors, good hospitals and good recreational facilities all moved away from the new migrants, away from the African Americans who had come so far to gain so little.

The technologies of the automobile and the suburb seem to have changed almost everything. They have helped change what it means to be a woman in a male-centered world; what it means to be a person of color in a culture of white supremacy; what it means to live in the city; and what it means to live in the country. More examples of the impact of new technologies abound. The point is, new technology alters the very meaning of our lives and institutions and it does so in unpredictable ways.

Although such alterations may never be predictable, they can be understood. The way to understand the impact of a new technology is to trace out how its new tool-skill combinations alter the roles performed by large segments of society. Cultural meaning and social role go hand-in-hand. As the social-economic roles many women perform have changed because of new technologies, so too have the cultural meanings of being a woman.

Technology, culture, and conflict

As the role of being a worker outside the home has gained at the expense of being a wife and mother inside the home, the values of women have also changed. Herein lies the origin of the great cultural conflicts that have rocked the United States in recent years. Significant numbers of women now possess and act out new kinds of values, values that seem very threatening to women who still possess and act out the old values, also very threatening to men who find that the new values of many women conflict with their values. Religious revivalism, misogyny, reactionary men's movements, and gay bashing have arisen in this cultural context.

The changing roles of many African Americans have changed the values of many African Americans. The changes seem threatening to some African Americans and to most European Americans. The new separatism in the black community and the new racism in the white have sprung up in this cultural context. Of course, many other factors are also involved, for culture is exceedingly complex. Nevertheless, the strong impact on culture of new technology cannot be denied. New technology introduces new meanings, beliefs, and values into the cultural mix of processes and factors. The direction of change is often unexpected. Technology is so thoroughly intertwined with culture, with meanings, beliefs, and values, that Richard Brinkman says,

> [C]ulture functions as a storage bank of man's accumulated knowledge and provides the mechanism or vehicle for passing this knowledge on from generation to generation. Culture provides a blueprint or code for human behavior and in this regard serves as man's social DNA.
>
> (Brinkman, 1981, p. 107)

Each generation tries to pass the values, meanings, and beliefs of their culture (the old learning) on to the next generation. But, new technology alters the roles that the new generation plays. The culture of the old generation is devalued and demeaned as a result, creating the generation gap – a kind of cultural lag.

How new technology affects vested interest and class structure

Recall that the upper class is the leisure class. Its members show off their exemption from work with conspicuous leisure and show off their ability to pay with conspicuous consumption. Members of the leisure class are not interested in working with the latest technology; but instead are interested in making more money and in improving their own status. Their privileged position is maintained by their vested interest in income. In the current period, that vested interest is crystallized increasingly in the form of absentee ownership of corporate stock.

If technology never changed, and if new institutions never arose, members of the leisure class could continue receiving their income and enjoying it without having to manage it. Individual fortunes might rise and fall, the number of observations falling within different statistical intervals of family income might rise and fall as well. Nevertheless, without new technologies or new institutions, there would be no structural change, no social evolution.

New institutions and new technologies induce structural change because they require new sets of skills and new authority relations between people participating in society's going concerns. As new technology continues being implemented, new sources of income emerge to enlarge some flows of commercial traffic and to shrink others. New relations to wealth begin to emerge. Joseph Schumpeter coined the phrase "creative destruction" to describe the changes that take place.

Health care is an excellent illustration. New technology and new institutions are transforming health care in the United States. On the technology side, new and improved surgical procedures, drugs, and therapies of all kinds have drastically increased expenditures on health care. Health care specialists are learning how to do more things for us and how to do old things for us much better. On the institutional side, Medicare and Medicaid have drastically increased government participation in health care. Furthermore, the rapid spread of the Health Maintenance Organization (HMO) has changed health care even more. A look at the HMO will illustrate a change in authority within the health care system. HMOs are raising the authority of some health care specialists at the expense of the authority of others. The patient's Primary Care Physician now acts as a gatekeeper to other health care specialists. If patients want to see the dermatologist because they fear they have skin cancer, they must first get their Primary Care Physician to refer them. Otherwise, the HMO will not pay for the dermatologist. Primary Care Physicians are gaining authority. Medical specialists are losing it. Can income and status be far behind? Furthermore, even the recommendation of the Primary Care Physician can be rejected by the insurance company funding the HMO. So the authority and profits of the insurance company gain over everyone else. And then, what about patients and their freedom to choose? It used to be that critics of so-called socialized medicine warned us that it would take away our freedom to choose our own physicians. Now, with privately managed care, we are free to choose, as long as the physician we choose is on the approved list of the insurance company and HMO.

Structural change means that some vested interests are destroyed; others are created. The whole system may begin to evolve as old vested interests become threatened and collapse and as new ones open up and become entrenched. New occupations rise as new tool-skill combinations are created by new technologies and new institutions. Old occupations fall. Perhaps, whole classes rise and fall with the new technology. New values, beliefs, and meanings begin to emerge in the culture. People experience new ways of doing things and new things to do. They drive cars instead of carriages. They party in the backseat instead of spoon on the front porch. They find new ways of getting incomes. Other people lose their old ways of getting income. Those who gain learn how to justify and defend the new relationships. Those who lose learn how to attack and criticize the new relationships. The justifications and the criticisms remold the culture.

The rise of the automobile is an example of a new technology that caused evolutionary change not only in industrial production and class relations but also in sexual morality, gender relations, family structure, community living patterns, and much else. The rise of the Internet is a more recent example of new technology giving rising to evolutionary change. The internet is not only remolding the structure of the economy by spawning new industries, new occupations, new vested interests, but it is also remolding the structure of the culture by spawning new values, new meanings, and new beliefs. A generation gap is already discernible and cultural lags are opening up between those who are and those who are not keeping up with high-tech developments.

How technology affects economic relations
– a Marxist view

Without technological improvement, as we shall see in this chapter, there would have never been any change in social structures. But, as we saw in Chapter 2, without a social structure there never would have been any technological improvement. So we must examine the interaction of technology and society. The Marxist literature is discussed in Sherman (1972, Chapters 2 and 3; 1987, Chapter 3; and 1995, Chapters 2, 3, and 4).

Primitive society

For millions of years, humanity lived in small bands of closely related people as an extended family (see the excellent book by Diamond 1997, for material in this section). Primitive technology consisted of crude stone tools, used to gather wild fruit and vegetables and to hunt wild animals. There were small bands consisting of extended families and there was little contact with other bands. Within the band, everyone worked together and ate the food together. In this primitive economy, there were no specialists and no leisure class because only if everyone worked together would enough food be found and taken to survive. A single individual could not produce a surplus above his/her basic needs, so slavery was not profitable and did not exist. There was no organized government; if a person performed very well in hunting, they might temporarily lead the hunt; and if they performed very well in gathering food, they might lead for a while in that activity. Since there was almost no private property worth anything, and since there was little contact with other bands, there was almost no warfare and no prisoners of war. A rare prisoner would be brought into the band, or eaten or simply killed.

Tools changed very, very little for millions of years, partly because no one had the leisure to specialize and invent at this low level of productivity.

The economic relations also did not change. If they did not all work together, neither the individual nor the band could survive, so the social relations were reproduced by harsh necessity day after day at that low level of technology.

Diamond sums up the social relations reproduced for several million years in the primitive communal society of the band as follows: "Hunter-gatherer societies tend to be egalitarian, to lack full-time bureaucrats and hereditary chiefs ... no ... specialists are possible at subsistence level" (Diamond 1997: 89–90).

Then, 7 to 13 thousand years ago (estimates differ widely, but Diamond says 13 thousand) there was the beginning of agriculture and herding in a few areas: the Middle East, Central America, and China. The process took a few thousand years because the primitive social system did not encourage the changes, but finally there was a settled, agricultural society in a few regions. But once humanity evolved to agriculture, Diamond says: "Once food can be stock-piled, a political elite can gain control of food produced by others, assert the right of taxation, escape the need to feed itself, and engage in full-time political activities" (1997: 90). The surplus produced by agriculture and herding means that the elite can also employ full-time warriors to fight, priests "to justify" wars and elite rule, metallurgists to make plows and swords, and scribes to record information on battles and ownership. Division of labor increases productivity, so slavery becomes profitable and prisoners of war are made slaves. The elite group becomes a slave-owning class. Diamond finds the first well-developed slave-based agriculture, with division of labor, including specialists, priests, and nobles, probably arising first in Mesopotamia.

It is worth emphasizing that the advent of agriculture did not merely improve productivity, but eventually changed every aspect of society. How exactly was each of the sectors of the social fabric of a non-class society changed by this one invention, that is, agriculture? First, it caused a cumulative change in other technology. Agriculture raised productivity, so the community could assign specialists in various crafts and support them from the surplus of agriculture. The division of labor allowed specialists to invent better tools, first better stone tools, then metallic tools. Thus, productivity was raised still further. Groups need no longer be nomadic, but could build towns on the basis of a stable agricultural product. People could accumulate some personal property in clothing, houses, and so forth. Population density could increase rapidly, supplying a labor force.

Pre-capitalist, class-divided societies

Slavery became profitable because a slave could now produce more in one day than the slave's own subsistence. It also became profitable to make war for others' property and for slaves. The prisoners of war were no longer killed, eaten, or freed – they were sold into slavery. Thus, the class relations were changed so that there were slaves and masters, though in some areas there were also free citizens who did not own slaves. But slave owners were the ones who accumulated large amounts of wealth and ran the political system. Thus, there was a ruling class with leisure time.

Class division and slavery requires force and violence to hold the slaves, as well as to resolve property disputes between slave owners. So there were police and armies, judges and kings. In addition to force, it was necessary to have myths to convince people of the righteousness of their society. So there were priests and monks and nuns. In terms of culture, the rulers also had the leisure time to have some of their number create art and mathematics and philosophy. The role of political institutions is discussed in detail in Chapter 5.

Ideology and mythology changed drastically. No longer was the collective good of the whole tribe in hunting or gathering food a supreme goal strongly enforced by society. Now the deeds of rulers were enshrined and the behavior of rich men often discussed and emulated to the best of people's ability. Although there were remembrances of the earlier collective ethic in Greek and Roman myths and traditions, the slave societies became strongly individualist in their actual ethical behavior, at least among the ruling classes. The role of ideology and myth is discussed in detail in Chapter 4.

Thus, particular class relations gave rise to a major change in technology, which brought about further changes in technology, changes in ideology, changes in institutions, and changes in class relationships. On the basis of the new institutions and class relationships, there would be a new and dramatically different path for technological development.

As noted in the previous chapter, division of labor enabled these early slave based societies to accomplish great feats. Pyramids could not have been built without thousands of slaves, agriculture to feed them, and a social system and army to coerce and coordinate the slaves. While the early slave societies made great advances (writing, metal tools, architecture, and art), it was also pointed out in the last chapter that slavery in the later Roman empire eventually led to stagnation of the forces of production. The reasons for the stagnation are discussed in Chapter 8 of this book. For the full and complex story of the ancient civilizations, built in some part on slavery, the transition to feudalism in some areas, and the operation of serfdom under the feudal system, the best single Marxist source is Perry Anderson (1996).

Most systems of serfdom, or mixed slavery and serfdom (of which there were many), were subject to some periods of stagnation. But the west European form of serfdom and feudalism gave a few more incentives to serfs and lords than some other systems. So after a thousand years or so of feudalism and serfdom in western Europe, there had accumulated very, very slowly some of the forces of production necessary for capitalism and some of the elements of capitalist class relations in some areas. Chapter 8 will summarize some of the very extensive and controversial Marxist literature on the transition from feudalism to capitalism While most of the debate is left to Chapter 8, a few preliminary points need to be noted here. First of all, the process included many revolts or class conflicts between the serfs and the lords. Second, it included several political revolutions led by the emerging capitalist class or bourgeoisie, including merchants, lenders, master craftsmen, and eventually small manufacturers. Knowledge of this experience was one thing that led Marx and Engels to claim that class conflict is the driving force of social evolution. As we shall see in Chapter 8, the bourgeoisie eventually revolted against feudalism because they found that the class relations and political institutions of feudalism constrained their activities and reduced their profits – they were aided against the old feudal ruling class by the peasants and by the newly emerging urban working class (still mostly artisans and crafts people).

Capitalism

In the last chapter Marx and Engels were cited – in half a sentence – as saying: "The bourgeoisie cannot exist without constantly revolutionizing the instruments of production ..." (Marx and Engels 1848: 12). In other words, the class relations of capitalism are such that capitalist entrepreneurs – the bourgeoisie – are forced to rapidly improve technology. But the complete sentence from Marx and Engels says: "The bourgeoisie cannot exist without constantly revolutionizing the instruments of production and thereby the relations of production and with them the whole relations of society" (Marx and Engels 1848: 12). Whereas the first part of the sentence says that the class relations of capitalism determine its technology, the second half says that technology determines its class relations (and the rest of society). As Marx always emphasized the role of class relations and class conflict in evolution, some writers alleged that he was a "class reductionist", who reduced every explanation to class. However, since Marx emphasizes how technology undermines and eventually changes class relations and society, many writers have said that Marx was a "technological reductionist", who reduced all explanations to technology. Obviously, both assertions cannot be correct because you can't say that X determines everything and at the same time that Y determines everything – the truth is that neither assertion about Marx is correct.

The Marxist position may be stated more carefully as follows: First, the class relations of capitalism (or any stratified, class-divided society) shape new technology determining its form and direction at any given time, whether it will go forward rapidly, or whether it will stagnate. Second, whatever technology emerges, it then has an effect on the class relations and the rest of society. If society produces a rapid development of technology, then it slowly undermines the old class relations and old social relations and old myths and replaces them by new ones. But we shall see that a third point is necessary: when it comes to the basic structure of economic institutions and class relations in a class-divided society, such as who holds power and who gets exploited, any possible change meets immense resistance from the old ruling class and generally requires a revolution to accomplish it. The first proposition was examined in Chapter 2; let us examine the other two hypotheses.

In the routine working of a capitalist society, technology is embodied in capitalist investments in new capital. Most capital investments are merely used to replace worn out plant and equipment. Some portion, however, in an expansion is not just reproduction, but is net addition to new plant and equipment. The capitalist orders whatever level of technology is currently available within his/her budget limits. Thus even when something is labeled "replacement" by accounting, it may actually involve new technology. If nothing new is on the market, then profit maximization determines that replacement will be at the same level of technology. But every large firm has its own research unit. Thus, it will often use new technology in the replacement of capital or in the expansion of capital.

If the firm is competitive, it will be forced to use the best available technology. If it has monopoly power, it may stick with an outmoded technology for a long time. One should keep in mind that the reproduction of capital is different from the reproduction of technology, since the amount of capital may remain the same while the technology is new.

The capitalist system is usually reproduced in new capital, new technology, and the old class relations without recourse to force and violence. But repression, force and violence will be used when needed in the eyes of the ruling class, that is, when they feel threatened by a real or imaginary threat. Thus, force was used against the socialist government in Spain in the 1930s to install the dictatorship of Franco; more than a million Communists were killed in Indonesia in the 1960s to install the dictatorship of Suharto; the President and many others were killed in Chile in the 1970s to overthrow the legally elected socialist government and install the dictatorship of Pinochet, and many other such cases. Repression was used against the US Left in the 1950s (when this author was given an Undesirable Discharge from the US Army for political reasons, later changed to Honorable Conditions as a result of a successful class action suit in the US Supreme Court in the 1960s). It is easy to understand how a static society is reproduced; the question is why it ever changes.

61

Marx's writings on social evolution are scattered throughout his work and not collected at any one point. Engels, in *The Origin of the Family, State and Private Property*, does discuss technology throughout the book in terms of its evolutionary role. The classic Western Marxist anthropological discussion of the role of technology in evolution was V. Gordon Childe in his book *Social Evolution* (1948). The Marxist literature since then on the role of technology in evolution is discussed in Sherman (1972 Chapters 2 and 3, 1987 Chapter 3, and 1995 Chapters 2, 3, and 4).

Obviously, technology influences capitalist society. In the modern capitalist world, think of the enormous changes in behavior and institutions that have been wrought by computers, automobiles, contraceptives, radio, television, airplanes, and so forth. But each of these innovations had its shape determined by the social-economic environment of given class relations.

Incremental change in capitalism

An excellent book by Greenbaum (1995) argues that computers have caused change in the relationship of workers and bosses in offices, but that the direction of change has been determined solely by the profit drive of business. Computers in the 1950s were huge, expensive and not very reliable, so only expert programmers ran them. Then generation after generation became smaller, more powerful, and more reliable. This eventually allowed their widespread use by clerical and professional workers. Greenbaum (1995, Chapter 2) shows how computers in the 1950s and 1960s were seen as the solution to all problems in the office. Managers wanted to cut costs by more and more sophisticated tools and less and less sophisticated workers. By the 1970s, according to Greenbaum (1995, Chapter 4), managers dreamed of making office work like factory work, closely controlled and monitored. But the dream remains somewhat elusive. Computers were designed to help routinize and divide tasks. Eventually, however, it was found that extreme routinization and division of clerical labor actually reduced efficiency. At first there were typing pools in the basement, with computers designed for this use. But it was eventually found necessary to restore many private secretaries – and even cheaper to teach many lower executives to use their own computer. By the 1990s professionals were doing all their own typing, while secretaries were limited to managers. More and more pieces of white collar work were cut into small pieces, routinized, and automated.

Then by the 1990s PCs were designed for networks, so the whole labor force could be connected. In the 1990s it was also discovered that productivity can stay high with the use of computers by the worker at home. The productivity is enforced by piecework under the name of projects with deadlines. The only drawback is the total isolation of the worker from companionship of other adults all day. Computer hardware and software are designed for the tasks wanted by business, not for the convenience, comfort or safety of workers. In other words, the class relations of production determine the various options affecting the forces of production, such as hardware, software, and job organization.

It must be stressed that the short-run incremental change of technology is directed in ways that are decided according to the existing class relations, but in the long run the continued change of technology and the other forces of production may lead to a whole new situation. In other words, each individual firm tries to shape technology to its advantage, but the aggregate flood of new technology is not controlled by any firm or planned by any agency. Thus the continued advance of the forces of production – even though it has been created by the existing class relations in a direction thought to be helpful at each moment by each firm – may eventually lead to major pressures for change in existing class relations and economic institutions (as we shall see below).

Resistance to change in class relations

The usual tendency of the dominant class – including the major corporations in the United States – is toward retention of the status quo in economic institutions and class relations because that is the source of their power and wealth, so it will be shown below that there is usually resistance to institutional change. We have seen that the class system is usually kept from change by routine economic forces, political institutions, and myths, but that force and violence is used to maintain the status quo if peaceful means don't work.

Improved technology is beneficial to the short-run interests of those members of the dominant class who first introduce it. Once the class relations of capitalism have produced new technology, technological change has caused capitalism to go through a number of stages, but it is still capitalism.

In the United States, capitalism was mainly underdeveloped and agricultural from the Revolutionary War to the Civil War. Most of the people were still farmers, neither hiring employees nor being employed by capitalists. But by the Civil War, industry had grown substantially in the North. After slavery was defeated, industry grew very rapidly in the United States, so that the era of small farms and small business was left behind and giant firms with monopoly power dominated the economy by the early twentieth century. This stage has been called monopoly capitalism.

Many of these changes came gradually and peacefully. As an example, in the mid-nineteenth century most people in the United States were still small farmers self-employed. But this slowly changed as a result of technological change and the accumulation of capital in giant firms, where former farmers had to learn how to be industrial workers. By the mid-twentieth century most people were workers, employed by capitalist industrial and service firms. The change from agriculture to industry and service as the majority of value-producing economic sectors obviously reflected an enormous change in the forces of production. The result was a complete change in relative class power, though no change in the basic relations of capitalism occurred.

Within the change from agriculture to industry in the United States, the vital change by the time of the Civil War was the rise of Northern industry to a greater economic power than Southern slave plantations. Both Northern industry and Southern slavery tried to expand into the West, bringing conflicts as in Missouri and Kansas. The basic change ending slavery in the South was resisted violently by the southern slave owners and required the bloody class conflict known as the Civil War, leading to the eventual eradication of the slave owning class. The industrial revolution in the United States thus included both a technological revolution and a dramatic change in social and class relations. It might be said that the class relations of Northern capitalism led to the industrial revolution in the Northern United States, which eventually caused a change in class relations (the end of slavery), but that change was not smooth and automatic; it required the long and violent Civil War.

The Great Depression of the 1930s led to considerable increase in government intervention in the economy. Then the Second World War caused an enormous growth in government. After the second World War, in addition to the continued military drive, technologies such as nuclear energy and space exploration required continued government intervention. So we went from a stage of monopoly capitalism to a stage of monopoly-with-government capitalism.

Finally, with the aid of the information revolution of the 1980s and 1990s, as well as the demise of the Soviet Union, capitalism has spread to be truly world wide and integrated in many ways. For example, all the stock markets of the world are closely tied together by the information network, so when one collapses, they are all immediately affected. Furthermore, each industry in the world-wide market is rapidly coming to be dominated by just a few firms, so there is world-wide oligopoly and monopoly power. Individual governments and individual labor movements, who wish to make progressive changes, face the power of the giant international firms. This is still very much a capitalist economic system, motivated by unlimited private greed, but it is a new stage of capitalism with new dynamics. Thus, the present stage of capitalism is characterized by global integration, government intervention, and monopoly power.

Major reform in capitalism

Let us turn to the US New Deal of the 1930s as an example of institutional reform in a complex class-divided society. It is a classic example of the lag between the productive forces and the class relations. In the orthodox, neoclassical view, such a long continuing depression is not easy to explain. In their view, there is no involuntary unemployment and the system only declines because of outside shocks. This leaves nothing much to be explained or to worry about – because the system should adjust quite rapidly. But institutionalists and Marxists are all agreed that it was the institutions of capitalism that gave rise to the Great Depression. The institutionalist, Wesley Mitchell, showed how each stage of the capitalist business cycle derives from the dynamics of the previous stage. John Maynard Keynes and Karl Marx both showed that aggregate demand may be well below aggregate supply, causing a depression, as a result of the internal dynamics of capitalism.

In the late 1920s production was rising, profits were rising, and the distribution of income was getting worse. By 1929, there was insufficient aggregate demand (while unit costs did not change much). Why was there a deficiency of aggregate demand? Marx explains aggregate demand in terms of class income. Workers are exploited and the rate at which they are exploited determines profits as well as wages in the aggregate. The increasing productivity gains went automatically to the corporations under the capitalist rules of the game. Workers had to negotiate or strike to get their share – so workers lagged behind and had to play catch up; thus the share of labor declined in the late 1920s. But this causes a problem for consumer demand. The ratio of consumption out of profits is far lower than that out of wages because capitalists have far higher incomes and can use much of them to save and perhaps to invest. Thus the structure of class relationships and the power of opposing classes caused a limited aggregate demand in 1929. Workers are always playing catch-up by negotiation or strikes. Thus the ratio of wages to profits declines in every expansion, causing aggregate demand to be limited. The worsening profit outlook (as all other factors influencing profits remained about the same) reduced investment. The lower investment led to a recession, which was exacerbated by financial panic into the Great Depression. This is a highly oversimplified description, but the economics of capitalist depressions are examined in detail in Sherman, 1991. The only important point here is that the class relations of capitalism were such as to hold back production, investment, and technological growth for ten long years.

As a result, the relatively peaceful class relations of the 1920s were ended and class conflict broke out in the form of strikes as well as political turmoil. The Socialist and Communist parties increased their votes many fold, while the Democrats won a landslide victory in 1932. There followed a series of radical reforms: unemployment compensation for unemployed workers, social security for old age, maximum hours for work, minimum wages for work, and legalization of union bargaining and strikes. These reforms – caused by a structural tension leading to a class conflict – changed the structure of the US economy to a significant degree, but they did not change the basic institutions and relationships of capitalism.

Some readers may think that the Great Depression is irrelevant ancient history. But the underlying class relations and economic institutions of capitalism have continued, so the problem has also continued. It is shown every time that a recession results in a fall in production and a rise in mass unemployment. It is also shown in a story in the *Los Angeles Times* in 1999 subtitled "American farmers are in a financial crisis; while supply is up, the demand for products is down" (Simon 1999: 1). The story carefully explains that improved technology has increased the production potential of American farms, but crisis conditions in economies of Asia, Africa, and Russia mean that people just do not have the money to demand more food and in fact are eating less food. Of course, there are millions and millions of people going hungry in the world (even in the United States) and some dying of starvation every day, but they have only the desire for food, not the monetary demand. By contrast, the richest capitalists no longer count their money in millions, but in billions – and the three richest men in America have as much money as the Gross Domestic Product of the poorest 45 nations. The world is now mostly capitalist, so this disparity and tension is due to the class relations of capitalism which are impeding the forces of production in this dramatic way.

Two revolutions

Finally let us examine revolutionary change in institutions in the case of the rise and fall of the Soviet Union – this example is discussed in detail in Sherman, 1995, Chapter 10. In 1917, Russia was a weak and backward society ruled by an almost absolute Czar. The countryside was still semi-feudal with great landowners and very poor peasants, many organized into villages collectively liable for taxes and rents. Agricultural productivity was far lower than any other European country. More than 80 per cent of the population were peasants. The cities held some large factories and the beginnings of an industrial working class, but most of the factories were owned by foreigners from Germany, France, and England. Only 10–15 per cent of the population was literate. These social-economic conditions held back potential growth and improvement of technology. Defeat in the First World War, peasant revolts for land, and lack of food in the cities sparked a revolution, first a democratic and capitalist revolution, then a socialist revolution. The class relations of a semi-feudal, semi-capitalist society had prevented

Russia from having a rapid increase of its forces of production. This led to class conflict, which – under the stress of war – ended in a revolution.

The economic backwardness, Civil War, and foreign intervention led to a repressive dictatorship and an over-centralized, dictatorial-run, government-owned economy. This economy did succeed by draconian measures in developing the Soviet Union into the second largest economy in the world, but at the cost of human misery and deepening repression. The economy was able to cope less and less well with the needs of a complex productive system.

Modern complex systems cannot be run efficiently by dictatorships, especially with over-centralized planning. The leadership recognized the purely economic side of the problem as early as the 1960s and attempted decentralizing reforms, but the ruling class of middle-level Party leaders, bureaucrats, and industrial managers successfully resisted all attempts at reform through the 1960s, 1970s, and 1980s – because any real reform would greatly reduce their power. By the end of the 1980s the growth rate had dropped so low that the ruling class was forced to deal with the problem – and the working class was becoming restive. Finally, most of the ruling class decided that they could profit as well or better under capitalism and suddenly many commissars became capitalists. A counter-revolution ended the state-run economy and attempted to install a capitalist system from above – but the attempt resulted in a backward, crisis-ridden type of capitalism.

What led to the counter-revolution of 1990 and the restoration of capitalism was the fact that Soviet political-economic institutions and class relations became a barrier to further progress in technology, so this triggered class conflict leading to this new revolution in Russia.

Conclusion

Different Voices

Our discussion of technology and social evolution has been in two different voices – the Marxist and the institutionalist. But then the extraordinary complexity of social evolution justifies using two of them. How else could we emphasize class and the broad sweep of historical change – done so well in the Marxist voice – while also emphasizing vested interests and institutions – done so well in the institutionalist voice? To do justice to a complex song, a duet presentation is better than a solo one.

Same song

In spite of our conceptual (tonal) differences, we are singing the same song. In Chapter 2 we agreed that economic relations and much more influence technology, including the direction of technology and its rate of growth (ranging from rapid to negative). Also in spite of our conceptual differences, in Chapter 3 we have agreed that technology influences economic relations and much else, often undermining social relations, sometimes in the direction of collapse or radical change.

These are important notes in an evolutionary song (theory), common to both voices. But they are not the whole scale. Many more notes could be added. In Chapter 4 we examine the role of myths and in Chapter 5 we examine the role of the political process.

4

ENABLING MYTH

This chapter is on enabling myth, again as a dialogue. Those who want further institutionalist discussion of enabling myth should consult Dugger (1994), while those who want further Marxist discussion should consult (Henry 1990: 11–18). In this chapter, we first examine how enabling myths affect society, then ask how society affects enabling myths.

How enabling myths affect society

We divide this question into three parts: the effect of myths on economic relations, the effect on political and social institutions, and the effect on technology.

How do enabling myths affect economic relations and vested interests? – an institutionalist view

The contents of enabling myths are stereotypes, blindspots, and double standards regarding such types of inequality as class, race, gender, nationality, religion, and sexual orientation. In stratified societies, the myths carry significant emotional charge for those who believe them, the charges being either positive or negative. Scapegoating provides the negative charge; emulation provides the positive. The emotional charge they carry makes enabling myths powerful social control mechanisms that strengthen the economic relations of the status quo and that solidify the power of the vested interests.

Members of the upper strata might become renegades and attack the system if they come to believe that their privileges and powers are not deserved. Furthermore, members of the lower strata might become revolutionaries and attack the system if they come to believe that their burdens and weaknesses are not deserved. Enabling myths help the patriarchs, white supremacists, capitalists, jingoists, religious fanatics, and gay bashers to justify their unequal position in society. Renegades are made unlikely when these enabling myths teach the powerful and the privileged that they are superior. Revolutionaries are made unlikely when these enabling myths teach those people with the least wealth and power that they are inferior.

Convincing those on the bottom is the more difficult of the two. Enabling myths help keep the poorest, most despised, and weakest people at the bottom by raising doubts and creating blind spots in their own minds about whether or not they deserve their lowly position. Do they deserve it because of their inferiority? Well then, perhaps they should just be quiet and endure their exploitation and humiliation. Could it be that they do not deserve such poor treatment, but receive it anyway because the society in which they live is unjust? Well then, perhaps they should struggle against their oppression. But then, if enabling myths say that nothing ever changes, why try? If society does not evolve, then will the last ever become first? Will there ever be equal treatment?

Enabling myths are a part of a society's dominant ideology that support the divisions of a stratified society. They are a form of learning that enables the people at the top of the social pyramid to feel superior and the bottom inferior. (A general theory of inequality is in Dugger 1996a, b. See also Sherman 1996.) People must be taught the why and wherefore of social stratification. Such knowledge is not a part of human nature, but of human culture and must be taught to succeeding generations. Enabling myths are not due, however, to a conspiracy. It is more complicated than that. Patriarchs or capitalists do not simply get together and make up some falsehoods to tell to the women and workers to convince them of their inferiority and of the futility of trying to improve their lot. Enabling myths are products of cultural evolution, not conspiracy.

When carefully analyzed and studied in their social context, enabling myths can seem irrational and even silly. Nevertheless, these myths are not to be treated lightly. They are not on the same level as fairy tales told to children. They are not merely the stuff of laughter and prank. They are the stuff of oppression and death. They are powerful means of controlling whole masses of people. Enabling myth is similar to propaganda, in that both are means of social control used by the powerful to control the powerless. However, enabling myth is far more permanent and penetrates far deeper into the culture of a people than the propaganda used by a particular political regime. In this respect, enabling myth is more like folklore, for both enabling myth and folklore penetrate deeply into culture and they both arise from deeply within culture. (See Arnold 1966 for an interesting study of the US)

Thorstein Veblen's *Theory of the Leisure Class* provides an excellent institutional analysis of emulation. Emulation provides the positive emotional charge of envy to people on the bottom who look up at those on the top. Emulation causes the oppressed to want to be as much like their oppressors as possible. Emulation replaces the urge to revolt against the top people with the desire to climb into their ranks. It is the strongest of all social control mechanisms. When people are harmed by vested interest, emulation leads them to want their own vested interest. It is not the vested interest to which they object, but their own lack thereof.

While emulating applies to looking up the social scale, scapegoating, on the other hand, applies to looking down. Emulation is envy and is directed toward status, wealth, power and privilege. Scapegoating is contempt and is directed toward humiliation, poverty, weakness, and deprivation. To he who hath, it shall be given; from him who hath not, it shall be taken away!

Whenever something goes seriously wrong in a society – a war is lost, unemployment goes up, poverty worsens, families disintegrate – people look for the reason. More than that, they look for who is to blame. Generals never lose wars. At least, they are too powerful to have the blame placed on them. It is always the soldiers or the civilians or the liberal politicians who lose wars. Or at least, they lack the power to avoid the blame – they become scapegoats. Corporate leaders never cause unemployment by laying off workers. Or at least, they are too powerful to have the blame placed on them. It is always the workers who are too lazy or their unions who are too demanding that cause unemployment. Or at least, they lack the power to avoid the blame – they become scapegoats. It is never the excessive demands of work or the complete loss of work that causes family disintegration. (It is hard to tell which is worse for an employee's family – being exploited by a capitalist employer or not being exploited by a capitalist employer.) It is the laziness or the promiscuity or the drinking or the drug taking or the excessive spending of the family's breadwinner that is to blame for the family's problems. Or, at least the breadwinner lacks the power to avoid the blame, so they are scapegoated, particularly if they are female and black. It is as if a new crime has been invented for African-American women – the crime of having a child while black. (You are, of course, familiar with the new crime invented for African-American men – driving while black.) Is there a pattern here? Gunnar Myrdal's *American Dilemma* provides the standard institutionalist analysis of scapegoating.

Scapegoating is particularly unsavory. For example, elite German men, having lost the First World War, looked downward with hatred and lies toward Jews, scapegoating the Jews (who had nothing to do with the German loss) for their own loss of privilege, power, and machismo. The Germans who scapegoated them eventually murdered millions of innocent Jews in the Holocaust – the Nazi "Final Solution" to the "Jewish Problem."

Power determines who is scapegoated and who is emulated. Bottom groups are scapegoated because they are powerless, not because they are the cause of some social shortcoming. Lacking power, people in the bottom groups have difficulty defending themselves from scurrilous attack. They also have difficulty in promoting an effective counterattack. In the reverse way, people in top groups are emulated because they are powerful, not because they are the cause of some social success. Mark Nathan Cohen, with a broader stroke, explains:

> Because questioning the system itself has always seemed too threatening to the maintenance of our system of beliefs, we have been forced to redirect our anger toward handy scapegoats. That means that we not only have to choose people to act as scapegoats; we have to invent ways to justify our choice.
>
> (Cohen 1998: 203)

Emulation and scapegoating differentiate the deepest feelings of the members of stratified societies and split the flow of feelings into two directions. Emulation directs deep positive feelings upward toward the higher strata. Scapegoating directs deep negative feelings downward toward the lower strata. This means that on one hand, enabling myths about the good qualities of the upper strata tap into and reinforce a stream of deep positive emotions. While on the other hand, enabling myths about the bad qualities of the lower strata tap into and reinforce another stream of equally deep but negative emotions. Those who would pursue equality by attacking vested interests and established economic relations swim against the strong social currents of these streams.

Enabling myth based on emulation is institutionalized in the concrete form of a leisure class (Veblen 1975). Members of the leisure class claim their membership through honorific connections to the means of production, not through direct work with the means of production. Honorific connections to the means of production make it possible to take credit for the work of others, and, very important, to extract income from that work. Honorific connections are about ownership, not workmanship. Ownership engages with deeds and mineral rights, with shares of stock in corporations, with bonds and mortgages on valuable property, with beneficial interests in trusts, with inheritances and bequests from ancestors, and with foreclosures and sales of other people's property. All such are honorific. Creating, destroying, and transferring these honorifics (meaning objects that bring honor and prestige) take much ingenuity, time, and effort. Nevertheless, doing so is not considered in the same light as the ingenuity, time, and effort put out by a carpenter, electrician, or cook.

In short, the leisure class produces honor and income for itself, keeping itself in the upper strata of society. The working class produces the products and performs the services needed to keep the society going materially. So, enabling myths must convince those who do the work that they do not deserve all the credit or the income for doing so. Rather, the members of the leisure class are designated by the enabling myths as the deserving ones. The lower strata must be continually scapegoated to seem unworthy, while the upper strata must be continually emulated to seem worthy. That is the great service performed by enabling myths to the reproduction of the status quo of stratified societies.

What is enabled?

Enabling myth enables social stratification. (This includes the colonization of one society by another. See Memmi 1967.) Stratification creates inequality by dividing people into the powerful and the privileged upper strata, and the powerless and deprived lower. Stratification is profoundly complex in modern societies, being based on a number of intersecting and reinforcing divisions.

First, stratification is based on relations to the means of production, on class. The leisure class owns the means of production. Its members receive credit for the work of others, (emulation) and receive income without working themselves. The working class owns no means of production. Its members receive blame for laziness and prodigality (scapegoating). So, when they are laid off from work, whether or not it was their fault, the myths of their society teach them to blame themselves for being lazy, not to blame the owners of the corporation that laid them off for being greedy. Furthermore, when they run out of personal saving during their unemployment, the enabling myths of their society teach them that they ran out because they did not save enough while working, not because their employer did not pay them enough for the work they performed.

Stratification is also based on what is popularly referred to as identity politics. In stratified societies people are divided into top and bottom groups according to a whole array of allegedly important characteristics: race, gender, ethnic/national origin, religion, and sexual orientation. Often these divisions reinforce one another, leading to multiplied exploitation and oppression, as in the treatment of African American women. (Further discussion of these divisions is in Dugger, 1998; Cohen, 1998; Peterson and Brown, 1994.)

How do enabling myths affect economic institutions and class relations? – a Marxist view

An important myth in the capitalist United States is that all of the poor live in poverty because they are lazy. This is a very persistent myth, but it is false in the following ways. In the first place, many of those below the poverty line work full time year around at tedious, hard, or unpleasant jobs. Second, many are disabled, so they cannot work for that reason. Third, many are young mothers who cannot get full time jobs for that reason. Fourth, many are involuntarily unemployed because the capitalist system generates recessions. If one believes that the poor are just lazy, then it is easy to cut off welfare, as conservatives have tried to do for many decades. If the poor are lazy, then it is easier to argue against minimum wages, as conservatives have always done.

There is also the myth that the unemployed are lazy and do not wish to work. But in 1929–1931 millions of Americans went from being employed to being unemployed until, according to official data, 25 per cent were unemployed. Did one out of four American workers become lazy all at the same time? The advertisements for jobs are cyclical, so there are many ads for workers at the peak and very few at the trough of the business cycle. Thus it is not that workers suddenly do not wish to work, but rather that no one wants them to work. Moreover, there have been many newspaper stories about plants that offered a few jobs and had workers lined up for blocks. Does that sound like lazy people? But when the rich wish their legislators to cut unemployment compensation, such myths enable them to do so.

Economics is full of myths. One lovely example is the Natural Rate of Unemployment. The implication of this semantic phrase is the myth that every society is subject to the same given rate of unemployment, regardless of system or circumstances. So there is nothing one can do about it. The actual technical meaning is the much narrower one that a particular rate of unemployment is required to prevent inflation. (For a thorough and detailed discussion of the literature from several points of view, see Symposium 1997.) This proposition has a weak theoretical basis and extremely dubious empirical basis, as shown by James Galbraith in Symposium (1997), yet the myth persists. This myth enables defenders of the status quo to argue that whatever rate of unemployment exists is natural and cannot be reduced without dire consequences.

Racism – the notion that one group is inferior to another – and sexism – the notion that one gender is inferior to another – can be proven false. Why do these myths persist? In a Marxist approach, we can only understand the answer to this question if we specify the institutions of the society about which we are talking. For example, in all societies based on the institution of slavery, we find that racist myths are dominant. Such myths of racism enable the dominant slave owning class to rule and to continue to reproduce the system of slavery. The myth of racism is propagated by the organized religious system, the education system, the media of communication, and the political system. But this leaves a mystery: why do these political and social institutions propagate the myth of racism? The myth of racism is very helpful to the interests of those who own slaves, so they will push it in any forum that they control. In every society based on slavery, the slaves have no power and the slave masters have all of the power. Thus the slave masters in the US South before the Civil War controlled the powerful religious system which did much of the education and was the most powerful media of communication, as well as any other schools or newspapers. Obviously no slaves participated in the political system, so the masters held power there as well. In both ancient Greece and the old South there were the forms of democracy, but the slaves were excluded. So those who controlled all of the dominant means of communication had an interest in perpetuating the myth of racism and had the power to do so.

In the twentieth century, probably the most notorious example of an enabling myth was Hitler's use of anti-Semitism. Hitler told the German bankers that all of their troubles were due to Jewish Communists. Hitler told the German workers that all of their troubles were due to Jewish bankers. These false and contradictory propositions helped enable Hitler to seize power in capitalist Germany. Since the problems of Germany were all caused by Jews, they were all arrested, put in camps, and mostly executed. Since all Jews were Communists and trade union leaders and in close conspiracy with those who were not Jews, most non-Jewish Communists and trade union leaders were also arrested and mostly executed. This allowed the fascists to consolidate political power by wiping out the large Communist and Socialist parties and to take over the leadership of the most powerful capitalist enterprises in the name of rooting out Jews and treason. By wiping out the trade unions, they greatly increased the profits of German capitalist firms.

Most racists are also sexists. Hitler's favorite slogan was that women should be with children, church, and kitchen (kinder, kirche, and kuche). This would enable superior German men from the superior Aryan race to have a supply of meek and subordinate women. The myth was propagated by the all-male leadership of the German fascist party. It was also propagated by all of the German media, which were controlled by the fascists.

In the contemporary capitalist United States, a great many conservative politicians have been elected by declaiming against African Americans, either directly or by innuendo. "Have you lost your job? Then we will stop the affirmative action program that gives your job to African Americans." This is pure myth, since most African Americans have the worst jobs in society and the unemployment rate among African Americans is double that of white workers. Yet this seemingly irrational view is very rational and profitable for those who get elected by it. It is also a very useful tool for those employers who split white from minority (African or Latino American) workers by using the myth of racism. The power of this myth helped Southern capitalists have almost no unions for many decades. Lack of unions meant higher profits. It should be stressed that racism has very seldom been a conscious conspiracy; it is rather that the institutions such as the media are an integral part of the capitalist system and would never oppose any basic facet of its supporting ideology.

Similarly, in the modern capitalist United States, many myths are spread against women, all of them demonstrably false. They persist because (a) some male politicians can beat women politicians in an election, (b) because women can be paid lower wages, (c) because they promote male dominance in the family, and (d) because the myths of sexism divide the working class into conflicting male and female groups and thus weaken it. The divisions weaken unions and reduce the power of strikes, just as they divide and weaken all progressive political activity. The myths of sexism are spread by the media, the churches, and the political system, and the educational system.

Just as is the case with racism, these myths are not spread by a conscious conspiracy. In the first place, the executives who make the decisions in the media, the educational system, the churches and the political system are mostly white males. These white male decision makers do not need to be told to be racists and sexist, nor do they need to make conscious decisions to be racist and sexist; these myths are not casual beliefs, but are their deeply held values. Secondly, all of these institutions as well as the corporations are integrated into a whole, so racial and gender discrimination are institutionalized and linked to all the other institutions. What does that allegation mean? For example, women mostly have more trouble than men in raising money in political races; part of the reason is that most wealth is controlled by males with sexist prejudices, who really are convinced that women will be weaker candidates and will do a less efficient job if elected. They also believe that women will be "soft" on the poor and the disadvantaged so women may vote for more money to help these groups.

Another example of the interacting nature of US capitalist institutions are the obstacles faced by minorities in the educational system. Seldom does anyone in power anymore say consciously that I am going to stop minorities from getting an education. But minority families have less wealth and income. Therefore, they have less money to send children to college. Moreover, most minority families still live in roughly segregated areas, segregated not by law or violence, but by money. In those poorer areas, the schools are generally worse because there are fewer tax dollars, fewer available good teachers, and less monetary support for higher cultural activities. So minority children get a poorer elementary and secondary education, which makes it more difficult to get into universities or to do well in universities. No conscious decision is needed to maintain this institutionalized racism – rather, conscious decisions are necessary to break the pattern. But getting white male politicians who make the decisions – and corporate executives who control the money that finances the politicians – to make conscious decisions to take affirmative action to break the institutionalized and integrated pattern of racist and sexist discrimination is obviously very difficult.

It should not be forgotten that each immigrant group to the United States faced prejudice and discrimination. There are myths that all Irish are too loud and are buffoons, while all Italians are dirty and careless. Such myths of inferiority of one group to another by ethnicity enable employers to split workers and thereby weaken and defeat union efforts to organize for better conditions or higher wages. Such myths have also allowed conservative politicians to split voters and thereby win elections, which then increases the support of the economic status quo.

There is a myth that US democracy is perfect, so everyone has an equal voice in running the government. Does everyone own an equal number of TV stations? Does everyone have an equal ability to give thousands of dollars to candidates or to lobbyists? The fact that people have entirely different amounts of wealth under US capitalism means that an unemployed worker does not have the same political power as a billionaire like Ross Perot.

In Northern Ireland, Protestants know that Catholics are evil and inferior, while Catholics know the opposite. In Israel, Jews know that Arabs are evil and inferior, while Arabs know the opposite. In India, Hindus know that Muslims are evil and inferior, while Muslims know the opposite. In all of these cases, such myths and prejudices enabled the British to divide the people of these colonies and rule for a long, long time – bringing a great deal of economic gain to British capitalists.

How do enabling myths affect political and social institutions?

This topic is discussed in detail in Chapter 5.

How do enabling myths affect technology?
– an institutionalist view

Enabling myths can slow down the spread of new technology or distort the development of new technology. Remember that new technology is applied from the community's joint stock of accumulated knowledge. So when most people in the United States believed that a Communist invasion of their country was likely, they supported massive spending on military research and development. The arms and the space races against the Communist menace distorted the accumulation of the community's stock of knowledge. We scared ourselves (or let the Communists scare us) into learning more about the means of destruction and less about the means of production. The result of the allocation of our resources was fairly straightforward – growth in military technology was accelerated; growth in civilian technology slowed. Even a decade after the fall of the Soviet Union, we continue to allocate many of our scientists and engineers to the arms and space race, even though the race is over and we won. We have developed a blind spot in our vision as a nation. We cannot see that we are wasting our resources running a race that we already won. (Further discussion is in Melman 1997.)

Another blind spot has affected medical technology. For many years little research effort was devoted to the cardio-vascular health of women. It was thought, mistakenly, that women were just not very susceptible to cardio-vascular disease. When AIDS first began to spread, little effort was devoted to research into women and AIDS because it was thought, mistakenly, that women were just not very susceptible to AIDS. The result of generations of biased allocation of research effort has been a gendered distortion of medical technology. The same bias can be found along class lines. Medical research is directed toward therapies and cures for diseases and conditions suffered by those who can afford to pay for health care. The health problems of the poor get far less research. The same is frequently true for the health problems of people of the "wrong" color, of the "wrong" sexual orientation, and of the "wrong" ethnic/religious background.

Vested interests are involved in each of these cases of blind spots and distorted priorities. The military-industrial complex that President Eisenhower warned us about has a strong vested interest in continuing the arms and space race eleven long years after we won it. (This is being written in 2000. The Soviet Union collapsed, for all practical purposes, in 1989.) Whole complexes of male researchers, male grant-evaluators, and male-dominated insurance companies and HMOs have vested interests in male-oriented medical research. Whole complexes of research institutes, private laboratories, university departments, and corporate research facilities are funded by the profit from selling health care to those who can afford to pay. Those who cannot afford to pay fund none. And in our society, you do not get more than what you pay for.

How do enabling myths affect technology?
– a Marxist view

The choice of technology is almost never limited to one possibility, but usually has a range of competing technological alternatives. For example, power can be generated from a plant run by atomic power or power may be generated by use of solar power. This choice is surrounded by myths. On the one hand, when atomic power first appeared, it was said to be the answer to all our prayers. There would be unlimited cheap power for industry, free from coal-smoke. There would be tiny atomic motors to run automobiles. But this simple solution was found to be mythological. Instead it was found that atomic power was quite expensive to build and maintain – and that atomic power could result in terrible accidents, killing many people and harming thousands. Obviously, anything is possible, such as invention of a cheap and safe fusion power, so we should not rule out possibilities by reason of sweeping myths, but should keep a flexible outlook – always asking what is best for the people as a whole, rather than the corporations.

It has often been said, by those with a vested interest in the status quo, that such and such could *never* be done. For example, some scholars who had built their reputation in other ways, said that Egyptian hieroglyphics could never be translated – but they were translated. Some, who owned other transportation, said that people could never fly, but the airplane was invented. Some automobile companies are always saying that automobile pollution is as low as it can go, but enough pressure always convinces them that it is possible to go lower. So one should never believe the myth that such and such can *never* be done.

How society affects enabling myths

We divide this question in three parts: how economic relations affect myths, how social and political institutions affect myths, and how technology affects myths.

How do economic institutions and vested interests affect enabling myths? – an institutionalist view

Enabling myths support a society's basic institutions and vested interests. Enabling myths do not emerge because of conspiracies of the top strata against the bottom strata, but they emerge because such myths enable those with vested interests to feel good about themselves and enable those without vested interests to accept their fate. If there is anything "natural" about stratified societies, it is this: enabling myths are a natural support of them.

Since our society is based on market capitalism, the market and capitalism are its most important economic institutions and the strongest interests in our society are vested in the control of markets and in the ownership of capital. "Naturally" then, the most important enabling myths of our time have to do with markets and with capital.

Market myths

A market is an arena of exchange, a social space designed to facilitate the circulation of goods and services through the economy. Markets help move wheat from the farmers of Fargo to the cereal manufacturers in Battle Creek to the bowl of your kid sister in Dallas. They also help move shoes from sweatshops in Jakarta to shopping malls in Chicago to feet in Cicero. They do so through collective action that establishes and enforces standards, routines, rules, and laws governing how the ownership of specific goods and services changes hands. Markets must have standards, routines, rules, and laws. Without them, markets break down into an infinite series of disputes between different sellers, between different buyers, and between buyers and sellers.

A market is an institution that has been slowly built up out of the numerous settlements of disputes about standards, routines, rules, and laws. The settlements come in three forms. Disputes are settled by court decisions. The decisions accumulate into a body of law made up primarily of precedent-setting cases. Disputes are settled by private agreement. These agreements accumulate like court decisions, but they accumulate into routines and working rules instead of common laws. Disputes are also settled by new legislation. New legislation frequently establishes a new framework that serves as a starting point for the accumulation of court decisions into common law and as a new starting point for the accumulation of private agreements into routines and working rules. Every private agreement, court decision, and new piece of legislation rewards some interests and punishes other interests. The rewards are vested in the way the disputes are settled – creating vested interests. The most important two features of markets are that they are evolutionary and disputatious. The working rules, standards, routines, and laws that keep them agoing have evolved over many generations of experience in settling disputes. Markets do not come to us by instantaneous creation. They come to us by continuous evolution. Markets are not characterized by natural harmony. They are characterized by disputes.

Nevertheless, we can deny their evolutionary nature and mistakenly assume that markets are spontaneous, that they spring up quickly, automatically, and by themselves. This is the myth of spontaneity. It is a powerful enabling myth that became important after the Soviet collapse in 1989. It helped American economists to keep a straight face when they told policy makers in centrally-planned economies that they should immediately dismantle their planning bureaucracies and privatize the factories. The policy was called shock therapy and as soon as it was applied, the advisors promised, markets would spring up spontaneously to transform the stagnant economy into a dynamic new system. Of course, what usually happened was a little different than promised – the economic system usually collapsed and a long process of evolution began. (Further discussion of transformation problems is in Hall and Elliott 1999. Discussion of market mythology in the formation of the US economy is in Bourgin, 1990.)

Markets did not pop up like toadstools after a rain, but in spite of what happened to the livelihood of many of the people, shock therapy did help open the door of many centrally planned economies to US trade and investment.

Another market myth is Say's Law of Markets. According to it, the market system maintains natural harmony. The market system can experience overproduction in one market, but not in all markets. We might experience a temporary surplus in one market, as people stop eating donuts and start eating cereal but not a prolonged surplus in all markets. A temporary surplus in one market – donuts – is not a problem because the price will fall in that market and resources will move into another market – cereal – where the demand is greater. If people are without jobs for a long period, it is because they are too lazy to adapt to the need for cereal makers instead of donut bakers. If we are really infected with the bleeding heart, the only aid we should give the unemployed is help getting new training. Replacing their lost wages with unemployment benefits or giving them welfare payments will corrupt them, will make them into a permanent underclass. If left alone, the market system will bring them back to their senses and maintain natural harmony.

This myth is in the interest of taxpayers who want to stop paying taxes to support welfare and unemployment benefits. It also is in the interest of employers because it reduces the alternatives faced by their workers – work or starve would be best for the employer. We learned the hard way that Say's Law was a myth. We learned it 60 years ago during the Great Depression. It taught us that people do not just stop consuming donuts so they can consume more corn flakes. (In depression and recession, they stop consuming donuts and corn flakes, both.) Several recessions since the Great Depression have reinforced our learning. Nevertheless, Say's Law is still giving us Alzheimer's Disease. We seem to be perpetually forgetting what we learned in the Depression and what we have been reminded of by the many recessions since then. We constantly forget that overproduction in many markets at once does happen and we constantly forget that unemployment does spread widely, and not because of a widespread breakout of laziness. So in recent years we have gone along with cuts in unemployment benefits and welfare, and we have blamed the unemployed for being lazy.

Capital myths

Capital myths support capitalism and mostly overlap with market myths. So a few lines illustrating them will suffice. An interesting capital myth is the one claiming that capitalist entrepreneurs shoulder the burden of uncertainty for their society when they choose to undertake their perilous profession. If we looked more carefully, we could all see for ourselves what an uncertain life is led by most owners of corporations as compared to most workers for corporations, particularly when we observed which of them – worker or owner – becomes unemployed, disabled, or involuntarily retired the most frequently.

Another interesting one is the one about the capitalists who shoulder the burden of saving for their society when they choose painfully abstaining from consuming goods and services instead of pleasurably consuming them. (No donuts or corn flakes for Donald Trump. He righteously saves his pennies to build new casinos for us, instead.) So he needs all the tax breaks, subsidies, favorable regulations, zoning changes, and sympathy he can get.

How do economic institutions and class relations affect enabling myths? – a Marxist view

Enabling myths, like all other myths, are not just a few false words thought up by a small cabal or conspiracy of evil men. Rather, a myth is pervasive in the society because it is embedded in the dominant institutions and correctly reflects the dominant ideology. Enabling myths reflect the basic interests of all the institutions of capitalism and the elite who run those institutions – including the media, the education system, the religious institutions, and the political system. Very few people consciously say I will spread some false myths; rather, they are sincerely believed and taken for granted by most people living within the institutional matrix of capitalism.

How are myths created? They are created every day routinely in the media, the schools, the churches, corporations, and by the government. The ongoing process is best illustrated by a concrete example. The economics profession tells many myths: that there is competition, so there is very little monopoly; that aggregate demand adjusts to aggregate supply, so there is no involuntary unemployment; and that every person receives their fair share of income according to their product (including billionaires who get $200 million a year from merely owning stocks and bonds).

Economists believe these myths themselves, but they are not born that way. Each economist is trained by an older generation that teaches their myths. Although economics students sometimes resist the myths at first, they usually internalize them to pass the doctoral comprehensives – or else they flunk. Then they become Assistant Professors, who need money from foundations (that require acceptance of the myths), who need to get articles in major journals (that require acceptance of the myths), and who need the votes of senior faculty to get tenure (and senior faculty require acceptance of the myths). Of course, the heads of foundations, the editors of journals, and the senior faculty all believe these myths quite sincerely, so they do not need to conspire to enforce them. Thus each individual economist is shaped by a whole set of institutions to believe in, expand, and teach certain myths.

Marx was very much alive to the perceptions of the economy, perceptions by workers and perceptions by capitalists. Every prominent Marxist thinker, such as Antonio Gramsci in the 1930s, referred to Marx's observation that the dominant ideology is always the set of myths and ideology that is in the interests of the dominant class in a society. It would be silly to imagine a society in which the most pervasive ideas and myths ran counter to the interests of those with the power and wealth in society. A recent Marxist work that pursues the theme of convenient social myths is that by John Henry (1990).

Each society has different myths. Anthropologists tell us about the myths of primitive societies and historians tell us about the myths of slave and feudal societies. By definition, in a capitalist society there is a small group of people that owns all of the physical capital (plant and equipment) and that hire other people to do work for them. The owners of capital then own the product that is produced by those who work for them. They sell it and make a profit. Production continues only so long as they expect to make a profit. This is a pure model of capitalism. In reality, some people have a foot in several classes, there are a number of classes besides capitalists and workers, capital is not owned mostly by individuals but by giant monopoly corporations, and government plays a vast role in the economy. But this brief definition will allow us to proceed to discuss the myths of our capitalist society.

All day long, at work, at school, and in the media, we are immersed in a torrent of images and concepts about the world. Some of this flood of views, and propaganda may be called enabling myths. These are myths that try to channel social evolution in some direction by making us believe something that may support our current institutions – such as the notion that everyone earns exactly what they deserve (including billionaires). All of the institutions of capitalism ordinarily and routinely, without any conspiracy, teach enabling myths to the oppressed to keep them that way. The members of the upper class, if well adjusted and content with themselves, also sincerely believe the enabling myths – and they have the power to control the institutions that promulgate those myths.

Why do such myths persist and why are they reproduced from year to year? Because they are helpful to some powerful group. A later section will show that myths in the forms of race, gender, and class prejudice help mold political, social and economic institutions to the interests of the ruling class.

There is a myth that the market is perfect, so consumers get exactly what they want. But consumers usually do not have much knowledge about the quality of competing products, except via advertising, which is often false information. The myth that the market is perfect can also be used to argue that all public health care is bad because it interferes with the market. This myth was spread widely by advertising during the debate on health care in President Clinton's first year in office. It helped to enable conservatives to defeat even the most mild steps toward universal health care – leaving millions of the poor with no health care and leaving extra millions of dollars in the pockets of the rich because they did not have to pay any more taxes.

There is a myth that people get rich by hard work and success in the competitive market place. But the data indicate that the best way to get rich in the United States is to have rich parents. If your parents are millionaires, you have both a good education and a lot of money to start a business career. Such myths enable those who benefit by the system to preserve the system.

Finally, it is worth noting the myth that the capitalist market system has always existed with a few minor detours. But very primitive tribes must work collectively to survive and there is very little property, so the notion of private property hardly exists – and there is no exchange with outsiders, so there is no market and no capitalism. Such primitive, non-market societies existed for about 98 per cent of human existence.

For most of the feudal period, most people lived in isolated feudal manors that were largely self-sufficient, so there were few markets. Market days might be once or twice a year, very special occasions, so there was no routine market exchange and no capitalist class. In this sense, conservatives deny evolution because they wish to preserve the status quo by convincing people of the myth that it has always existed and always will exist. Whereas the fact that evolution exists is a mighty weapon for radicals who wish to see the world change.

Enabling myths help to support the rule of the elite who exploit others. Thus myths in the US South said (as in ancient Greece and Rome) that some men were masters while some men (and women) were, by nature, slaves. It followed that in this society work was viewed as something to be done by slaves or the lowest of free men. Work was not something a respectable member of the Southern elite ever did. The Southern slave-owning rulers were concerned with the art of governing, so they wrote on that subject and they did make some practical improvements in governing and in military affairs. But since work was off limits for the slave-owning class (with even supervision often left to others), it followed that many of them had little practical experience in the technical operations of agriculture or industry. Since they received income without productive work, and since their myths said that was just and proper, they did very little innovation in the productive process. Thus both class relations and the consequent ideology or mythology tended to hold back technological progress.

Under slavery, other myths were widespread that protected the masters from the slaves. One of those was the racial superiority of the ruling class and the inferiority of the slaves. This myth not only helped rationalize slavery for the masters, it also helped to convince those citizens who were technically free but poor and powerless that they were much, much better off than the slaves and even better off than they actually were. The free non-slave-owning farmers of the old South believed they had not only limited material income, but also psychic income from being free citizens of the South. Even if some citizens had a worse material plight than some slaves, they were loyal to Southern slavery.

Some myths may also be used by revolutionary classes to further a revolutionary change and their own ascendancy to power. Thus before and during the French Revolution, the bourgeoisie (merchants and manufacturers) and their myth makers claimed that if only the king were overthrown and a republic established, there would be liberty, fraternity, and equality in France. From this time on, there is confusion between the capitalist economic system and political democracy. Most people today, for example, believe that in Eastern Europe communism was replaced by a "democratic economic system." Nevertheless, under capitalism, democracy is limited to the political sphere at best and has nothing to do with democracy in the economic sphere. In a capitalist firm, the boss has the power. So if a worker completely disagrees with the boss, the worker is fired – that is not a democracy. After the French Revolution, the capitalist class held exclusive economic power, having ousted the feudal landlords, and it also exerted overwhelming political power from then till now.

So it was a myth that the French Revolution would bring economic equality, but a very useful myth. Whenever the bourgeoisie decide to get rid of a dictatorship, such as the Soviet one, they tell everyone that "democracy" (by which they mean political democracy plus capitalism) will automatically help everyone to achieve equality. The myth says that capitalism is democracy. This is a very powerful myth in favor of revolution wherever there is some form of dictatorship and a non-capitalist economy.

Thus myths play a vital role in reproducing the status quo and upholding ruling class power in the usual non-revolutionary times. But in revolutionary times myths also play a vital role in bringing about a revolutionary change in social institutions. Antonio Gramsci frequently observed as the theme of all his writing that in the more or less lengthy transitional period from the status quo to revolution the two sets of myths frequently confront one another through their human, class protagonists.

How do political and social institutions affect enabling myths?

This topic is discussed in detail in Chapter 5.

How does technology affect enabling myths?
– an institutionalist view

A simple answer to this question, a kind of first approximation, is to say that new enabling myths evolve along with new institutions and new technologies (Ayres 1978). New technologies and new institutions create the need for new enabling myths.

New technology changes the way people think because it changes the way people make products, perform services, distribute goods, and consume. New technology and the accompanying new way of thinking can either reinforce or weaken different forms of inequality and vested interest, depending on how people control, use, and adapt to the new ways. In recent years many new technologies have made it easier for people to get around. So people with various handicaps have insisted on taking advantage of the new mobility. As they pushed themselves into the mainstream of life, they dispelled all sorts of myths about themselves.

The effects and social ramifications of new technologies are extraordinarily wide and powerful. They are both intended and unintended. They are both beneficial and detrimental. They harm some groups and benefit others, creating new myths for the support of the newly benefited and destroying old myths that no longer protect the newly harmed.

Furthermore, new technologies are used far beyond the workplace itself, and involve changes in more than just the means of production. New technology can originate in many different places, as well. Although new technology has to do with means, it does not always originate in the workplace and may have nothing to do with the means of production. After all, modern societies have the institutionalized means to do many things. The means of production and distribution are institutionalized largely in the corporation. The means of consumption are institutionalized largely in the family. The means of coercion are institutionalized largely in the state. The means of deception are institutionalized largely in the mass media. New technology can originate from any of these areas and can have impacts on the way we think about any of them as well. In her study of the role of women in cotton production in the American South, Ruth Allen provided us with the following insight regarding how a new consumer's good (the automobile) changed human relations within the family:

> Under the old carless regime, the masculine members of the household got out their horses, saddled them, and rode away unquestioned. There was no room to take the wife, daughter, or sister; and there was no room for argument or protest. There is room in the car, and when the car goes the wife and daughters get in, and again there is little room for protest. The man has lost his liberty. No longer is "going to town" the open sesame to a few hours of absolutely uncensored life. A greatly privileged class is passing, and it may be by such seemingly unimportant changes as this that civilizations are undermined and social systems fall.
>
> (Allen 1933: 40-41;
> quoted in Bernasek and Kinnear 1995: 81)

A change in technology calls for a change in enabling myths. Under the old carless regime, as Allen described it, one set of patriarchal enabling myths was used to keep women in their assigned place. But with families having cars, a new regime of patriarchal enabling myths was needed to keep women down.

Of course, new enabling myths may not spring up fast enough or be effective enough to contain the liberating effects of some technologies. Then, more profound upheavals may begin to threaten the foundations of the social edifice. Such certainly was the case of the factory and the wage labor system. It gave rise to a whole set of new enabling myths that replaced those of the medieval society and its handicraft system.

What new technologies sometimes do is let genies out of bottles. Then, what new enabling myths sometimes do is push them back inside. Examples abound: The printing press let mass literacy out of the bottle. For quite some time it roamed free. But finally, freedom of the press pushed it inside a newly constructed bottle. ("Freedom of the press" meaning the enabling myth that supports crass commercialization, and concentrated ownership and control of the mass media.) The automobile let many women and African Americans out of their bottles. After the Second World War, the feminine mystique became the new enabling myth for the social control of uppity women. Feminists have fought it ever since. For the social control of African American mobility, we have the new crime of driving while black.

New technology always introduces new forms of myths and ideological struggles because it always introduces new things to struggle about.

How does technology affect enabling myths?
– a Marxist view

In the most primitive technological period, which covered most of human existence, most myths sought to explain nature. Nature was dangerous and mysterious to primitive peoples. So their myths included Gods of fire, water, thunder, and lightening. If one correctly portrayed a mastodon in song and dance and pictures, then one might control it and kill it without losing members of the tribe. So myths about nature helped to give confidence to the whole tribe – or to reinforce the power of a witch doctor.

When technology changed and far more private wealth became available, both institutions and dominant myths changed. The higher productivity made slavery profitable for the first time – whereas before a slave could have produced no more in a day than his or her own subsistence. When human institutions changed from primitive collectivism to slavery, the dominant myths changed drastically. No longer was nature the main enemy, but rather the enemy became other groups with property to be looted or human labor power to be exploited. So we find myths about the inferiority of other tribes and ethnic groups.

No longer was the collective good of the whole tribe a supreme goal strongly enforced by society. Now the deeds of rulers were enshrined, for example, the pharaohs were considered divine by a strongly enforced mythology taught by priests and supported by soldiers. The behavior of the rich and powerful was said to be divinely ordained, so such behavior was often discussed and emulated to the best of people's ability – though there were often laws which prohibited the lower classes from imitating certain behavior of the upper classes. Although there were remembrances of the earlier collective ethic in Greek and Roman myths and traditions, the slave societies became strongly individualist in their actual ethical behavior, at least among the ruling classes.

The institutional structure was one in which men ruled slaves and slaves produced wealth. So women were said by myths to be inferior to rationalize their subordinate position. Furthermore, to pass on private property in ancient Rome, it was important to determine a legitimate heir, which meant prohibiting women of the ruling class from having sex freely with others than their husbands. So the law prohibited such sex by women of the ruling class, enforced by the death penalty against slave men, and myths came to be popular about the wonders of virginity and abstinence from illegitimate sex by women – though not by men – so the double standard for sexual behavior first arose. Thus, the social mores and social myths completely changed as new institutions were built on new technology.

Conclusion

Institutionalists and Marxists agree that social myths help enable favored groups to remain on top and justify the status quo from year to year. We also agree that when technology and social relations change, new myths emerge. Finally, we agree that in struggles over what institutions will die out or spread, myths play a mighty role, with enabling myths defending the status quo against egalitarian reform or revolution.

5

DEMOCRACY

This chapter deals with political processes and evolution, particularly with democracy. For more from the institutionalist literature see Dugger and Waller (1992). The Marxist literature is discussed in Sherman (1972 Chapter 9, 1987 Chapter 8, and 1995 Chapter 9).

How society affects democracy

We define democracy, then ask how it is affected by economic relations, myths, and technology.

What is democracy? – an institutonalist view

Democracy is not the rich individual's freedom to decide where to invest their money. That is plutocracy, confused nowadays with democracy. Plutocracy is rule by the rich. Democracy is rule by the people. Democracy depends on the capacity of the people to decide how to pursue the common good. In stratified societies, where most of the people are held down by inequality, democracy is a process of becoming, rather than a state of being. Democracy is not a *yes* or *no* thing, but a matter of degree, which keeps changing as the process continues. The democratic process includes more and more previously excluded people as political participants. The most important features of the democratic process are enlarging the quantity of people participating in the political process and improving the quality of their participation as well. The democratic process does at least four things:

1   It extends the right to vote and actual voting to more and more groups who used to be excluded because of their gender, class, race, religion, or whatever.
2   It spreads knowledge about political issues and reduces the range of corruption, irrationality, and myth in public life.

3   It spreads actual participation as elected and appointed government officials to members of more and more groups.

4   If it proceeds far enough, the democratic process comes into conflict with the divisions of stratified societies.

That is, democracy and inequality are incompatible. In fact, to become fully developed, the democratic process would require the transformation of stratified societies into egalitarian ones. In our case, it would require an egalitarian transformation of capitalism, racism, sexism, homophobia, and jingoism (Bowles and Gintis 1987, Bowles, Gintis, and Gustafsson 1993, Carnoy and Shearer 1980, and Dowd 1997). If you take social evolution seriously, as we do, the possibility of just such a transformation must be taken seriously as well.

Continuation of the democratic process is not assured. Please remember that evolution does not mean progress. From the evolutionary point of view, the political process can move in any direction; can run in either forward or reverse so to speak. If it runs in forward gear, we will call it the democratic process. The democratic process is increasingly inclusive. If it runs in reverse gear, we will call it the aristocratic process. The aristocratic process is increasingly exclusive. The democratic process forms a people who collectively decide their own fate; the aristocratic process forms an elite that decides for the people. The democratic process is geared to spread out decision-making and include more and more people. The aristocratic process is geared to pull in decision-making and exclude more and more people. Plutocracy (rule by the rich) is the aristocratic form taken in our time.

What is democracy? – a Marxist view

We may distinguish formal democracy and effective democracy. Formal democracy means that the society follows all the formal rules of multi-party elections with universal suffrage and free speech for all minorities. Effective democracy means that most of the people can easily participate in speech in the media and in election campaigns *on an equal basis*. In reality many capitalist societies have had formal democracy, but very little effective democracy because the power of wealth controls to a large extent both elections and speech in the media.

Before discussing the degree of effective democracy, it should be emphasized that one should not sneer at formal democratic procedures. Many leftists – but especially Soviet Marxists – have sneered at formal democratic processes as hiding a lack of effective democracy. But the history of the Soviet Union proves the vital importance of formal democracy. The Soviet Union had universal suffrage in elections, but only one political party, the Communist Party. Free speech could only be used to support the Communist

Party. So in reality there was very little effective democracy and a great deal of repression and terror and dictatorship. So formal democracy is essential as a necessary, but not sufficient, condition of effective democracy. We shall see later why it is not a sufficient condition for effective democracy. If socialism is defined as effective democratic control of the economy, then formal democracy is also a necessary condition of socialism. One might have said that the Soviet Union had a purely formal socialism in that there was no private ownership and the means of production were owned and controlled by the government, but the government was not controlled by the people, so the Soviet Union lacked effective socialism as it lacked effective democracy.

It will be argued below that the United States has formal democracy, but a low degree of effective democracy because of the enormous power of the wealth of a small elite in the political process. The fact, however, that the United States does have formal democracy is enormously important, as was illustrated in the 1950s, when all of the norms of formal democracy were violated. Thousands of people lost their jobs, the Communist Party was effectively outlawed in spite of formal democracy, many people went to jail, and two people were executed as a result of those violations. Under any economic system, one must always fight to maintain the most extensive possible formal democratic rights as a necessary precondition of effective democracy.

How do economic institutions and vested interests affect the political process? – an institutionalist view

Politics and economics are perennial factors in the larger evolution of society, with one and then the other being the dominant factor. At the opening of the new millenium, economics is dominating politics as a global plutocracy is emerging. Today's globalization process spotlights the dominant influence of economics on politics. In globalization, economics is in the saddle and it rides humankind. Four economic institutions are driving plutocratic globalization. They are the European Union (EU), the World Trade Organization (WTO), the International Monetary Fund (IMF) and the World Bank (WB).

The WTO evolved out of an earlier organization – the General Agreement on Tariffs and Trade (GATT). After the Second World War ended in 1945, GATT became very successful in bringing down the level of tariffs on most internationally traded products, particularly on those produced by large, international corporations. GATT was so successful that by the 1980s it became increasingly clear that tariffs were no longer the major hindrance to the continued growth of the international corporation. Tariff barriers to trade were way down, but different regulations in different countries had

91

become regulatory barriers to trade. International corporations found that their products were often kept out of lucrative new markets by the way those markets were regulated in each host country.

For the corporations in the European Union, the problem was known as the "harmonization" problem. The different countries of the Union needed to harmonize their regulations so that the laws, standards, rules, and routines of each were the same. To do so, the European Union developed its own administrative bureaucracy and its own dispute resolution apparatus (judicial system). By harmonization, the European Union reduced the regulatory barriers between its member countries, and promoted more growth between them.

GATT needed to do the same thing for its members, to continue the expansion of trade between its leading corporations. But GATT took a different road than the European Union. GATT formed a new organization with an administrative bureaucracy and a dispute resolution apparatus of its own. That new organization was formed in 1995 and is the World Trade Organization (WTO).

The road taken by the WTO gives powerful economic interests dominance over local and even national politics. The WTO chose deregulation instead of harmonization to resolve disputes. A famous dispute involving sea turtles illustrates the *modus operandi* of the WTO. In the United States, the political authority had made commercial shrimpers fix their nets with expensive contraptions that allowed sea turtles to escape the net. This saved the turtles from drowning and the political authority from further environmentalist and humanitarian criticism. However, it also kept out of the US market the shrimp still being caught by foreign operators who did not fit their nets with the turtle-saving contraptions. In response, the non-complying operators took their case to the WTO and it resolved the dispute over market exclusion by declaring that the turtle-saving requirement was a regulatory barrier put up by the US to keep foreign shrimp out of their market and had to be dropped. Why did the WTO not harmonize fishing regulations for the global economy by insisting that everybody's turtle-drowning nets be fit with the turtle-saving contraptions? The WTO does not take the high road to harmonization. It takes the low road to deregulation. The dispute resolutions of the WTO cut back on political regulation in the name of free trade. The WTO's deregulation opens up the people and the environment of the evolving global economy to significant abuse. The WTO does not take the high road and raise political regulations up to the same standards in the name of harmonization. It is not protecting the people and the environment from abuse. Turtles have no vote in the WTO. Neither do you, or I.

Although turtles have no vote in affairs of the European Union, the people do. The EU has a European Parliament, elected by the people of the member states. To promote growth, the EU leans toward harmonization. The WTO has no such parliament elected by the people of the member states. It leans toward deregulation.

Two more economic institutions have powerful influences on the politics of globalization – the International Monetary Fund (IMF) and the World Bank. As with the WTO, they are not designed to represent the interests of turtles or of you and me. They too are pushing very hard for deregulation of the evolving global economy instead of harmonization.

The World Bank and the IMF were established at the end of the Second World War. They were intended to help mold a peaceful path down which the world economy could evolve. Governments sponsor the World Bank. It borrows in the private bond markets of the industrialized countries – primarily the United States, Europe, and Japan. Then it lends to the non-industrialized countries – India, Nigeria, Pakistan and such. The lending goes to finance irrigation projects, transportation projects, and other infra-structure. The projects are usually government-sponsored. Governments also established the IMF. It has a large fund of gold and foreign currencies contributed to it by the member countries. The fund is used to make loans to countries that are trying to stabilize the exchange rates of their own currencies. At first, the World Bank and the IMF operated somewhat indep-endently. Now, they operate more or less in tandem. The United States and its allies dominate both institutions.

Frequently, underdeveloped countries import more than they export and they frequently have massive debt payments flowing out of their economies and into the richer economies. The net importing and the debt payments are constantly in danger of pushing the exchange rate of their currencies down to unacceptable levels – down so low that they cannot afford to pay their debts or to buy essential imports from the developed countries. Their exchange rate problem periodically comes to a head with a massive flight of funds from the country, putting the country's financial system in crisis. Here is where the IMF and World Bank come into play. They offer large loans to stabilize the currency and the financial system of the country in crisis, but they also insist on something in return. They insist that the country in crisis deregulate its financial system, so foreign (US) banks and investors can buy up whatever they want and can withdraw their funds from the country whenever they want. They also insist on an austerity package designed specifically for the country in crisis. The austerity package usually involves a balanced budget for the government, a high interest rate for the banks, and a recession for the economy.

In short, the IMF and the World Bank have become the equivalent of international loan sharks. They impose harsh loan conditions on debtor countries that have little choice but to accept. Those harsh conditions cripple the debtor's economy and force open the debtor's door to foreign investors.

The economic interests represented by the WTO, the IMF, and the World Bank are shaping the evolution of the global economy. To some extent, the European Union is taking a different path in Europe, but elsewhere the path involves deregulation of international investors, rising global inequality, and accelerated growth of large international corporations. Economics is dominating politics. The global economy is ruled by the rich, and is evolving in directions favorable to them, at least for now.

How do economic institutions and class relations affect the political process? – a Marxist view

The Marxist literature on democratic processes, undemocratic processes, and the state begins with several of Marx's pamphlets. The most famous Marxist writer on the state was Lenin, who has inspired whole libraries full of Marxist literature following Lenin's lead or highly critical of Lenin. The extensive debate in the Marxist literature up through the 1960s is discussed in detail in Sherman (1972 Chapter 9); the later radical and Marxist debate is presented in Sherman (1987 Chapter 8); and the further debate is updated in Sherman (1995 Chapter 9).

The common Marxist beginning point is that the political process tends to reflect the basic class structure of society. Thus, in the US South before the Civil War, slaves could not vote and most Southern legislators were white, male, slave-owners. In the modern United States, economic power is highly concentrated in a small elite group, but so is political power concentrated in the same group, either directly or indirectly.

Capitalism is incompatible with democracy

Robert Kutner contends that "A capitalist democracy exists in necessary tension between the contradictory principles of one citizen/one vote and one dollar/one vote. Money buys nearly everything else and keeps trying to buy what should not be for sale in politics" (Kuttner 1998: 345). A pure market capitalist system means that you can buy anything, so there would be no limits on political spending. Some conservatives advocate this on the basis that anyone should be able to spend in the market and that political spending is free speech. If we really abolished all regulations on political spending and lobbying, then a corporation could spend a billion dollars to get a President and Congress elected. Ten corporations could surely spend so much money that they would win in the present situation. Thus, all of politics would be bought by money instead of being decided by the democratic votes of people – even if the form of voting remained. Or there could be two parties, each funded with billions of corporate dollars, still not democracy but the form would remain. Capitalism thrives alongside the form of democracy because the democratic form provides very useful legitimization and promotes the myth that everyone is equal politically. It is the content of democracy that capitalism undermines.

If this sounds like science fiction, then consider the facts. In the United States, every citizen has the right to vote, so isn't it contradictory to say that political power is lodged in the hands of a small minority? Voting is one tiny part of the political process and it is shaped by the institutions that shape the individual.

The voter is not from outer space, but is influenced by family background, race, gender, and class, all of which are internalized in one's psychology. Voters' information comes partly from experience, but partly from the media, from religious organizations, and from the educational system. For most voters, 30 seconds on television provide the basic data on most issues.

This brings us to the question: who controls the media, religion, and education? Religious organizations are usually raising money, so the influence of the wealthy is very great. Private education is controlled by rich trustees, but public education is usually also controlled by rich trustees or regents, appointed as favors by governors or state legislators. The media are owned by corporations and the wealthy. Moreover, media are guided by advertisers and sponsors to some degree. So economic power is felt in the media in at least two ways. The dominant media in a capitalist country do not preach socialism or revolution, but support the status quo and call for incremental reforms under some circumstances.

Wealth also plays a role within the political parties by influencing the choice of candidates. And once a candidate is elected, most politicians spend remarkable amounts of time raising money. But only the wealthy can contribute large sums of money – while most workers, all of the poor, and all of the unemployed, usually contribute nothing. Contributors have access to politicians and exert influence over them. Finally, any one wishing to get ahead in a corporation must support the status quo in the economy as a whole.

A good example of how the power of the capitalist class is expressed in Congress is given by Robert Reich. Reich (1997: 91), who was then Secretary of Labor, describes a discussion he had with Marty Sabo, who was then Chairman of the House Budget Committee. Sabo explains to him why the House Democrats will vote to cut spending on all social and education programs even more than Clinton recommended. According to Reich, Sabo says:

"The freshmen Democrats are all deficit hawks. But it's not just the freshmen, a lot of other Democrats are spooked" (page 91). Reich asks what has spooked them? And Sabo replies (according to Reich):

As long as the Republicans were in the White House, the business community didn't talk about the budget deficit. It ballooned. They didn't care. They spouted that baloney about supply-side economics. For the twelve years that the debt mounted, there was a conspiracy of silence – Reagan and Bush, the Democrats up here on the hill, big business. No one said a word. Defense spending exploded. Business liked that too. And the silence gave Democrats the cover to expand Medicare and a few other things.

(Reich 1997: 91)

So no one really "conspired," but interests went in the same direction. So what changed?

Sabo says (according to Reich):

But then big business discovered last summer that there might be a Democrat in the White House come November and Democrats running both houses of Congress. That ended the conspiracy. Business figures they won't get more military spending and certainly no more tax cuts for corporations or for the wealthy. So they did a U-turn. Suddenly all they want to talk about is the national debt.

(Reich 1997: 91)

But if the Democrats are the liberal party and if they have a majority and the President, what is the problem?

According to Reich, Sabo says:

We're owned by them. Business. That's where the campaign money comes from now. In the nineteenth century we gave up on the little guys. We started drinking from the same trough as the Republicans. We figured business would have to pay up because we have the power on the hill. We were right. But we didn't realize we were giving them power over us. And now we have both branches of government and they have even more power. Its too late now.

(Reich 1997: 91)

An excellent book by Congressperson Bernie Sanders (1997) shows in detail how some elections can be won by socialists in the United States. Yet he also shows in great detail all of the pressures exerted against socialists by business, the dominant parties, and the media. The same book by Sanders (1997) also shows how socialists can build coalitions in Congress to win a few battles. But he also provides fascinating detail on how Congress is controlled by the corporations and the wealthy.

It should be noted that the effect of the dominant ideology is not just that voters follow ruling class values, but also that half the voters are convinced it is not worth voting even in Presidential races – and only a third vote in off-year Congressional races.

For all of these reasons, vested interests usually work automatically in the media, the religious system, the educational system, and the political system to preserve the status quo and to reproduce it from year to year.

How does myth affect the political process?
– an institutionalist view

After examining myths and apparently irrational behavior, it will be shown how these affect the political process.

How can the irrational be rational?

In the institutionalist section above, you were introduced to the World Trade Organization (WTO) and its parent the General Agreement on Tariffs and Trade (GATT), the European Union (EU), the International Monetary Fund (IMF), and the World Bank. These international institutions were established to eliminate the kinds of economic conflicts that contributed to the Second World War. The GATT and then the WTO were intended to promote peaceful trade relations. The IMF was intended to stabilize the crisis-prone system of different currencies and exchange rates that had disrupted trade and financial relations between countries since the First World War. The World Bank was intended to finance the development of the underdeveloped countries by helping them build infrastructure.

These institutions were all rational responses to international problems. They were established by the democracies that had triumphed over Nazi Germany and Imperial Japan in the Second World War. But, with the exception of the EU, they now appear to be profoundly irrational. The IMF now destabilizes poor countries in crisis. The World Bank is now an international loan shark for countries with no alternatives. The GATT–WTO is now deregulating the global economy. Why in every case, except for the EU, has the rational become irrational?

The question comes up because we still tend to think of evolution as progress. However, the recent evolution of the global economy, under the influence of the WTO, IMF and World Bank, has not benefited the common people. It is not progress, but it is evolution anyway. Besides, in a narrow self-interested sense, irrationality is rational if it results in someone else's ox being gored. The WTO, IMF and World Bank are goring the people's ox in their direction of the global economy. But they are also feeding the international corporation's ox. Integrating separate national economies into a single global economy creates winners and losers. The winners have been rich and powerful. The losers have been poor and powerless.

Artificial selection and conscious decisions

Human volition or agency – individual choice of specific actions – is the driving force behind the evolution of political culture. This, you could say, involves artificial selection instead of natural selection. Humans are not marionettes, whose actions are chosen by some kind of natural force operating above their heads that pulls their strings making them jump and twitch. Instead, humans choose their own course of action. However, they do so in a particular cultural context containing both rational and irrational elements. That context frames in their own individual and group interest.

For an example, let us turn away from the global economy and look at the United States. Over the last two generations or so in the United States, the evolution of political culture has taken some fascinating turns due to humanly chosen responses to unsettling events. Political culture in the United States has paid lip service to democracy but has long been dominated by individualistic values, strong jingoistic meanings, and by the beliefs of white supremacy and male patriarchy. It is within this elitist political culture wrapped in pretty democratic packaging that individuals in the United States have made millions of choices, artificially selecting their evolutionary path, as it were. Those choices were in response to a series of unsettling events and these choices put the United States on a path that has taken it to the far right of the political spectrum. Three elements were involved:

1 The political culture,
2 The precipitating events, and
3 The responses to the events.

The values, meanings, and beliefs of the political culture

The values of the US political culture are individualistic. They include a fear of big government, a corresponding rejection of the welfare state, an individual achievement orientation with no corresponding societal obligation, and a simplistic kind of knee-jerk response to most social responsibilities that goes this way: "my property, my income, my choice – leave me alone." The meanings of the political culture are jingoistic. To most people in the United States, their nation means the ideal nation toward which all others strive. To be the United States means to be the nation that has repeatedly saved great parts of the world from dire peril through waging gallant wars.

In this jingoistic view, the US saved Asia from the expansion of the Japanese Empire (the war waged by China is ignored). It also saved Europe from the Third Reich (the war waged by the Soviet Union is ignored.) And the United States saved the whole world from the international Communist conspiracy (all other factors are ignored.) So the United States means more than just a "city on the hill." It means the nation that saves the world whenever the world is in dire peril – a kind of superman among nations – a supernation.

The beliefs of supernation are supremacist across a wide range. In the 1950s those beliefs included the following: Americans were believed to be superior to the citizens of all other countries. White people were believed to be superior to all black ones. Male patriarchs were superior to all females. Heterosexuals were superior to all homosexuals. And, in large segments of the US population, Christians were believed to be superior to all others. These beliefs were not held by all Americans and were seldom enunciated so bluntly as they are here. In fact, they were seldom discussed at all in polite circles. The pretty democratic paper that packaged the elitist culture deflected such discussion. However, politicians put their careers in jeopardy if they directly violated the elitist elements in the culture. Even though silent beliefs, they were central to political culture in America during its golden age – the 1950s.

The political culture of supernation was dominated by the kinds of beliefs required to maintain the stability of its stratified society. They involved far more than just class. They were supremacy myths that kept whites up and blacks down; men up and women down; Christians up and others down; owners up and workers down, straights up and gays down; Americans up and foreigners down. In the 1950s, to challenge those beliefs was to be un-American. Nevertheless, they were all challenged in the 1960s, and by Americans. (Things change, don't they?)

Political events: supernation challenged

A number of events beginning about two generations ago in the 1950s and 1960s seriously challenged the political culture of the United States. A whole series of internal social upheavals took place: the civil rights movement and court-ordered school desegregation, the women's movement, the American Indians Movement, the student free speech uprisings, the peace movement, and gay rights. These internal upheavals threatened all of the supremacy beliefs, calling into question what it meant to be an authentic American. Furthermore, these upheavals were not along simple class lines, but threatened to upset a wide range of inequalities in society, in addition to class. The internal threats were insulting to many white American male heterosexuals whose narrow definition of their own centrality lost its exclusive claim to authenticity. A whole counterculture arose within the very heart of America that challenged and insulted white supremacy, male supremacy, American supremacy, Christian supremacy and heterosexual supremacy. The pluralistic nature of democracy was in danger of being taken seriously by significant numbers of Americans. Equality was afoot.

Compounding these internal events were a number of international events that were perceived as terrible blows to Americanism: True Americans believed that they watched helplessly as China and then Cuba joined the international Communist conspiracy. They believed that America barely reached a stalemate in Korea. And they believed that America suffered its first defeat ever when it lost the war in Vietnam. The latter event was the most divisive of all because the counterculture seemed to openly support what was supposed to be the national enemy.

In reaction against the counterculture's taking democracy seriously, white supremacy, homophobia, jingoism, male patriarchy, racism and Christian militancy all became far more sophisticated politically and entrenched culturally. White supremacists no longer attacked blacks directly, but accomplished their goals indirectly. That is, black people were not burnt up by lynch mobs. Instead, black churches were burnt down by unknown perpetrators. Furthermore, welfare was cut, public education defunded, and affirmative action dismantled. Uppity minority students got their punish-ment, as the reactionary revenge began the destruction of public education in America. Uppity minority workers got their punishment, as employment (last hired first fired) was cut and real wages pushed down as the Federal Reserve began in the 1970s its two-decade fight against inflation. The spiritual seekers of the counterculture got their punishment as narrow religious fundamentalism became a potent political force for spiritual conformity. The fresh air that the counterculture blew into the American bedroom and closet quickly turned stale as male patriarchs tried to put women back in their place and tried to put homosexuality back in the closet. Women's clinics were bombed, abortion doctors murdered, gay people attacked. Massive tax cuts were handed out to the rich to ease their pain (balance the budget)? Enormous increases in military spending were insti-tuted by the Reagan administration to atone for Vietnam. Iraq was bombed back to the stone age as an object lesson to all foreigners who would chal-lenge Americanism. Militia men sprang up in the angry heartland. A US veteran of the Iraqi war took his reactionary anger as deep into the heartland as possible – to bomb the Murrah Building in downtown Oklahoma City. Extraordinary increases in spending on jails, prisons, and penitentiaries took place. The war on drugs was declared and quickly filled them all up. Capital punishment was reinstated across southern and western swaths of the angry land in 1976. The NAACP (National Association for the Advancement of Colored People) Legal Defense Fund has counted 474 executions as of August

10, 1998 and reports that 3,474 people await execution on the death rows of thirty-eight states and jurisdictions [Levinson, 1998]. Chase them down beat them up, convict them, and execute them. Let god sort them out. And god, of course, is a true American.

These rightist responses have not been carefully thought out by individuals or by a cabal so as to benefit the capitalist class. There is a capitalist class, and it most certainly has benefited by the reactionary tide. Nevertheless, these rightist responses took place because of the complex interplay between the elements of political culture, the events of the time period, and the choices of individuals caught up in the cultural sequence of events and interpretations. Social movements rather than class conflicts defined most of the issues. (Further discussion is in Mayo Toruno 1997: 585–593.)

How do myths affect the political process?
– a Marxist view

After examining myths and apparently irrational behavior, this section explores how they affect class consciousness and the political process.

How is irrationality rational?

At first glance, a great deal in our society seems ludicrously irrational. For example, millions of people are unemployed, even though there is a great deal of work that could be done. There is the irrational notion that some groups are superior to others. There is the irrational notion that men are superior to women. There is the vast amount of crime and violence in the society, including not only felonies on the street, but also violence against women in the home, crimes against children, corporate crimes against worker health and safety, and so forth. Yet in each of these cases, such as racial discrimination, some group profits from the seemingly irrational views and behavior.

For example, the average model of women's clothing is underweight by the usual medical standards. Surely, it is irrational to have women's clothing modeled by a group of unusually skinny women. Yet capitalists who sell women's clothing are convinced that the clothing will sell better if the models are below normal weight, so they expect to make more profits by utilizing such under-weight models. The point is to convince women that they should all have a slender look. This slender look will win them all the men they want and everything else they want. Moreover, this advertising has been remarkably successful. It has certainly convinced most young girls of this irrational concept. Thus, a remarkably large percentage of all young girls are on diets! We conclude that many seemingly irrational concepts in the society serve to bring in high profits.

One basic irrationality is the fact that many people, even in the United States (not to speak of millions in the third World), go hungry or are badly undernourished – yet the United States produces far more food than it can sell. The issue of want amid plenty is carefully discussed and measured in Janet Pappendieck, 1998. It is worth noting that this seeming irrationality is a basic part of the logic of capitalism, since food cannot be given away to the poor without lowering the price and profits of those who control the food supply.

The Surgeon General of the United States says that cigarette smoking is very bad for your health. Yet the government of the United States gives subsidies to the tobacco industry to produce this harmful product. Surely it is irrational to encourage a harmful product! In fact, it is irrational from the view of society, but it is rational for some groups in capitalism. Tobacco farmers want to make profits and do not care about the effects of their product – the same way as those capitalists who make nerve gas or atomic bombs do not care about the effects of their product (unless it bites them). Why does government give money to produce tobacco? One reason is that the tobacco industry gives enormous sums of money to Congresspeople. Moreover, Republicans – and most neo-classical economists – believe that it is proper to produce whatever consumers want to be produced (though tobacco is not an instinct at birth, but a taste acquired by advertising, like most things).

Another apparently irrational action is the decision of the Supreme Court that money equals free speech. After the Watergate scandal, Congress passed reforms to limit the amount of money an individual could spend in a political race. But some millionaires wanted to spend their own money on their campaign in unlimited amounts. The Supreme Court held that they could spend all they want because they are using it to speak to the electorate and free speech is protected by the First Amendment. Thus, money equals free speech! This argument is clearly irrational from the viewpoint of society since it allows money to decide elections, contrary to democratic fundamentals. Yet it is rational under capitalism, since it fits the ideological view that anything can and should be bought – and it fits the class structure of power that gives that power to the dominant capitalist class.

On a television talk program (February 25, 1997) one United States Senator endorsed this Supreme Court decision, repeating many times that money is free speech – and claiming that Senators spend very little time getting money donations (contrary to the other three Senators on the program). His irrational position spreads a myth that earns him contributions and gets favors for the contributors that result in profits.

Another newspaper article (Clifford 1997: 1 and 20) says that a suit has been filed by an individual to stop the environmental regulation that is preventing Lake Tahoe from death by pollution. Her suit alleges that she has the constitutional right to do anything she wants with her own land and that the compensation offered is insufficient. To allow individuals to kill an extremely beautiful lake because they happen to own land there is surely irrational for society. But under capitalism it is rational to protect the rights of individual property owners against society because they represent the capitalist class and its right to do as it pleases with its property.

A man was given a sentence of life in prison for stealing a single slice of pizza (Krikorian 1997: 1 and 10). The man was a convicted felon. Nevertheless, to send someone to jail for stealing a slice of pizza is irrational because the punishment does not fit the crime, but to send someone to prison for life for stealing a slice of pizza reveals a sick society. Of course, it is rational from the ruling class view to have laws as tough as possible to protect their property. It is worth noting that the United States, the epitome of capitalism, has the largest numbers of prisoners in the world!

Myth and alienation

Large numbers of people in the United States feel loneliness and helplessness. They feel isolated and separated from other people, from their friends and family and fellow workers, and even from themselves. This is called alienation and has been discussed by many Marxists (see e.g. Bertell Ollman 1971).

What are the causes of alienation? Of course, those who live in poverty and/or unemployment have this feeling – and it is very strong in those addicted to drugs. But the feeling of alienation is spread far wider than those groups. Many of the employees of large corporations think of the corporation as a faceless giant that enforces ridiculous rules, pays no attention to their tiny part of the product, and does what it pleases with the final product – over which the employee has no control. Employees also know that they may be fired in periods of widespread unemployment, so they feel helpless relative to the corporation and to the job market. The institution of the market means that every worker is a rival of every other worker for jobs and promotions – this makes for separation from other people. The institution of the market also means that you get goods impersonally – or if you have no money you are denied goods impersonally – and it means that many consumers also face the faceless corporation with very little power. Thus the institutions of the market and the corporation are prime causes of alienation.

But there is also political alienation because people feel they cannot affect the giant faceless government. Many are convinced that the rich and powerful control the government, so the average individual can have no effect on the government. So they do not vote. Even in Presidential elections about half the people do not vote – and even less vote in other elections. Moreover, the pattern of who votes and who does not is not random. That half of the population that never votes includes most of the poor, the unemployed, welfare recipients, and millions of lower paid workers. Most of the affluent do vote. The myth that all politics is useless and corrupt and that one can have no effect on politics is a powerful weapon helping to deliver the government to the interests of the capitalist class. The myth is strongly supported by the media, who do not report most movements to change policy on the issues, but do report all of the nonsense and corruption which is found among many politicians. Notice that the excuse for corruption is often that everybody does it – or that I am just supplying a demand (a market excuse).

The market pressures everyone to look out for themselves instead of cooperating with others. The myth is that there is no alternative to a dog eat dog type of world. This powerful myth tends to prevent workers from organizing in a cooperative way to fight corporations in the economic arena – and it tends to prevent workers from organizing to fight corporations in the political arena. It is all hopeless anyway, so let others try; I'll spend my time trying to get rich by myself.

Class consciousness and political decisions

In the viewpoint of contemporary critical Marxists, an important role in institutional change is played by class-consciousness, the conscious decisions of individuals that are heavily influenced by their class positions, but also by all the other institutions discussed in the previous section. Since individuals are influenced by so many disparate factors, any given individual may hold any conceivable view, regardless of their class position. For example, Marx and Engels came from affluent, elite families and were not from working class backgrounds. But if we examine the average consciousness of an entire group, such as landlords or tenants, we will find that the average view does support their interests, such as being for or against rent control. Similarly, although there are exceptions, lowering the tax on capital gains is supported mainly by the elite who have very large capital gains.

Most Marxists, such as Wolff and Resnick (1986), define a class as a group of people who share similar objective relationships to the production of goods and who appropriate their incomes in similar fashions – a definition based on objective criteria. Such a class sometimes has a common consciousness of their position and their interests – but sometimes they do not – so the subjective criterion of a common consciousness may not always be present. The terms "objective" and "subjective" may be clarified by example. Suppose that I am a tenant; I have an objective interest in having rent control;

but I may believe subjectively that rent control is un-American and wrong.

The great Marxist historian, E. P. Thompson, always emphasized the importance of class analysis, but he also always emphasized the subjective and historical definition of class, emphasizing that class is not just a structure, but is something that happens consciously between real, live humans:

> Class happens when some men, as a result of common experiences (inherited or shared), feel and articulate the identity of their interests as between themselves, and as against other men whose interests are different from (and usually opposed to) theirs. The class experience is largely determined by the productive relations into which men are born – or enter involuntarily.
>
> (Thompson 1966: 9; parentheses in original)

Thompson showed how the British working class came to have a certain viewpoint or consciousness based on the awful working and living conditions of the time as well as all the current religious mythology of that day that was part of everyone's upbringing. Thompson fought against two kinds of errors: against those people who said class is not very important, but also against those who said that only objective interests are important and there is no need to worry about the psychology of people (see the interesting and thorough discussion of Thompson's views in Ellen Wood 1995). There is nothing necessarily contradictory in looking at both objective relationships and individual consciousness of class at the same time; indeed most contemporary Marxists would insist that both are necessary to understand politics and social evolution.

On the one hand we can thus predict that a ruling class will tend to resist change in political institutions that brings other classes or groups more power. On the other hand, this is true only on the average of all its individual members, but we also know that some of those individual members will behave differently. Those groups emerging into a stronger position will – on the average for all of their component individuals – try to change political institutions to get more power, pushing forward the democratic process. For example, in the early nineteenth century the local and state business elites in the United States tried to keep property qualifications for voting, so that those without property could not vote. On the other side, industrial workers tried to remove those obstacles to the democratic process. Similarly, the old Southern elite fought tooth and nail after the Civil War to prevent African Americans from voting. And some business interests opposed the vote for women because they were worried about having to raise the wages of women to equality. In each case, there was a conscious effort by some groups, based on their interests, to maintain the status quo and hold back the expansion of the democratic process; while there was a conscious effort by other groups, based on their interests, to expand the democratic process.

Consciousness is a vital part of the political process, but it is not determined randomly in a vacuum. Rather, it is influenced by all of the class relations and institutional structures that affect people's lives. Evolution takes place because groups do act in ways that are somewhat predictable, even though some individuals act differently.

How does technology affect the political process? – an institutionalist view

The maintenance of the political process means more than just the maintenance from year to year of particular branches or structures of government – the Supreme Court, the Congress, or the Presidency. Maintaining these kinds of structures over time is important, but far more important is the passing on from generation to generation of the values, beliefs, and meanings that give support to and flesh out the political structures and processes of a political system. It is in the reproduction of values, beliefs, and meanings that a political culture is carried forward, and doing so is profoundly important. It is the political culture that evolves and it does so through a complex interplay between the democratic and hierarchic processes and the technologies and events that alter them.

The ways and means of mass communication are the most important technologies that have impacted political culture in recent generations. The change of political culture under the impact of new mass communications technologies has resembled the feigned retreat of a brilliant general facing a superior, but overconfident foe. The brilliant general has been leading the aristocratic army against the seeming advance of the democratic army. The seeming advance has been driven by new technologies. The feigned retreat has captured the new technologies and turned them to aristocratic account. The retreat is actually an advance. Can anything appear more dialectical/ diabolical?

The first engagement in the protracted war over the technology of the mass media involved the invention of the printing press. At first, the printing press seemed to further the cause of the democratic army, making it possible for more people to learn to read and to become more informed about the issues of the day. The printing press also curtailed monastic control over classical texts. But in their feigned retreat, the aristocratic army poisoned the press on which the people had come to depend for their opinions. Freedom of the press, it was slowly learned, was great, but only if you owned one. Otherwise, the printing press and the freedom to use it came to increasingly centralize the control of communications. Increasingly, the village story tellers, wandering minstrels, travelling lecturers, priests, preachers, and other decentralized "opinion makers" were replaced by the impoverished author, newspaper reporter, and editor – all working for the owners of ever larger and ever more centralized newspapers and publishing houses. It matters little whether today's reporters, journalists, editors, and newspersons are personally liberal or conservative. What matters is that independent freelancers have been replaced by dependent lackeys.

A few generations after the printing press and reading had become widespread, the right to vote was extended beyond the propertied classes. Eventually, even women and former slaves acquired the right to vote in most countries. The centralization of mass communications by the printing press had proceeded so far that most of the formerly excluded folks did not vote radically differently from the propertied classes. Most of them had been taught the meanings, values, and beliefs of the aristocratic political culture by the new technology of centralized mass communications. They voted accordingly.

A similar sort of thing took place with the introduction of radio and television. The new broadcast communications technologies looked like they could open up whole new worlds of music and culture to people from all walks of life. And they could have. But they did not. The new broadcast technologies did not fill the homes of the common folk with the beauties of opera and symphony or with the profundities of high culture. Instead, to centralization and privatization of the means of communication was added intense commercialization. Furthermore, commercial television, far more than commercial radio, radically altered the election process. It replaced the importance of political party members and their participation in campaigns with the importance of financial interests and their payment for expensive television advertisements. Now elections are really not exercises in democracy, but contests of plutocracy. The prize goes to the advertised personality (formerly political candidate) who has raised the most money for advertising and has projected the most appealing image to the voters.

Hail Ronnie Reagan. Celebrities, or those who can afford to become celebrities, are our new political leaders. But they embody the meanings, values, and beliefs of supernation's political culture, adapted as it is to the new technologies used to broadcast mass communications.

Of course, the evolution of political culture continues and no one can predict whether aristocracy will continue gaining over democracy or whether the tables will turn. We will just have to see what happens.

Interesting trends

Institutional structures are important in the evolution of a political culture. The mass media is only one such structure. The judicial system is another, and here we find an interesting trend in the United States that favors democracy. New scientific knowledge of the effects of smoking on human health has changed the political culture through the judicial system. Largely ignored by the mass media, and stymied by most of the formal structures of government, the tobacco fighters turned increasingly to the courts and sued the tobacco concerns for damages. Armed with new information, the tobacco fighters won a whole series of legal victories and put the tobacco industry on the run. The Health Maintenance Organizations (HMOs) that have been denying many Americans the quality health care they think they deserve are coming under the same kind of legal attack as the tobacco companies. Although generally quite conservative, the US judicial system has become a democratic channel for the people to attack injustice through the class action suit.

The political culture is not determined simply by new technology and the struggle over its use. Evolution in political culture can come through the mass media, the courts, the legislative branch, or the executive branch. Franklin Delano Roosevelt's New Deal involved all the branches or structures of government. His "fireside chats" mobilized the mass media. Roosevelt himself transformed the executive branch. The legislative branch also participated in transforming the structure and function of American government. Although the Supreme Court at first resisted the New Deal, as Roosevelt's appointments came to dominate the Court, it too began transforming the legal structure and political culture of the United States. Evolution can also come through the efforts of mass movements – civil rights, women's movement, peace movement and all the rest. Even the military influences the evolution of political culture. The mass participation in World War II introduced servicemen and servicewomen of many nations to a wide range of new people and new ideas. The Vietnam War profoundly altered US political culture.

How technology affects the political process
– a Marxist view

The direction of change in democratic institutions will be influenced not only by class interests, but also in some ways by technological changes. Each new expansion of the technology of communication and information transmission has been greeted by a belief that it would automatically increase democratic knowledge and participation. But in reality, new technology is usually controlled by the ruling class and is used to their benefit. Thus, it used to be the case that a candidate needed enthusiastic supporters to go door to door. But technological advance has made that largely obsolete because the most important thing is to spend millions of dollars on slick television advertising. The sociologist Robert Lynn (famous as co-author of the study on Middletown) came to the conclusion that: "The problem we face today is that, in an era that increasingly lives by science and technology, business control over science and its application to human needs, gives to private business effective control over all the institutions of democracy, including the state itself" (Lynn, quoted in Noble 1979: 109). Only a change in social circumstances that forces the middle and working classes to fight to change the situation will eventually lead to greater democratic participation utilizing the new technology.

How does the political process affect the rest of society?

Here we consider how the political process influences economic relations, social myths, and technology.

How does the political process affect economic institutions and vested interests? – an institutionalist view

The political system is the ultimate power in society. It controls the use of violence. The force of arms is its ultimate power. At any one time, however, it may seem to just passively reflect the interests of dominant economic classes or groups. So its power, at any one point in time, may seem to come from that class or group of top people and to serve that class or group of top people. But there is more to the state than that. It is a sleeping tiger. The power of the state is more than derivative. It is also original. It is powerful even when it stands against a dominant class or group. Furthermore, the state is more than a hireling. It does more than just defend the interest of the owner against the worker, the master against the slave, the patriarch against the woman, the white man against the black. It promotes its own interest, as well. Its wars against other states sometimes benefit and sometimes harm powerful interests inside its own society. In war it may turn against its own corporations, drafting their executives and confiscating corporate assets. Its role in resolving disputes between different private interests makes it an ever-present force in the evolution of society.

In an evolving society, economic interests do not stay in a natural harmony or balance. Instead, though common ground often can be found, there are always winners and losers in evolution. So over time, disputes are inevitable and in the absence of social controls, there are no natural limits to how far the disputants will go in pursuit of their own interests. Absent state control, they may end up killing each other over a pittance. The mass media is full of such stories. Peaceful resolution of disputes requires the power of the state. If the state cannot or will not settle a major dispute between two private parties, one of the disputants themselves may usurp the power of the state and impose a settlement by force of arms. During prohibition, Al Capone did so with respect to the liquor business in Chicago. Disputes arose between bootleggers over their sales territories. Since the liquor business was illegal, the political system could not be called in to settle the disputes. So, Al waded in and settled the disputes with great finality. Had he been able to maintain his own use of violence against the objection of the government of the United States, Al Capone would have become a kind of state himself – the King of Cicero, perhaps. The point is, when disputes arise, and they always do, a special kind of power is called into play. John R. Commons called it "sovereignty" (Commons 1961: 684–96).

Sovereignty is the power to settle disputes. It is a state power, and its exercise makes the state a driving force in social evolution. In exercising its sovereignty the state can work through its executive, legislative, and judicial branches.

Presidential appointments and directives to administrative agencies at the Federal level and gubernatorial ones at the state level can change the way disputes with labor unions, say, are decided. President Reagan, for example, destroyed the Air Traffic Controller's union when they went out on strike during his first term of office. His action set a new course for the evolution of labor-management relations in the United States.

New legislation can cause drastic change. Such was the case with the new laws passed during the New Deal that revolutionized banks, stock markets, retirement pensions, agricultural stabilization programs, labor relations, and much else in an attempt to fight the Great Depression. The New Deal set the whole economy off on a different evolutionary path.

Court decisions also initiate change, as in the decisions handed down in sexual harassment suits, and in the tobacco wars. Sexual harassment decisions have put the relations between men and women in the workplace on a totally different footing than before. After the tobacco wars, product liability and class action suits will never be the same. The giant corporation that harms others is now a little less secure in its vested interest to profit at the expense of whomever. Perhaps movement down a more socially responsible path will begin. Or perhaps the power of class-action lawyers will be curbed and the path of least resistance will beckon once again.

The future is largely unpredictable. But this much can be predicted: the political system will have a powerful effect on the evolution of society.

How does the political process affect economic institutions and class relations? – a Marxist view

Politicians pass laws. Many of these laws regulate the economic relationships of society. Thus, at first glance it appears that laws are the sole determinant of economic relations and economic institutions. For example, in the US South before the Civil War, the laws stated that slavery was legal, that the master could buy and sell the slave, could punish the slave, and could sell the slave's family at a whim. In the modern United States, under the laws passed by the political process, slavery is illegal, but capitalism is legal. A capitalist can buy the labor power of an employee for a certain number of hours and the capitalist can sell the product of the employee's labor. In the former Soviet Union, the laws made capitalism illegal and made a government-owned economy legal; most production took place under a law passed by the political process. So it seems that laws determine economic relations.

But reality is far more complex. At any given time, the political process and the laws it passes are interdependent and interacting with the economic process and its relations and institutions. For example, it is true that the US government passes laws to tax corporations, thus affecting economic relationships. On the other hand, one strong influence on the Congress people who pass the corporate taxes are the corporations. Those corporations spend millions of dollars to affect the Congress and the tax laws that it passes. So at the same time that politics and laws affect economic relations, those same economic relations affect politics and laws.

Moreover, in the evolutionary process, change generally occurs in economic relations and is only reflected in laws with a short or long time lag. For example, in the feudal period, all of the laws concerning economic transactions were usually decided by the feudal lord on each manor. The laws passed by the lord were mostly concerned with what the serfs on his estate must do or not do. The serfs were under the lord's control, so this was a simple situation. What about laws governing the transactions of merchants with feudal lords? For a long time, there were no merchants because everything was made on the estate. When trade became significant, there were no laws to protect the merchants from arbitrary decisions of the lords. Eventually, however, the merchants fought for and achieved a whole new body of law concerning trade and the protection of contractual obligations – so the trade and the merchants came first, followed by the commercial law.

Similarly, after a revolution has eliminated a whole economic system and substituted a new one, the old laws are tossed out and new ones are put in place. For example, after the Civil War destroyed slavery in the US South, capitalism became the dominant economic system throughout the United States. Only then was the Thirteenth Amendment passed to outlaw slavery – after that economic relation had almost all been eliminated by force. Of course, a revolution happens through the political process – so one could argue that the political change preceded the economic change, which preceded the legal change. For example, Abraham Lincoln was elected President of the United States in the political process, which led to the political revolution known as the Civil War, which destroyed slavery, which set the stage for the Thirteenth Amendment. In truth, economic change leads to political change, which may lead to further economic change – the interaction between politics and economics is endless and any beginning point one chooses is arbitrary.

It is worth briefly examining the main ways that the US government affects the US economy. First, there is enormous spending for military purposes, which is the result of intensive lobbying by giant corporations and results in amazingly high rates of profit. Second, federal, state, and local governments spend huge amounts of money for roads, which carry the goods and services sold by corporations, and which earn high profits for the corporations that build the roads – again as a result of corporate lobbying and election of the friends of corporations. Third, government spends money on education, which educates employees to have the skills required by corporations; while the heads of corporations sit on many of the governing boards of educational institutions. Fourth, governments collect taxes – written by legislators who are under the influence of the big corporations. Taxes are used to support the military, the police, the roads, education, and so forth. This is how the political process affects the economy under capitalism, but remember that the process was very different under feudalism or under the Soviet system.

How does the political process affect myths? – an institutionalist view

Enabling myths are the content of social control and social control is necessary in a stratified society. Such myths are about the superiority of people occupying the top strata and the inferiority of people stuck in the bottom. Unless those in the lower strata can be convinced to be content there or at least to be fatalistic about their lowly position, they will try to change it. Enabling myths justify the inequality of the society and reduce the strife between the top and the bottom. Justification for the stratification is institutionalized in all of the major social organs, particularly in the education system.

Resistance to enabling myth rises and falls. The result is a continual battle for the hearts and minds of the members of society. In our time, the left pushes for equality; the right for inequality. In recent times the left seems to be the flightier of the two. In the United States, the purely indigenous Old Left of Big Bill Haywood and the Industrial Workers of the World wilted under the heat applied against it during the First World War. Then, the Old Left gained strength in the Depression of the 1930s. The Old Left of the Communist Party, however, began fading in the 1950s as

Khruschev's revelations about Stalin's excesses took their heavy toll. But then the New Left of Ken Kesey and Tom Hayden rose very quickly in the 1960s, only to fade almost as quickly in the 1970s. All through the 1980s and the 1990s, in the absence of an effective left, the right wing has been fanning the flames of classism, racism, sexism, jingoism, and homophobia. New enabling myths have been created in the form of such whoppers as "Bell Curves," purporting to "prove" the intellectual inferiority of African Americans (Herrnstein and Murray 1994) and "Tenured Radicals," purporting to show that subversives who cannot be fired from the American academy are waging war against Western Culture (Kimball, 1990). Both of these myths involve scapegoating. The first is a myth impugning the intelligence of minorities; blaming them for their own dispossession. The second is a myth impugning the integrity of egalitarian academicians, blaming them with trying to poison free inquiry in the academy.

As long as we have entrenched inequality of any kind, we will have such enabling myths, for new ones will just keep popping up after old ones are debunked.

How does the political process affect myths?
– a Marxist view

It is easy to allege that myths are reproduced because they are useful to the ruling elite, but that is not a proof. The most important task is to show the mechanisms by which myths are reproduced. In normal times all of the institutions of society contribute to reproducing the dominant myths year after year. Of course, the dominant myths normally reflect the interests of the dominant class. If the dominant myths are contrary to the status quo, then we are in a stage of dis-equilibrium and revolution.

The education system teaches the dominant myths (such as a belief in "free" market capitalism) at many different levels in many different ways. One of the earliest critiques of the ideological role of education was Veblen's *The Higher Learning in America*, which he seriously considered subtitling, "A Study in Total Depravity" (Veblen 1965: 261).

Organized religion preaches the dominant myths, for example, the desirability of slavery in the South before the Civil War and the claim that it was divinely ordained. The news media – TV, radio, and newspapers – report the news in a way that is completely biased in favor of the status quo, although they claim to be objective and neutral.

None of this is surprising. The dominant myths support the status quo. The present social-political-economic system – the status quo – is very desirable and profitable to the vested interests of the dominant class. The dominant class controls the education system, organized religion, and the news media. The political system also ordinarily is controlled, directly or indirectly, by the dominant class, so it too supports the dominant social myths.

How does the political process affect technology?
– an institutionalist view

As explained by Clarence Ayres, to a limited extent, the evolution of technology is a self-contained process (Ayres 1978). It is driven by the prior accumulation of tools and skills in the community's joint stock. Technology has been evolving faster and faster because the accumulated stock of technology that fuels the evolution has been getting larger and larger. Each new generation adds more to the stock because it was handed more by the previous generation. The result is a self-augmenting process of cumulative evolution (a redundant phrase) where the forward movement of one generation becomes the starting point for even faster movement by each succeeding generation.

However, the political system strongly affects both the rate of change and the direction of movement of technological evolution. The political system funds and administers research and education. It also establishes laws and adjudicates disputes that determine how new technology is fit into the existing system of vested interests and going concerns. State policies on research, education, and new technology require brief discussion.

State research policy

The central government and the decentralized state governments in federal systems all fund research projects and administer various kinds of research institutes. The mix of military and civilian projects that are funded strongly affects what kind of science and technology is promoted. The way in which secrecy issues and ownership issues are handled can slow down or speed up the dissemination of science and technology. If advances in science and technology are locked up as state secrets, then dissemination will be slow. Dissemination will also be slowed down if such advances, funded by the public, are strictly controlled through tight licensing agreements. Ideal conditions would include no military projects and no state secrets, plus free use to anyone of any new advances in technology.

Details make a difference. Grandiose projects that catch the public imagination are favored by politicians, but not necessarily by scientists. So when politicians choose which projects to finance, the giant and the spectacular take precedent over the small and mundane. So the US and the USSR spent many billions of dollars and rubles on the race to the moon. But getting a man there was so unimportant scientifically, that once the US won the race and televised several of its moon landing spectacles, nobody has bothered to return a human to the moon in nearly three decades. Been there, done that.

When scientists instead of politicians choose which projects to finance, a different sort of bias comes into play. Scientists rely on the peer review process – a panel of distinguished researchers is chosen to review the research proposals of their peers. Peer review favors conformity over diversity. Projects that conform to the basic approach already taken by the reviewers are funded. Projects that take a strikingly different approach are not. The conforming projects validate the reputations of the reviewers, while the diverging projects challenge existing reputations with new approaches.

State education policy

Education systems are usually state-funded and state-administered, although some private education also takes place. The wider and the more equal access to education is, the more people can contribute to the growing community stock of knowledge. Class, race, gender, religious, and other barriers to education all slow down and distort the ability of new people to contribute.

Educational content is extremely important. Education that simply indoctrinates acceptance of social norms and established authorities contributes nothing to the evolution of technology. Education that teaches classism, racism, sexism, homophobia, jingoism, and religious intolerance deducts from the community's joint stock of accumulated knowledge. It teaches us to know things that just are not so.

State technology policy

New technology has to fit into the existing ways of doing things. A new way to do something or a new thing to do has to be pushed into the established system of vested interests in the old ways to do things and the old things to do. New technology generates conflicts. The laws, rules, and procedures for handling the conflicts are strongly influenced by state policy regarding for example property rights, intellectual capital, and patents. A new technology frequently destroys the value of an old property right. New mining techniques destroy the value of mines that cannot be adapted to them. A new technology requires new human skills and makes old ones – old human capital – outmoded. A new technology may also make an old patent outmoded, or may infringe on existing patent rights. All these examples of the new versus the old result in disputes that usually end up in court for resolution. Just how the state and its court system handle them will affect the evolution of new technology. In conclusion, the influence on technological evolution of the state and the political system is profound.

How does the political process affect technology?
– a Marxist view

US politicians spend money for dams, battleships, hospitals, roads, and space ships. Obviously these political decisions change the composition of the labor force, the use of raw materials, the accumulation of capital, and technology. All of the technology that went into the atomic bomb and the early nuclear power industry was paid by the US government, so politics obviously affects technology.

The question becomes more difficult, however, when we ask why these particular political decisions about technology were made. For example, how and why were the pyramids built? First, note that a primitive hunting and gathering society could not have built the pyramids – it would have lacked a government that ruled a large population and a class relationship that ensured a supply of cheap labor. In ancient Egypt, there was slavery, so a strong government was needed to prevent slave rebellions. A strong government was also needed to fight with other governments over expansion of land and slaves. The Pharaoh was given absolute power – and then to make the government more powerful he was held to be the divine son of a god. This myth afforded strong support of the political and economic status quo. Then to extend the myth within the context of the whole religious mythology of Egypt, it was decided to protect the immortal body and soul of the pharaoh by protecting him for eternity in a huge pyramid. The pyramids also added to the awesome and impressive might of the Egyptian government. In order to build the pyramids, thousands of slaves were used as cheap labor. Thus the needs of government in a given class relation, plus the necessary religious myths, plus the labor supply afforded by the class relations, were all necessary to the building of the pyramids and the new technology that was developed during their creation.

Conclusion

In the evolution of democracy, institutionalists emphasize cultural meanings, values, and beliefs – the political culture. Further emphasis is placed on political processes of change, on the effects of new technologies, and on cultural sequences of events. The political processes of change can exclude (aristocratic) or include (democratic) participation. The state can work both ways. It can democratically respond to the demands of the downtrodden and turn subjects into citizens. But it also can aristocratically respond to the complaints of the privileged and turn union members into corporate servants. Significant technological changes in communications over the last several generations have worked toward greater exclusion. New communications technologies have centralized and concentrated the control of the means of communication. Freedom of the press is great, if you are one of the very few who own one. The 1960s demonstrated that cultural events really matter and that individual responses to them in the context of mass movements can add up to extraordinary change – to revolutionary evolution.

In the Marxist view of democracy, the question is whether the institutions of capitalism are compatible with democracy – and the answer is that only a very limited amount of democracy can exist under the rule of wealth. Great stress is laid on the economic power of the capitalist class and its ability to control the political process directly and indirectly. Direct means include contributions to political parties and candidates as well as lobbying. More important are indirect means including the ubiquitous structural threat to withdraw capital and/or jobs, the use of the communication institutions (media, education, religion) to spread helpful myths, and the day to day presence of capitalism that convinces people it is the only possible reality. Variety and change in political institutions result from the cumulative effect of new technology, changes in relative class powers and changing myths. Some types of new technology are given harmful applications or are sabotaged by the ruling, corporate class. New technology – such as television and computers – is controlled by the capitalist class and is utilized, not only to make profit, but to control the democratic process, so the process is evolving toward less and less democracy as capitalists can buy more and more of high-tech political process. Marxists do not, however, see capitalist control as complete or eternal, but rather emphasize the conflict of the capitalist class with the middle strata and lower strata of the working class over every issue in the democratic process. Changes in relative class strengths may also eventually lead to democratic evolution.

The two views – institutionalist and Marxist – are not necessarily opposed. They do emphasize different aspects of political democracy at the opening of the new millenium. They both, however, incorporate myth and irrationality into their explanation of democracy and change, and they both bring conflict of interest into their analysis. Neither is static. Both are evolutionary, but neither sees natural harmony evolving as an automatic element of democracy.

Part III

PROCESSES

6

STRUCTURAL CHANGE

We begin with our agreements, then look at some of the differences in our approach to structural change.

Common ground: agreement on the causal elements, processes, and definition of evolution

In Chapters 2 through 5, we explored the causal elements of our theory of social evolution. We found that institutionalists and Marxists disagreed on several of the detailed concepts and approaches to social evolution, but we also found that we agreed on the basic causal elements in social evolution. We agreed that economic relations (Chapter 2), technology (Chapter 3), ideology (Chapter 4), and polity (Chapter 5) were the important causal elements in social evolution. In the next three Chapters – 6, 7, and 8 – we discuss important processes in social evolution. We agree that three general aspects of the processes of evolution are particularly important: (1) structural change, (2) social tension, and (3) social conflict. Of course, we also continue to disagree on various specific details.

In Chapter 1 we started out our conversation with agreement on a definition of social evolution. Structural change was central to our definition of the evolutionary process.

Reality of structural change – an institutionalist view

Social structures and institutions

Social structure means the same thing as social institution. Both are habits of thought learned by individuals and are shared by members of the same society. These habits of thought are also guides to action because they give meaning and value to human relationships and help channel relationships in socially approved ways. In concrete form, these habits of thought become

121

organizations such as the family, the church, the school, the government agency, the court, the political party, the corporation, and the union. The word "structure" refers more to this organizational aspect of habits of thought, while the word "institution" refers more to the values and meanings aspect of habits of thought.

Habits of thought can be as informal as the little practices a family has established in its celebration of birthdays or as formal as the laws a nation-state has established in its regulation of banks. They are rules of thumb that channel human choices in the way that drop-down menus channel computer use. They are social norms, the software of a society. Norms do not have to be followed, but if they are not, certain unfavorable results can occur. The individual always has a choice. You do not have to follow the menus and default settings of your computer program. But if you do not, you may have to rewrite the program on your own or you may find that the computer does not work as expected. As long as your computer is not doing too badly, it is easier to just follow the menus and accept the default settings.

The social institutions or social structures of a society are what make one society differ from another because they engender different human relationships. Just as computers think and act differently when loaded with different software programs, individual people think and act differently when born into different societies. They do so, not because human nature varies from one society to another, but because social structures and institutions vary. However, this is not to say that the individual is just a passive product of the social structures and institutions into which they are born. Those structures and institutions are themselves the product of many generations of individual and collective actions.

Structural change – cumulative and nonrepetitive

In the process of structural change, the actions of the current generation always begin with the product of the preceding generation. Each succeeding generation starts at the point where the preceding generation left off. The process is cumulative. A simple illustration will help clarify the point: two generations ago, Texans started air conditioning their homes by sticking window units in their bedrooms. The next generation of Texans went further and put central air conditioning in their homes and added air-conditioners to their cars. The up and coming generation of Texans has air conditioning built into its habits of thought. They cannot go back two generations to the time when folks sweltered all night long during the summer and woke up wet and exhausted every summer morning. So if the current generation of Texans were asked to save energy by turning off their air conditioning, they just will not do it. Instead, in addition to air-conditioned homes and air-conditioned cars, they increasingly insist on air-conditioned everything. They will not go back to the good old days of an open window. If we lived in Houston, none of us would. We would want to air condition the very sidewalks. We may have to. (Global warming?)

In the process of structural change, we do not go back to home base and repeat. There is no home base. The process of structural change is not repetitive. We do not go back to some fixed point that is common to all generations, back to some constant human nature and repeat. There is no constant human nature. Not even the human gene pool is constant. Again, the point can be emphasized with an example from the evolution of the personal computer and its software. Each generation of software programs builds on the previous generation of programs. Succeeding generations of programs do not return to the original operating systems for a place to start. They build on the latest operating systems. Change in program systems is not repetitive. It does not go back and repeat the old patterns. Besides, the hardware has changed so much that the software cannot go back. Just as there is no constant human nature, there is no constant computer model. The new ones have been changed forever.

History does not repeat itself. History cannot repeat itself for the same reason that you cannot step into the same river twice.

Structural change and scientific law

In social science, the regularities that we can observe in human relationships are called "laws." When we observe regularities in human relationships, we are observing the product of shared social structures and social institutions. So as social structures and social institutions change, the regularities we observe in relationships also change. The laws of social science change as the structures and institutions of society change. They all evolve. This may not be true in the physical sciences, but in social science, law is not constant. Each set of social structures and institutions – each society – generates its own set of regularities, of laws. Structural/institutional change causes change in the regularities, in the laws, of a society. Evolution means that not only structures and institutions change, but the laws and regularities change as well. Laws are not constants in social science because structures are not constant in society.

The law of demand is not the same as the law of gravity. Although we should expect falling objects to follow the same law 500 years ago as they do 500 years in the future, we should not expect markets to do so. (Further discussion of laws in social science is in Mills 1959: 148–164.) The law of demand says that, holding other things constant, when the price of a commodity rises the quantity demanded will fall. Of course, that is true, but trivial. It is not a universal law on the same level as the law of gravity because in the law of demand we do not expect that the constancy requirement will be met. The law of demand is not universal because over the course of a thousand years (not that many generations) so much about the market system will change – let alone the market for a specific product – that who knows what major things will happen to the demand for a hamburger. Of course, when the price goes up the quantity demanded will still go down, but by then, do you really think that we will even be eating ground up dead cows with e coli mixed in? By then, the law of demand with respect to hamburgers will be moo(t). Sorry. I couldn't help myself. But, a thousand years from now, objects will still fall through space and they will still follow the law of gravity.

The fact of structural change is the only constant in social science. Human societies have undergone the most profound kinds of evolution and continue to do so. Hunting societies have evolved into herding societies and then into farming societies. On the Great Plains of the United States and the prairie provinces of Canada, tribal peoples used to stampede whole herds of buffalo off the edges of certain elevated plateaus. The fall killed even the strongest bulls. After the stampedes, generation after generation of buffalo hunters harvested thousands of pounds of meat every year at the base of these special "falls." The buffalo harvest fed and clothed all the peoples of the tribes. Certain regularities of the harvest and its distribution were the results of the habits of thought passed on from one generation to the next. Those habits of thought helped to determine who got what cuts of meat and other parts of the buffalo.

Today, on that very same North American prairie, generation after generation of wheat farmers harvest tons and tons of wheat every year. The distribution of the harvest feeds millions of people all around the world. Certain regularities of that current harvest and distribution are also the results of habits of thought passed from one generation to the next. But the regularities, habits of thought, and the very people themselves have all evolved into something completely different. Now, mortgages, property rights, legal contracts, insurance policies, and such all help determine who gets what share of the annual harvest. And now, the shares are given out in money instead of body parts.

Beginning in medieval Europe, the handicraft system evolved into the putting-out system and the putting-out system evolved into the factory system. (The putting-out system involved merchant-capitalists leaving raw materials with workers in their cottages and returning later to pick up the finished products that the workers made from it. The factory system brought all the workers together in one place and put them under the watchful eye of the capitalist-overseer.) The industrial revolution changed almost everything. And even now, the leading industrial country of the world (the United States) is de-industrializing. Economic structures have changed so drastically that while once kindly Geppetto made one-of-a-kind Pinocchio by hand in his own little shop, now giant US toy-maker Mattel has the interchangeable parts for millions of Barbies assembled for it in Chinese factories and marketed all over the world.

Stateless and classless societies have evolved into societies stratified into classes and ruled by nation-states. The buffalo hunters of the North American plains had no need for the state. They did not group themselves into classes. Their contempt for people who did was unbounded. But such people proved to be the hunters' destruction.

Societies in which the people provisioned themselves with no thought of property rights have changed into societies in which many of the people think of little else. Once simple harvest traditions decided who got the buffalo tongue and who the liver. Now distribution of the (wheat) harvest takes a little more. It (apparently) requires the help of a far-flung system of corporations, government agencies, banks, insurance agents, courts, prisons, jails, police departments, Bureaus of Investigation, and Marshall Services; all of which require staffing by a whole army of corporate and government bureaucrats, judges, bailiffs, lawyers, sheriffs, investigators, prison guards, jailers, and probation officers.

There are many other profound changes to think about. The structure of the family has changed drastically. Only a few hundred years ago, many infants did not survive into adulthood. Now, many adults fear that they will live too long – so long that they use up their savings and fall into destitution. The structure of the military has changed drastically. Only a few hundred years ago, when men went to war they had to hack off each other's arms and legs with sharpened lengths of steel. Killing was hard and dirty work. Now, they can incinerate themselves by the millions with just the push of a button. Killing is now easy and clean. So, of course, we do much more of it.

Resistance to structural/institutional change

Clarence Ayres would have explained many of the structural changes above as due to the forward thrusting of new technologies against the backward pulling of old institutions. Explaining the opposing roles of new technology and established institutions in causing structural change was one of the major contributions made by Clarence Ayres in his *Theory of Economic Progress*. Structural change was a result of two counteracting forces – the forward thrust of new technology versus the backward resistance of old institutions. Ayres made technology the exclusive dynamic factor in structural change.

Nevertheless, changes in any of the causal elements we discussed in Chapters 2 through 5 can initiate structural change. After all, technology does not initiate everything. (See Ayres 1978, Tool 1979, and Peterson 1994.)

Structural change and progress

Social evolution is continual because change never stops. But is change all that is meant by social evolution? Change means doing and thinking differently. Progress means doing and thinking better. Progress means movement upward in some scale of value, from a less to a more valued position of human welfare. If we look back one thousand years to the turn of the second Christian millenium and compare human welfare then with human welfare now, at the turn of the third Christian millenium, most observers would agree that progress has taken place. Life expectancy for most humans has gone up. Infant mortality has gone down. Nutrition has improved. Sanitation has improved. Clothing and shelter have improved. Literacy has spread. Small pox is gone. Tuberculosis still kills and may kill even more, but its rate is down. Other basic improvements have also been made. Until recently, perhaps until the nuclear age, most institutionalists believed that progress would continue. They almost believed that it was inevitable. But in recent years, this faith has begun to falter. We believe that societies will continue to change, but we are not sure that the change will be progress.

The importance of time and place

Neoclassical economics, the mainstream economics of the textbooks, makes a big mistake. It ignores structural change. It treats all times and places the same. Neoclassical economists have no excuse for their mistake either, because a whole school of economists taught them better, over a hundred years ago. That school of economists is known as the German Historical School. (Further discussion is in Mitchell 1969: 523–597.) With the German Historical economists, the institutionalists share an appreciation for the importance of time and place. One obvious example of the need for historical specificity in economics is the free trade doctrine. As the German scholars realized full well, free trade was great for the British industrialists of 1870. British industries were firmly established by then so they enjoyed all the advantages of increasing returns. In their competition with the British behemoths of the time, the Germans were handicapped, even in their home market. On top of that, the British navy protected British industrial exports in most foreign markets. So free trade was a recipe for the permanent under-development of German industry. The German historical economists knew it. They knew that economics was relative to time and place because different times and places were characterized by different social structures. They knew that economic relations and policies must be continually re-evaluated in the light of changing circumstances. Economic doctrine and theory must evolve along with changing circumstances. In their arguments against the free trade doctrine, German Historical Economists tried to teach the English, but the English Neoclassicals would have none of it.

Now, for what seems the same reason (national interest), the American Neoclassicals will have none of it from the economists of the underdeveloped world. The Americans insist on the universality of the free trade doctrine, the same as the English did a century or more earlier. But, of course, history never exactly repeats itself. Much has changed over the last century. New national powers have risen and fallen. New international institutions such as the World Trade Organization, the World Bank, and the International Monetary Fund now make American hegemony different from the old British Empire. But the nation with the strongest vested interest has promoted free trade before.

The reality of structural change – a Marxist view

In the Marxist view, there is real structural change in basic institutions and class relationships from one society to the next. Therefore, laws of social dynamics apply only within each society on the basis of its specific institutions and class relations – this is called the principle of historical specificity. Contrarily, orthodox, neoclassical economics is ahistorical. It claims that its laws are valid for all societies – so even the best neoclassical accounts have a very limited notion of evolutionary change (see e.g. Nelson and Winter 1982).

Ahistorical social science, however, distorts social understanding because it assumes that the same basic laws apply to all societies, whether they are hunters and gatherers with primitive communal institutions or capitalist systems with complex industry. It is important that social science should always be historical and evolutionary.

To be historical and evolutionary in approach means acknowledging that each type of society has its own laws. Social-economic laws – or social regularities – are specific to particular societies. Different societies behave differently. Thus, the Soviet Union, under central planning from 1928 to 1988, suffered no unemployment – but it was centrally planned under a dictatorship with little freedom, much inefficiency, and extensive corruption. Thus there were very real problems, but they were quite different from US problems.

Of course, any two societies may have some particular thing in common. For example, both the US and Soviet systems made use of money and paid workers a money wage. On the one hand, the reality of basic structural change in institutions makes necessary the use of historical specificity, the realization that new institutions make old laws and understanding totally obsolete. On the other hand, there may be some continuities between a group of societies, for example, among all stratified and class-divided societies. Thus, the fact of fundamental structural change does not rule out an understanding of how evolutionary change occurs in all stratified societies. Because they do have some things in common, we can describe some very general processes which have some points the same in all of this type of society. The common points do not give us specific laws, but do make it possible to have some common approaches, so that at least we can ask the same questions in each of these societies. These common questions about evolutionary processes in all class-divided societies are discussed in the next two chapters.

Incremental change and revolutionary structural change

There is always some incremental change going on in human societies. But relatively rapid and drastic structural change is rare. Of course, revolutions do not come out of nowhere. If one wishes to explain a truly revolutionary change in human society, then one must always examine very carefully the incremental changes that led up to it. On the other hand, no incremental change in human history has ever gone on forever. When one spots clear trends in a society going on for a long time then even if the society looks stable, one should ask what kind of revolutionary change may occur – otherwise one will be taken by surprise. Once a revolutionary change does occur, just about everything usually changes. Many incremental trends cease and there are whole new incremental trends. Thus, to understand any incremental trend, one must situate it within the fundamental institutional structure caused by the previous revolutionary change. For example, one cannot understand incremental trends in education without knowing whether the educational system is part of a feudal or a capitalist society. One cannot understand trends in racial prejudice or in gender prejudice without knowing whether the society is built on slavery or on capitalism.

Let us list some incremental trends in US capitalist society. One trend has been in the percentage of women at work in paid jobs (besides their unpaid home jobs). This very gradual upward trend lasted for many decades until in the 1960s a majority of women in the working ages had paid jobs. Having reached that threshold, the new position of women in class relations caused new self-perceptions, new perceptions by men, a new movement with a major struggle, and new laws.

An incremental increase in the size of corporations in the nineteenth century, accelerated by the victory over slavery, led to highly concentrated industries by the beginning of the twentieth century. From a country with only small business establishments, the United States, after decades of incre-mental change, found itself in the very different situation of having giant corporations, with a few large corporations dominating each industry. The trend toward more concentration and monopoly continued throughout the twentieth century, so by the beginning of the twenty-first century there are super giant firms worth billions and billions of dollars and spread out over the entire world. From high concentration in each industry in each country, there is now a high level of economic concentration of power in each industry in the world market. Thus, purely incremental changes led to the evolution of capitalism from the stage of small enterprises to the stage of large monopoly enterprises – and further incremental change led to the stage of super giant global firms. These changes in capitalism brought about enormous changes in every aspect of life, including the direction and pace of technology.

It is vital to understand that incremental changes caused by the specific dynamics of capitalism lead up to every apparently sudden change in the capitalist economy. In the United States economy, there is often the percep-tion that there are no problems at all and that smooth growth will continue forever. Then, seemingly out of nowhere, the economy reaches a peak and goes into a recession or depression. But economic contractions do not come out of nowhere. They are completely explicable by a careful analysis of the incremental trends that led to that peak – in which certain proportions slowly change and get further and further out of balance. In most business cycle expansions, for example, the ratio of labor income to national income slowly declines, the ratio of consumption to national income slowly declines, and the ratio of raw material costs to consumer prices slowly increases. Then as if suddenly out of nowhere profits begin to decline, followed by a crash. If orthodox, neoclassical economists do not pay attention to the internal dynamics of capitalism that lead to the incremental changes in these proportions, they are quite surprised by the crash – and always claim that it is caused by some external shock to a smoothly functioning economy.

One could list many other incremental changes reflected in important trends in the United States, such as the increase in educational achievement; the steady decline in the percentage of farmers; the yearly rise in the percent-age of people in the service industries; the yearly rise of people in prison; or the trend toward increasing inequality since the early 1970s – or the global trend toward an increasing gap between the poorer nations and the richer nations. But let us now turn to the even more fundamental incremental trends that have led, not just to changes within one system, but to funda-mental evolutionary change through revolutions from one system to another. A warning is necessary, however, that each of these fundamental structural changes occurred at specific times and specific places; none of them meant a world-wide change in all societies at the same time.

The most primitive societies have no private ownership of the means of production, except such personal implements as bows and arrows – the whole tribe possesses the forest together and hunts and gathers food there collectively. That institutional system lasted most of human existence.

Then in a few places some thousands of years ago, including Mesopotamia, Egypt, Greece, and Rome the primitive society was replaced by stratified, class divided societies. In those societies, slavery was usually the dominant institutional system, but there were also free farmers, and often every type of servile category between free farmers and slaves – with every servile group exploited by the great landowners and nobility.

In Western Europe, the Roman Empire finally disappeared and slavery declined to a very small percentage of all workers – though some slavery persisted for centuries. The dominant form of economic relationship was the institution of serfdom. Serfs worked most of the year for the lords on the lord's land, but they were not owned in body like the slaves, and they had their own little plot of land for subsistence.

It should be emphasized that serfdom was very different from modern capitalism, since workers were bound to one piece of land and were not free to move – and they owed service to the lord of the land. Moreover, the lords often had to borrow money, so they made high interest rates illegal. Under capitalism, workers are free to move – if they can find a new job – and the more interest a capitalist makes, the more respectable they are. Although the change from feudalism to capitalism was incubated for centuries, its final coming was marked by revolutionary violence in the English Civil War of 1649 and the French Revolution of 1789.

In Russia, there was a socialist revolution in 1917. Unfortunately it did not bring democratic socialism, but rather a system of dictatorship with central planning that might be called the Soviet mode of production – a set of institutions that spread to Eastern Europe and to China and Cuba.

In Russia in 1990 there was a capitalist revolution. Unfortunately, it led to the CCC mode of production: chaos, crime, and corruption, with a slow drift toward a very backward form of capitalism. Alas, poor Russia!

In the United States, there have been several revolutionary changes. In the colonial period, the British controlled trade with the US, received rents from US holdings, and received taxes from US commerce. The colonial regime was overthrown by the US Revolution of 1776 and replaced by capitalism in the northeast, slavery in the south, and mostly free farmers in the west. The free farmers of the west were not capitalists because they employed no one except themselves and their families, nor were they workers because no one employed them. At the beginning of the nineteenth century most Americans were still in agriculture, some in slavery, a few employed by capitalists in the northeast, and most still independent, free farmers.

This changed gradually as there have been less and less farmers every year from then till now, so the US economy changed from 80 per cent in agriculture to one or two per cent. Most in agriculture today are farm workers, so the class of free, independent farmers has disappeared without a violent revolution – though with many vehement protests.

Slavery ended in the United States as a result of the Civil War. It was replaced in the South by sharecropping, a great advance over slavery, but still a system with much human misery. Only after the Second World War was sharecropping replaced by capitalist farming. The political power of the old Southern elite was hardly challenged until the intense battles of the civil rights movement in the 1950s and 1960s. Some of the ideology of racism that defended slavery still exists.

Lethal mistakes

Some readers may think that the argument about whether there is really revolutionary structural change of institutions in human social evolution is a purely academic and unimportant argument about ancient history. But ignorance or rejection of the idea of structural change has resulted in some quite lethal mistakes in the twentieth century.

As an example, in 1929 when the Great Depression hit the United States, President Hoover's economic advisors told him to do *nothing*. Why did so many orthodox neoclassical economists think that the best thing to do about massive unemployment was nothing? They held the view that under competitive capitalism, aggregate demand must automatically adjust to aggregate supply if the government does not interfere (called Say's law). Of course, the US economy did not automatically return to full employment and millions of people suffered from lack of food, clothing and shelter. The argument for this amazing doctrine – that demand would automatically come to equal supply, so nothing should be done about unemployment – was based on an assumption that economic laws are universal and apply to all societies the same way. Thus, orthodox neoclassical economists used examples and reasoning based on pre-capitalist societies. In the pre-capitalist feudal society of Europe, most feudal manors were very isolated for centuries, they had very little exchange with other economic units, they used no money but only barter of one good for another, and they did not produce for profit in the market but for internal use of the manor. Each year the lord put to work all of his serfs in full employment producing the things he thought were needed. If they could produce more than the minimum, then there would be luxuries. Since he was not worried about selling the goods, but only using them on the manor, there could be no crisis of overproduction of supply relative to the market demand. Capitalism, however, is a very different system with a different institutional structure and different class relations. Under capitalism, goods and services are produced only for the market, so there is a crisis if the market is lacking. And the demand under capitalism must be in money, so desire or need is not the controlling factor. Moreover, the monetary price in the market must be sufficient to produce the present rate of profit or else capitalists cut back production and unemployment ensues. The two systems are basically different.

Cyclical unemployment, as the great institutionalist Wesley Mitchell showed in many books (see e.g. Mitchell 1913, 1989) is a typical characteristic of capitalist institutions; it did not exist under feudalism (Mitchell is discussed extensively from a Marxist view in Sherman 1991). The characteristic evils and problems of feudalism – or of the Soviet system, which had inefficiency and corruption, but not unemployment – were very different from those of capitalism and from each other. If one makes a mistake and thinks that all systems are basically the same, then it is possible to make lethal mistakes. It was not just in the Great Depression, but in every recession or depression since then, orthodox US economists say that nothing should be done to end unemployment because the system will do it automatically – which always results in massive unemployment, higher rates of divorce and mental illness, and higher rates of crime and suicide – a lethal mistake indeed.

Conservative economists often reason from imaginary societie (with pre-capitalist characteristics) that are said to be "basically" the same as capitalism. Neoclassical economists have always used the model of Robinson Crusoe, a fictitious sailor who was supposed to be shipwrecked on an island, where he grew his own food. Milton Friedman, a famous neoclassical economist, uses a model that merely assumes that every household is an independent producer, who exchanges freely with other independent producers, "a collection of Robinson Crusoes, as it were. Each household uses the resources it controls to produce goods and services that it exchanges for goods and services produced by other households, on terms mutually acceptable to the two parties to the bargain" (1962, p. 12). *This is not capitalism*; it is a fictitious and imaginary economy used by Friedman – and many neoclassical economists – as a debater's trick (though many neoclassical economists undoubtedly believe it is really true in some sense). In Friedman's ideal world of millions of individual Robinson Crusoes, everyone has resources and can decide voluntarily whether to exchange with others. In the real world, enormous enterprises with enormous resources face individual workers with almost no resources. If there is any unemployment, and there always is under capitalism except in wartime, then a worker faces the choice of working for a capitalist (if a firm is offering a job at some wage) or being unemployed. Obviously, Robinson Crusoe is never unemployed, nor is a group of Robinson Crusoes, since they own their own island and can always produce for themselves if profitable exchange does not appear possible. Friedman then tells us that this institutional structure (a bunch of Robinson Crusoes) is basically just like capitalism, so there is no involuntary unemployment in capitalism.

Conclusion

Institutionalists and Marxists disagree on many concepts and on how to focus their approach on these issues, but we do agree that there has been both incremental change and fundamental structural change in evolution. We also agree that in stratified societies, there are often social tensions (discussed in the next chapter). Those tensions are sometimes resolved as they arise, in an incremental process. But, those tensions also can contribute to a much harder to resolve kind of conflict between those with an interest in the status quo and those who wish to change it. Such conflicts may lead to revolt against the system.

These tensions and conflicts may result in continuous incremental change or in discontinuous revolution. But evolution will lead, sooner or later, to fundamental structural change and fundamental structural change will lead to fundamental differences in human behavior. That is, social systems – sets of social structures – do change and such change also results in changes in human behavior.

Social tension and conflict occur more in stratified societies than in primitive, egalitarian ones. All societies have very different dynamics based on different basic relationships. There are no universal laws for all societies, but there are important questions to ask about every society and its possibilities for fundamental structural change.

7

SOCIAL TENSIONS

We begin with our agreements about social tensions, then each discuss the issue in our own ways.

Additional agreement: the formation of social tensions as an evolutionary process

Both institutionalists and Marxists see social tension as one of the dynamics of social evolution in stratified societies. That is, stratified societies do not evolve because of consensus, but because of tension. Natural harmony is not an evolutionary dynamic of stratified societies. Problems and disagreements continually arise, not naturally harmonious relationships. We continue our dialogue, exploring social tensions in this chapter.

Tensions and dichotomies in social evolution – an institutionalist view

Institutionalists working in the liberal tradition of Clarence Ayres see social tensions in terms of technology pushing us forward versus ceremony holding us back (Ayres 1978). From the technology side of the tension, the newly warranted knowledge gained by science and enlightenment undermines the old knowledge supported by superstition and tradition from the ceremonial side of the tension. Institutions resisted new technology because the new technology changed the ways people did things, and people loved the old ways. Institutional resistance, according to the Ayresians, was the backward drag of tradition. In this view, for example, the most important resistance to new medical therapies would come from the reverence for traditional healing therapies and fear of new and unknown ones.

However, those working in the radical tradition of Thorstein Veblen see social tensions in terms of industrial progress pushing us forward versus business greed holding us back. In the Veblenian, as opposed to the Ayresian view, institutional resistance to new medical therapies would come from HMOs (Health Management Organizations) and insurance companies who did not want to pay for "experimental" techniques. So according to the Veblenians, institutional resistance was the conscious defense of financial gain, not the backward drag of tradition. Nevertheless, vested financial interest would use whatever means it could to defend itself, including wrapping itself up in valued traditions. Veblen, when he put his famous dichotomy of business versus industry in general terms, emphasized the self-serving influences of sportsmanship, predatory exploit, and invidious distinction (inculcated through what he called imbecile institutions) versus the community-serving influences of workmanship, idle curiosity, and parental bent. In his preface to a collection of essays he wrote for the *Dial*, Veblen explained,

> [A] discrepancy has arisen in the course of time between those accepted principles of law and custom that underlie business enterprise and the businesslike management of industry, on the one hand, and the material conditions which have now been engendered by that new order of industry that took its rise in the late 18th century, on the other hand ....
>
> (Veblen 1964: v)

Veblen's dichotomy between business and industry is the tension between the selfish interest of the highly positioned individual and the common good of the community. A tension of this nature exists in all forms of stratified society – slavery, feudalism, capitalism, patriarchy, or in any form of national patriotism or religious intolerance. Veblen's grasp of human history was phenomenal, but he chose what he called the modern business system as the form of stratification on which to focus. Veblen believed that it was in the selfish interest of the businessperson to create some kind of a monopolistic position that allowed them to raise prices and restrict production. In business, Veblen argued, the powerful used false advertising, private collusion, manipulation of government regulation, and whatever other means they could to benefit themselves at the expense of the underlying population. To Veblen, business meant rent seeking, trying to get something for nothing through sharp practice and monopoly.

Business aimed at profit, not production. Sometimes profit and production coincided, but more often, they did not. Veblen knew that there was no invisible hand that would always guide the business pursuit of self-interest into serving the common good. The invisible hand was wishful thinking on the part of Adam Smith. Adam Smith's wishful thinking has become an enabling myth. The common good was served by more production of serviceable goods for the community. However, the business system was constructed out of institutions and it used technologies, both of which provided for the acquisition of more money by business people. Improving or harming the common good of the community was a byproduct, an unintended result, an externality of the business system. The common good was an afterthought. Needless to say, tension continually arose between the community and the business system (Veblen 1904 [1975]). And, it was the tension that caused change.

Radical institutionalists have updated their treatments but still refer to the tension between community values and business values as the Veblenian dichotomy. Community values include a stable industrial base that provides for stable employment at good wages for all of the members of the community, and a quality environment that provides for uninterrupted access to clean air, water, food, and outdoor recreation. Business values include the opportunity to earn high profits with minimum financial commitment, the right to open and close plants whenever and wherever, the right to use air, water, and soil without interference, and the right to hire and fire workers at will. The two sets of values are often at odds. Some of the most vivid contemporary illustrations of the tension between the two come from environmental issues. Nothing can organize the resistance of a community faster than the announcement of the planned opening of a toxic waste facility in the community.

Strong tensions are created by plant closings. When local plants are shut down or moved to low-wage countries, community resources can be stretched past the breaking point to deal with the unemployment and social disintegration that results. Do the owners of the plant owe the community any compensation for the harm done by closing it? If all of the costs of closing the plant are factored in, does it make economic sense to close it? Why should only the private costs to the plant owner be factored in?

Plant openings also create tensions. Who should pay for the subsidies used to attract the new plant? Does acceptance of the subsidies imply certain responsibilities to the community paying them? Do those responsibilities include paying a living wage to community members working there? Does the community acquire some kind of a stake in the plant by subsidizing it? Is the corporate owner of the plant the only one with a vested interest in it? When communities compete vigorously with each other for a limited number of new plants, does community authority undergo an erosion? Can local communities continue to raise the taxes and enforce the regulations required to maintain themselves as quality places to live?

The same sorts of tensions are raised when giant international corporations invest in poor countries. The poor countries compete against one another for the international investments. The countries are forced by the competitive pressure to offer greater tax concessions, regulatory concessions, and subsidies of all kinds. The countries push down their wages and suppress their labor movements to create more favorable business climates. Is this the meaning of globalization? Is it a new kind of imperialism where the imperialist is a giant corporation backed up by international institutions (the World Trade Organization, International Monetary Fund, and World Bank)? Is this the meaning of global competition – a race to the bottom in terms of wages, working conditions, union protections, and environmental regulations? Where will this new imperialism take us? To a global fascism? To a global revolution? First to the fascism and then to the revolution? Must we let it go that far?

Tensions and dichotomies in social evolution: class relations versus productive forces – a Marxist view

In order to explain how structural change occurs in the evolution of society, Marx discusses the interaction of ideology, political institutions, class relations (the relations of humans in the productive process) and the forces of production (labor, capital, nature and technology). He concludes from his studies that:

> At a certain stage of their development, the material forces of production in society come in conflict with the existing relations of production, or – what is but a legal expression of the same thing – with the property relations within which they had been at work before. From forms of development of the forces of production, these relations turn into their fetters. Then comes the period of social revolution. With the change of the economic foundation, the entire immense superstructure is more or less rapidly transformed.
>
> (Marx 1904 [1859]: 12)

What does Marx mean when he says that the frozen class relations of a mature, stratified society may come into conflict with the potential of the productive forces? He is saying that human relations and institutions may sometimes hold back industrial progress.

In Chapter 3 we saw one example that Marx had in mind, that the relations of serfdom in feudalism held back the industrial progress desired by the emerging bourgeois or capitalist class, leading to the English revolution of 1649 and the French Revolution of 1789. In Chapter 2, it was emphasized that, when the chains of feudalism were lifted in England and France, there was very rapid growth of technology, labor and capital, leading to the industrial revolution – which in turn changed all of society. But in a mature capitalist society, as we saw in Chapter 3, the rigid class relationships of capitalism created the Great Depression, in which production went backward for ten years, while technology stagnated for ten years. In Chapter 8 we shall also examine how the relationships of slavery in the Old South of the United States held back industrial expansion and led to the Civil War and the end of slavery, which then led to a vast expansion of US industry and amazing changes in political institutions, ideology, and all of society.

The tensions in society between rigid class relations and potential improvement of the productive forces lead to conscious class conflicts that account for reforms or revolutions (such as the New Deal or the French Revolution or the Civil War). In the present period, the striking difference between the rapid change of technology or forces and the lack of change in basic institutions and class relations is stated vividly by the historian, David Noble:

> Modern Americans confront a world in which everything changes, yet nothing moves. The perpetual rush to novelty that characterizes the modern marketplace with its escalating promise of technological transcendence, is matched by the persistence of pre-formed patterns of life, which promise merely more of the same.
>
> (Noble 1979: xvii)

Let us take contemporary examples of how capitalist economic institutions and relations hold back the productive forces of industry We have just had 25 years of stagnation in the whole capitalist world – in spite of striking advances in some kinds of technology. Thus the Gross Domestic Product (GDP) of 12 west European countries grew 3.8 per cent a year in 1950–1973, but declined to 1.8 per cent growth a year in 1973–1992. Similarly, the GDP of the United States, Canada, Australia and New Zealand rose at 2.4 per cent a year in 1950–1973, but declined to only 1.2 per cent growth a year in 1973–1992 (official OECD data reported in Hahnel, 1999). In much of the 1990s Europe and Japan were in recession, with high rates of unemployment. In 1997–1999, there was a very painful crisis in Southeast Asia, leading to falling production and rising unemployment.

The United States had a lengthy period of recession in the early 1990s including a production decline followed by a very weak recovery and high rates of unemployment – especially in California – for several years. In the late 1990s, the United States had a boom which improved conditions somewhat. But in spite of a slow rise of production in those 25 years in the United States, none went to the working class, because the real wage (adjusted for inflation) was no higher in 1998 than it had been in 1973. Since real wages fell for some of the period and did not rise over the whole period, while production did rise (albeit slowly) employers were making money.

Indeed the wealth and income of the top one per cent of income recipients rose spectacularly in this strange stagnation. Nevertheless, for the economy as a whole and for most people in it, the United States was in a stagnation as was most of the capitalist world in that quarter century – its productive forces held back by capitalist economic institutions and class relations.

Before the Russian Revolution of 1917, agriculture was remarkably backward with low productivity caused by the remnants of feudal relations with tiny peasant plots and collective village responsibility for paying off the burden of compensating the nobility for the official end of serfdom. Russian industry was mostly in the grip of foreigners – British, French, and German – who extracted immense profits from Russia and sent them abroad, retarding the growth of Russian industry.

As described in Chapter 3, the Soviet Union had extremely high rates of growth for many years after it tossed off the shackles of the old semi-feudal, semi-capitalist relations and got rid of foreign imperialist control of its industry. But it in turn instituted a more and more rigid set of institutions and class relations, which eventually began to hold back further growth, as evidenced by the slow decline of the rate of growth from the peak in the mid-1950s to the late 1980s.

Throughout the nineteenth and twentieth centuries, the Third world countries with most of the world's population were first kept in direct colonial rule, then kept in an almost equally burdensome neo-colonial rule. Under both colonialism and neo-colonialism, their exploitation and underdevelopment was guaranteed in somewhat similar ways. In the first place, corporations from the imperialist countries extracted extremely high rates of profit based on cheaply bought raw materials and cheap labor (under various types of coercion and anti-union laws). This process of profit extraction by foreign corporations with little development, did not change much in most countries after the change from formal colonialism to formal independence. This meant that the flow of profit and interest out of these countries throughout the twentieth century remained far higher than the flow of investment into them. Furthermore, within these countries for the first half of the century the colonial administrations ruled by force, including much corruption, extracting high taxes, but providing little education and very little infrastructure. When they became formally independent, many of these countries were purposely left with ethnic antagonisms and governments ruled with barren greed by the local elite backed up by the former imperial country, so the same retardation of economic growth prevailed. In brief, most of the world till the end of the twentieth century had class relations of an imperialist capitalism, with some remnants of feudalism in some areas, that held back the productive forces and led to continued misery, hunger, and under-development.

In these examples, Marxism sees a lag between the rapid advance of the forces of production (including technology) and the glacial pace of change in basic institutions and class relations. This lag or tension may show up as stagnation, depression, or many other types of economic crisis. Such an economic crisis may (but does not necessarily) lead to intensification of class conflict. An intensified class conflict may (but does not necessarily) lead to social evolution – in the shape of reform or revolution.

Fundamental structural change

The basic point – that the class relations may sometimes hold back the productive forces – is perfectly clear, but there are a number of controversial points that need further clarification. Is there exactly one set of class relations that will fit each set of productive forces and vice versa? Definitely not. With any productive forces, there can be many types of class relations that are possible. For example, in 1960, both the United States and the Soviet Union were highly industrialized. Yet the two had extremely different economic institutions, class relations, and laws of economic dynamics. The United States had private ownership of most factories and mines and land, whereas the Soviet Union had government or collective ownership of most factories, mines and land. The United States had a private capitalist ruling class, whereas the Soviet Union had a ruling class that consisted of party leaders, government leaders, and economic planners – only top managers were in both ruling classes. The US managers worried about how to sell their excess of goods midst a lack of demand, while the Soviet managers worried about how to meet production targets midst a lack of supply. Thus two very different systems had the same type of forces of production, differing only in amount.

It is certainly possible to imagine a set of class relations that are totally incompatible with given productive forces. To allow more romance, science fiction writers often imagine other planets with feudal systems, but these same writers often imagine technology far in advance of ours. Feudal lords with nuclear weapons are really a ridiculous notion. Since feudal power is decentralized among many warring lords, this would be very unstable. But more fundamental is the fact that nuclear weapons imply a whole large industry, which is owned by somebody making profits (if we rule out socialism). The owners would be powerful capitalists and would have great economic power implying great political power – hence capitalism and an end to feudal nobility.

The point of Marxism is not that capitalism is impossible with the present forces of production, but that it does an awful job. It is subject to recurrent depressions and mass unemployment, a quarter century of stagnation in the advanced capitalist countries, and continued extreme underdevelopment in most of the world. Moreover, it has extreme inequality, much poverty, environmental destruction, racial and gender discrimination, a high level of drugs and crime, and a large amount of alienation. It is worth fighting against such a system even if it will never just collapse by itself.

The notion of a tension between class relations and productive forces has very different meanings in different types of stratified, class-divided societies – and no application to a primitive society. So it is not a general law applicable in some precise scientific way to every society.

In fact some writers have said that there is a law of a tension between class relations and productive forces in capitalism, but not in other societies. An interesting and thoughtful consideration of these issues by Ellen M. Wood argues that: "The principle of contradiction between forces and relations of production may have a more specific and fruitful meaning if we cease to treat it as a general law of history – a law so general as to be vacuous – and regard it as a law of capitalist development" (Wood 1995: 135). Perhaps it would be clearest to put the matter this way: there is an important relationship between the class relations (basic institutions) of society and the productive forces (including technology) in all stratified societies. But the relationship, while important or even vital, is very different in each type of stratified society. So it cannot be made a general law with some precise content. What one can say – and it is very useful to do so – is that one should investigate these important relationships and tensions in every stratified society – so this is not a law, but an approach, a method, a central question to ask in all such societies.

The answer to the investigation in each case will be complex and different from other cases. Even in capitalism, it is true that the existing class relations and institutions lead to recessions and depressions, stagnation, and underdevelopment at certain times and places. But exactly how is a long and complicated story, built on many narrower laws of that system.

The specific differences between capitalist societies and pre-capitalist societies in this regard are striking. Under capitalism, there is a strong tendency toward very rapid improvement of technology and expansion of capital – except when these same relationships cause recession or depression, stagnation, or underdevelopment in the colonial and neo-colonial countries of the Third World. In pre-capitalist societies, however, such as slavery, sharecropping, or serfdom, we are far more likely to find the effect of rigid class relations to be long-term stagnation.

It is also essential to note that the relationship evolves within each society. In the early slave empires, slavery was a tremendous improvement over primitive relations in terms of increasing productivity, building mighty monuments and cities, as well as astronomy, law, and the arts. By the later

Roman Empire, however, slavery acted as a break on the productive forces, weakening Rome in many ways. Feudalism in western Europe began with a period of decline in production and technology and the arts with the chaos following the decline of the Roman empire. There followed very slow growth for centuries, but with enough growth in late feudalism to give rise to the beginnings of the bourgeoisie as merchants and master craftspeople. Capitalism ended the restrictions of feudalism and resulted in an explosion of growth known as the Industrial Revolution, with continuing technological revolutions to this day. Yet capitalist class relations and institutions have also resulted in the twentieth century in the Great Depression and other cyclical contractions, in the Great Stagnation of the last quarter century, and in continued underdevelopment of the Third World. An important exception in the Third World was the wonderful, uninterrupted rise of Southeast Asia, until it collapsed in a financial crisis. So the laws of capitalist development change to some extent in succeeding stages, though the basics remain the same.

Conclusion

Considerable disagreement exists between critical Marxists and liberal institutionalists over social tensions. The vested interests of the business system versus the common good of the community play little dynamic role in the theoretical system of Clarence Ayres. Instead, to him, tension was due to ignorance and superstition versus knowledge and technology. But considerable agreement exists between radical Veblenians and critical Marxists over the nature of social tensions and their role in social evolution. Both see a tension between vested interests and the potential for social and economic change beneficial to the majority of people on the globe.

8

SOCIAL CONFLICT

This chapter examines social conflicts in the process of evolution.

Even more agreement

Both of us, the critical Marxist and the radical institutionalist, agree that social conflict plays an important role in social evolution. But, as usual, we disagree on some of the particulars.

The role of conflict in evolution
– an institutionalist view

Preliminaries: social tensions and conflicts

Social tensions do not automatically break the continuity of social structures. Perfect tranquility is not required for the continuity of a social structure. In fact, social structures are resilient. But, they do break. A social conflict is a social tension that comes to a head. The conflict results in a discontinuity, a break in a social structure. If social tension can be resolved through some form of compromise and/or accommodation, then the tension never comes to a head in the form of an actual conflict and continuity is maintained. Even when tensions result in taking sides, if each side is willing to give a little, perhaps the opposing interests that give rise to the social tension can compromise. Even if one side is not willing to give an inch, perhaps the opposing side is willing to accommodate the stubborn side. Then continuity can be maintained.

But sometimes the social structure is not resilient enough and continuity is broken. Neither continuity nor discontinuity is inevitable in evolution. The American Civil War and the periods before and after it yield three interesting examples of how differently things can turn out.

The first example comes from the period before the War and involved the resolution of tension through compromise and accommodation. After the Declaration of Independence in 1776 in which Americans declared that all men were created equal, the slave labor system and the wage labor system lived cheek to cheek in the United States for over 80 years. The tension between equality and slavery threatened to come to a head several times, and compromises between slave labor and wage labor interests had to be written into the original constitution. After the constitution with its compromises was ratified, a number of additional compromises kept the tension between the free states in the North and the slave states in the South from leading to a break up of the nation. The Missouri Compromise of 1820 resolved the tension over admitting Missouri into the Union as a slave state. Next, a compromise over the "Tariff of Abominations" in 1828 resolved the tension for a while longer between the industrializing North and the cotton growing South. The continuity of the nation-state system established by the Declaration of Independence was preserved.

But the Compromise of 1850 over the treatment of fugitive slaves in the free states and over the expansion of slavery into the West could do little to reduce the growing tensions between the North and the South. Compromises had kept them together since 1776, but by the late 1850s the two sections resembled separate nations in everything but name. They had become conflicting social systems – one a social system based on wage labor and the other a social system based on slave labor. They could no longer compromise. The tension between the two led to greater and greater violence and came to a head in the Civil War. The war cost 600,000 lives. The continuity of the nation-state system established by the Declaration of Independence was broken. But slavery was abolished. Sometimes you cannot compromise; you cannot reform; you cannot accommodate.

The period that Southerners called the Redemption provides our third example of continuity and discontinuity in evolution. The Redemption is the period after Reconstruction. It involved a historic accommodation that forged nearly a century of renewed coexistence between industrial North and agricultural South. After the Reconstruction Era ended, a different kind of compromise and accommodation was reached between the northern capitalist elite and the southern planter elite. It left one elite in control of the northern industrial workforce and the other in control of the southern agricultural workforce. African Americans in the South were forced by the Ku Klux Klan into a new form of white planter domination, one that did not directly conflict with the capitalist domination of the industrial workers in the North. The Southern planters replaced slavery with a new system of domination that involved sharecropping, legalized racism, and extra-legal terrorism. As a result, the two different systems of economic inequality were able to coexist inside the same system of national laws. The South had lost the war, but it had won the peace. Southern planters re-established their domination of African Americans. Northern industrialists expanded their system of capitalist production with little Southern interference. The strong states' rights aspects of US federalism facilitated coexistence of the two. The Southern system of white supremacy even survived Franklin Delano Roosevelt's New Deal. Southern Democrats supported most economic aspects of their party's New Deal because it did not directly threaten their basic position *vis-à-vis* African Americans. Most African Americans were not covered by the New Deal's social security system nor by the New Deal's institutionalization of collective bargaining because they were still agricultural workers and agricultural workers were excluded from both social security and collective bargaining.

The story of the New Deal in the South is exceedingly complex. For example, Huey P. Long, populist Senator from Louisiana, broke ranks with other white politicians in the South. He withdrew his support of Roosevelt's program, but not because it was too liberal, but because he believed that it was far too timid. He organized his own program of radical wealth redistribution as an alternative to Roosevelt's reforms.

As Huey Long's left wing reaction to the New Deal illustrates, Coexistence did not go unchallenged, but it continued until the Second World War when war mobilization and accelerated mechanization of southern agriculture began setting the stage for what should be called the Second Civil War. Tensions came to a head in the Civil Rights Movement of the 1960s and the passage of federal legislation that effectively overcame the racist traditions of states' rights. Of course, even as this is being written (2000), recent conservative appointees to the Supreme Court of the United States are forging legal precedents to re-institutionalize states' rights. And, again, the story is complex. One of the leaders of the Supreme Court conservatives, Clarence Thomas, is an African American.

The evolution of the American system continues to be driven, with often astonishingly complex results, by the tensions and conflicts coming from the ways in which American society is stratified. Tension may or may not lead to conflict and discontinuity. It may lead to compromise and continuity. Neither result is inevitable. Both are part of evolution.

Evolution versus revolution

Sometimes, students of the issues involved frame them in terms of a dichotomy: evolution versus revolution. In this dichotomy, evolution is supposed to mean slow and incremental change involving the continuity of social structures and the use of peaceful compromise by the reformers. Revolution is supposed to mean rapid and explosive change involving discontinuity of social structures and the use of violence by the revolutionaries. Evolution is supposed to be the preferred method of change while revolution is supposed to be unacceptable and often ineffective, to boot. By implication, one should not encourage revolution. One should encourage evolution.

Such a dichotomy is misleading, however. Change is neither evolutionary on one hand nor revolutionary on the other. Instead, change is both. What we call social evolution includes sudden and discontinuous change as well as slow and incremental change. It also involves peaceful compromise as well as violent revolt. Furthermore, it is not so easy to make an *a priori* moral rejection of revolt or war as a method of change. Were the Southern Thirteen Colonies wrong to revolt against England in 1776? Were the Canadians the moral ones because they stayed loyal to the mother country? Were the Allied Nations wrong to go to war against Nazi Germany? Were African American slaves wrong to join the Union Army to fight their former masters? Were American soldiers wrong to fight against Japan? North Korea? North Vietnam? Kent State students? The history of social evolution is studded with just and unjust rebellions, uprisings, riots, wars and revolutions, with psychopaths, saints, thugs, courageous soldiers, and revolutionaries; also with periods of peace and incremental change, with visionaries, healers, poets, peacemakers, and stateswomen.

Compromise and continuity in social evolution

No one denies that inequality involves conflict. The historical record of it is too clear and too dismal. And yet, institutionalist reformers emphasize compromise and continuity rather than conflict and discontinuity.

John R. Commons was a professor of economics at the University of Wisconsin. Although not as well known as some, Commons was one of the most effective economic reformers in the United States. From the turn of the century to his retirement in the 1930s, he worked continuously for reform. In a curious historical twist, while the states' rights tradition of the US protected racist practices in some states, it sometimes protected the experimental reforms of other states. John R. Commons and Governor Robert M. La Follette were able to use states' rights to get the maneuvering room they needed to reform the economy of the state of Wisconsin. Many of his students and co-workers then took the reforms he experimented with in Wisconsin onto the broader national stage of Franklin D. Roosevelt's New Deal.

Commons devoted his life to making the existing economic system work better, not to making a new and better system. His efforts were directed at resolving tensions before they came to a head in conflicts. He promoted incremental change in the working rules that keep the conflicting interests contained in going concerns from destroying the going concerns.

He tried to reform industrial capitalism in Wisconsin. He campaigned ardently for union organization and for collective bargaining because he feared that the conflict of interests between industrial workers and industrial capitalists could tear the great capitalist corporations (he called them going concerns) apart. He was afraid that the goose that laid golden eggs for us would be killed in a struggle over who got the eggs. In particular, he feared that prolonged industrial conflict between labor and capital would cost the workers their livelihoods and the owners their wealth. Both sides to the conflict of interest would lose everything they had at stake, if they could not work out a compromise that would accommodate the interests of both of them. He promoted union organization and collective bargaining as the way to do so. What was needed, he argued, was an institutionalized system of collective bargaining between labor and capital that could forge a human-made harmony where no natural harmony existed.

Human-made harmony was reached through changing the working rules that kept going concerns agoing. He believed that this kind of incremental reform would keep conflict under control. Negotiations between union representatives and management would channel conflict into a very narrow range of issues concerning wage rates and working conditions. Such issues could be resolved peacefully within the institution of collective bargaining. Compromise would allow the goose of capitalism to continue laying golden eggs. (John R. Commons's *magnum opus* is Commons 1934 and is well worth the effort required to read it.)

Collective bargaining in the United States may owe its existence to reforms inspired by John R. Commons. Perhaps the capitalist goose does too.

Clarence E. Ayres was a leading liberal institutionalist of the Post War Era. He left the evolution of working rules and going concerns to John R. Commons. To Ayres, writing primarily in the 1940s, 50s, and 60s, evolution was not driven by the resolution of conflict within going concerns. Nor was evolution driven by conflict between the people at the top of the social pyramid and those at the bottom (men versus women, capitalists versus workers), or by conflict between the people at the top of different social pyramids (southern planters versus northern capitalists). Instead, Ayres believed that societies evolve because of the forward thrust of new technology pressing against the backward resistance of old institutions. Ayres called this backward resistance "ceremonialism," and he attributed the term to Veblen (Ayres 1978: xvi). Ceremonialism, Ayres explained, manifested itself in social stratification, social mores, tribal beliefs, emotional conditioning, and mystic rites. He did not emphasize the role of social stratification in ceremonialism. He emphasized emotional conditioning and tribal belief, but did not relate these to social conflict over inequality. He was an egalitarian (see Ayres 1946), but not a conflict theorist. He emphasized incremental change caused by the tension between tradition and technology, not explosive change caused by the conflict between the people at the top of the social pyramid and those at the bottom.

John Kenneth Galbraith is the most famous liberal institutionalist. He has emphasized how incremental change has transformed the motivation of the capitalist corporation. He has recommended Keynesian reform policies to stabilize the economy and an increase in public sector services to alleviate problems caused by raw capitalism.

The modern corporation, Galbraith argues, has developed a wide separation between the narrow interests of the capitalist owners and the broader interests of the productive managers. The owners want more profit from the corporation and are not that interested in the details or in the broader implications of corporate activities. The managers, on the other hand, want more production from the corporation and are very interested in both the details and the broader social implications of corporate activities. According to Galbraith, the managers have gained in discretion over the increasingly dispersed and absentee owners and are using their discretion to pursue their own agenda. That agenda represents a softening of the earlier drive for profit. Technological expertise, social respect, and ample managerial rewards are important to the rising managerial class. Galbraith calls them technocrats and he calls their class structure the technostructure. The rough edges of capitalism have been smoothed out by the technostructure. Class conflict has become outmoded. Tensions still exist between the technostructure, the absentee owners, and the public purpose, but with Keynesian policy maintaining full employment, with incremental reform where needed and with international peace, nothing need come to a head. (John Kenneth Galbraith has written many books, but the one that best summarizes his views on these issues is Galbraith 1973.)

Although they all emphasize different aspects of social evolution, the reform/liberal institutionalists share a view of the contemporary world. They believe that although the system is an unequal one, it will give us all more golden eggs if the government provides the spending required for full employment and the reforms needed to maintain continuity.

Conflict and discontinuity in social evolution

Radical institutionalists recognize that compromise and continuity are often found in social evolution. But, following Thorstein Veblen, they emphasize conflict and discontinuity. During the long intellectual night of the Cold War in the United States, writing about conflict and discontinuity was paramount to declaring oneself a Communist, so the radical tradition in institutionalism suffered a long period of stagnation.

To pick up the vital red thread in institutionalism we must go back to Thorstein Veblen himself, taking care not to ignore the openly critical works he published after the First World War. The titles of his last books indicate where his thoughts and experiences had taken him. He published, in rapid succession, the following books: *The Vested Interests and the Common Man*, 1919; *The Engineers and the Price System*, 1921; and *Absentee Ownership and Business Enterprise in Recent Times*, 1923.

The conflict between business and industry was a central feature of Veblen's thought. While other economists were fantasizing about natural harmony and perfect markets, in all his later books Veblen emphasized that business profit conflicted with machine productivity. He explained how, in the midst of the plenty created by the industrial revolution, a business had to cut back production in order to raise prices and earn profits because the excessive productivity of new industrial machinery was always threatening to swamp the market for industrial output.

Veblen saw that while leading inventors and engineers were constantly trying to perfect new technologies to produce more products, leading business people were constantly trying to form monopolies to keep up prices. Using the terminology of his day, Veblen framed his analysis of the resulting social change in terms of conflict between the self-regarding and other-regarding "instincts" of individuals. He also understood the growing conflict between the classes thrown together by the industrial revolution and by the European conquest of the New World. Veblen was among the first Americans to articulate where he came from and how he got there. In *The Instinct of Workmanship* he referred to three classes: the predatory or dynastic class, the owning or business class, and the engineering or industrial class. Veblen stated,

> The three conventionally recognized classes, upper, middle, and lower, are all and several pecuniary categories; the upper being typically that (aristocratic) class which is possessed of wealth without having worked or bargained for it; while the middle class have come by their holdings through some form of commercial (business) traffic; and the lower class gets what it has by workmanship. It is a gradation of (a) predation, (b)business, (c)industry; the former being disserviceable and gainful, the second gainful, and the third serviceable.
>
> (Veblen 1964: 184; parentheses in original)

The owning or business class has acquired property rights in the material equipment of the community. The community then foolishly (imbecile institutions) allowed the owners to appropriate the community's own joint stock of industrial knowledge. The owners now appropriate the community's knowledge in order to (mis)direct the industrial system's ample production into narrow financial channels. These channels yield the owners a pecuniary gain and the owners claim a vested right against all other claimants to receive that gain. Veblen referred to this class's vested interest as "the usufruct of the state of the industrial arts" (Veblen 1964, 220).

The faster the industrial arts created new products and new technologies, the harder the business class had to struggle to maintain high prices and profits. If the business class temporarily fell behind in its business of monopolization, the industrial system was thrown into a crisis. Falling prices and profits then forced massive declines in capital values and widespread bankruptcy and unemployment. In general terms, monopolization was always racing against technological improvement. Monopolization kept up prices and profits while technological improvement pushed them down. Here is a recent example of what Veblen was writing about. While new developments in drilling and recovery technologies have been driving oil production up and oil prices down, new monopolizing agreements among the Organization of Petroleum Exporting Countries (OPEC) have been driving the sale of oil down and the price back up (Circa 1999–2000).

What Veblen explained as the class usufructuaries of the business system had come into their cultural inheritance from an earlier predatory system and its class usufructuaries. Although the businesspersons now hold the New World in their calculating grip, they were not the first to grasp it. The members of the owning class are relatively peaceful, compared to the earlier dynastic class that seized the New World from its indigenous peoples in the first place. Their business ownership becomes safe and secure only after constitutions, separation of powers, and other limitations have chained down the violence of the dynastic class and its arbitrary exercise of state power. In addition to protecting the usufructuaries of the business system from attacks from above, constitutions, separations of powers, and other limitations on state power also protect against attacks from below, further entrenching the business system's status quo. As Veblen explained it, the business system resulted from an evolutionary sequence that began with a far more violent system of conquest. The more peaceful nature of the business system has allowed for a slightly freer development of the community's joint stock of knowledge.

This introduces the class that greatly interested Veblen – the professional class of "efficiency engineers." Its relation to the other classes and cultural sequences is understood by Veblen to begin with the fact that "the modern businessman is necessarily out of effectual touch with the affairs of technology as such and incompetent to exercise an effectual surveillance of the processes of industry" (Veblen 1964: 222). Veblen believed that businessmen recognized their own shortcomings. "So, a professional class of 'efficiency engineers' is coming into action, whose duty it is to take invoice of the preventable wastes and inefficiencies due to the business management of industry and to present the case in such concrete and obvious terms of price and percentage as the businessmen in charge will be able to comprehend" (Veblen 1964: 222). Someone must be competent in industrial ways of knowing. Since the businessmen are not, the members of this class emerge to keep the machines running. In his system, the "efficiency engineers" are both a class formation and a cultural sequence. First came the dynastic or ruling class – in Latin America they were the conquistadors, in the United States, the Indian fighters. Then came the business or owning class.

The last class to evolve is the efficiency engineers – Marx would call them the working class. Veblen did not believe that the class had its act together yet. In his time the technical experts who ran American industry had no real class consciousness. But he analyzed how they might acquire it. What, speculated Veblen, might evolve if they did? Quite simply, they would disallow the vested interests of the business system. They would act a lot like John Kenneth Galbraith's technostructure. Except that Veblen's engineers might turn out more radical than Galbraith's technocrats. Veblen's "Soviet of Engineers" would expropriate the vested interests and run the industrial system in the community interest. While Veblen's engineers would discontinue the old system, Galbraith's technocrats would soften its rough edges.

In his *Engineers and the Price System*, Veblen turned his eye from how the American business system evolved in the past to how it might evolve in the future. The book was ignored by liberal/reform institutionalists or was treated as a kind of extended irony or joke. But if it was a joke, then everything that Veblen wrote was a joke. Here is the ironic but serious ending of the book: After noting that the engineers still lacked any class-consciousness and after explaining that the underlying population was still deceived by the "Guardians of the Vested Interests," the phrase he used for the leading commercialized newspapers, Veblen concluded his book with

> There is nothing in the situation that should reasonably flutter the sensibilities of the Guardians or of that massive body of well-to-do citizens who make up the rank and file of absentee owners, just yet.
>
> (Veblen 1965: 169)

Veblen doubted that explosive, discontinuous change would occur any time soon in American business. He proved correct. But he also showed the conflicts built into the system and he showed serious reasons for doubting that the American system of business enterprise would continue forever. He will prove correct on that, too.

Conflict has many origins

Conflict and the resulting social change is generated by all the modes of inequality – not just the economic mode. Class conflict is well known and is the major kind of conflict arising from economic inequality. But it is not the only kind of conflict, probably not even the leading conflict if you use body count as the yardstick for comparison. That dubious distinction may belong to the conflict generated by the inequalities institutionalized by the nation-state system. National wars surely have killed more people than class wars. Religious and ethnic wars are also thoroughly murderous varieties of mankind's favorite bloodsport, with recent ethnic cleansings in Eastern Europe and sub-Saharan Africa significantly adding to the carnage.

Race and gender inequality can also result in more than ample corpse counts. The death rate from the latter has only recently been estimated by Nobel Prize winner Amartya Sen. Sen estimates that "excessive death rates and artificially lower survival rates for women" result in over 100 million "missing women" in Asia and North Africa. "Missing women" is Sen's phrase for women who would exist in a human population (but do not), if women were given equal care as men from inception to old age, instead of being given inferior care. Sen's estimate of "fatalities," so defined, may make gender inequality the most fatal form of inequality, even surpassing the more visible deaths caused by national wars (Sen 1999: 103–106). Inequality based on sexual orientation can generate fatal conflict as well.

The point is, a whole range of systems of inequalities contribute to social stratification and to conflict over it.

The role of conflict in evolution – a Marxist view

The best known statement of Marx and Engels in the *Communist Manifesto* says "The history of all hitherto existing societies is the history of class struggle" (Marx and Engels 1848: 9). Two different sources of class conflict can be distinguished: one in ordinary times and one in revolutionary times.

Ordinary class conflict

Every single day employees clash with employers over their wages and working conditions somewhere in the United States. Every day, there are fights in Congress about whether taxes should be cut (or raised) for the rich or the poor; a class conflict at the political level.

Every day, someone speaks on the reasons for a higher minimum wage or for a lower minimum wage; a class conflict at the ideological level. Every day the media assault us with arguments for or against health care insurance for the 44 million US citizens who have no health care; a class issue because all millionaires have health care, but many low-paid workers do not.

In ancient Rome there were many slave revolts. One of the most powerful was by Spartacus, a slave who led his followers to victory over two whole Roman armies before he was captured and crucified with all of his followers – (this story is immortalized in a wonderful novel and a movie, both called *Spartacus*, written by Howard Fast). Similarly, there were numerous revolts of the serfs in the middle ages, some involving pitched warfare and no mercy on either side with thousands of casualties.

The reason for these ordinary class conflicts is that the ruling class is exploiting slaves or serfs or modern employees. The mechanism of exploitation is very different in every case, but the result is that one class is extracting products from another class by custom or by law or by force. Whenever an exploited class protests in any significant manner on a large scale, it is often met with government force. Thus slave revolts in ancient Rome and in the old South, as well as serf revolts in feudal Europe, were met with all-out force and execution of every slave or serf who was involved or might be involved.

There have been thousands of strikes by US employees against employers – and force was used against the workers in many of them. Employers have used local police, state troopers, private police armed with machine guns, national guardsmen, and the US army to break strikes at various times. The US army was used against the American Railway Union workers' strike in the 1890s to put the union leaders in jail and completely broke a union of a hundred thousand men and women by persecution. The top leader of the railway workers was Eugene Debs, who was converted to socialism by the experience. Debs opposed the First World War as a conflict between capitalist classes in different countries, each trying to extend their influence and increase their profits. Debs was sent to prison for opposing the war, but he campaigned for President of the United States from prison and won ten per cent of the votes! (There is an exciting biography of Debs called *The Bending Cross* by Ray Ginger, but Debs is seldom mentioned in American history textbooks.)

In the 1950s a strike of Mexican American mine workers was met with force and a court order to stop the men from picketing. When their wives took over the picket line, the sheriff rammed a car against them and then arrested them – this true story is told in the powerful, moving movie called *Salt of the Earth* (one of the best available documentaries on race, class, and gender). Under Ronald Reagan, there was a strike of air traffic controllers, who said that there were too few controllers and this was dangerous – Ronald Reagan used a law to fire all of them.

Revolutionary class conflict

Sometimes in class-divided societies there is an unresolvable class conflict that is settled by revolution. This often results from a tension between rigid class relations (including frozen economic institutions and frozen political institutions) and the potential of the productive forces to improve society. This tension heightens and increases class conflicts, sometimes to the breaking point. For example, the US health care system presently has the technical capacity to give good health care to every child, woman, and man in the United States. If the profits of the insurance companies were all used to cover the uninsured, all 44 million uninsured could be covered by health care. So health care is not held back by the lack of productive forces; it is held back by US political institutions, US myths (created in part by enormous TV spending of the insurance companies) and US class relations (embodied in economic institutions). This gap between technical possibility and institutional reality makes people angry.

Similarly, millions of people die every year in the world from lack of food, while American farmers complain there is too much food to sell. This gap between the potential for everyone to have sufficient food and the reality of malnutrition makes people angry. The United Nations (see *Dollars and Sense*, Jan/Feb 2000, p. 42) has calculated that for just 40 billion dollars, or two-tenths of one per cent of world income, basic health care and basic education could be extended to every human being on earth, yet this is not done. The gap between potential adequate health and education and the miserable reality makes people angry.

Anger causes class conflict because the vested interests of the ruling class refuse to give up an ounce of their wealth and power without a fight. For example, a strike in the 1890s in Italy to reduce hours to 12 hours a day was met with force and violence – this is detailed in an excellent fictionalized movie called *The Organizer*.

It is the goal of Marxists to end all class conflict. To end class conflict, it is necessary to end all of the evils that drive people to fight for their food, clothing, shelter, health care, and education. It is necessary to end the domination of a ruling class that protects its wealth and power by the use of myths, coercion, and force. The only way to change these conditions is to change to a better society with completely different class relations, a society that Marxists call democratic socialism. Democratic socialism means the extension of democracy from the political sphere to include the economic sphere. This implies an end to enormous holdings of wealth and power, so Marxists are hated by the ruling class.

On the basis of existing structural tensions and unresolvable conflicts, I predict that capitalism will end sometime in the 21st century. Democratic socialism may or may not follow capitalism, depending on the circumstances.

Systematic questions and answers

Non-doctrinaire or critical Marxists do not transform these insights about evolution into iron laws eternally guiding evolution. They recognize that every particular type of society has its own specific laws – there are no eternal, transhistorical laws. But there are certain good questions to ask, certain points from which to begin our investigation of evolutionary (and revolutionary) events. This is because every stratified, class-divided society has some very general things in common, even though each has very different laws of development.

What is a class conflict?

In both Chapter 2 and above in this chapter it was shown that class conflicts result from the inherent clash between the vested interests of the ruling class in the current system of exploitation by giant corporation, that gives them their wealth and power, and the attempt of the workers and employees of the corporations to improve conditions and to gain more of their own product for a better life. These conflicts go on every day in some form in every business, in every legislature, in all of the media, and in the education system. This was spelled out in Chapter 2. Class conflicts also lead to total changes in institutional structure and class relations under certain circumstances discussed below. The power of class analysis is that it strips away all the hypocrisy and myths and lets political issues stand naked revealed as the fight of vested interests to keep and extend their power and wealth. For example, what else other than class conflict is the attempt to end all taxes on profits from the sale of stock – while leaving wages and salaries fully taxed?

What is a structural tension or unresolvable conflict, sometimes called a contradiction?

Class analysis teaches us that such conflicts as the Civil War in the United States do not drop out of the clear blue sky, nor are they caused by irrational petty conflicts between egotistic individuals – though such individuals play a role. Rather unresolvable structural conflicts result from particular class relations, such as the relations of slavery between master and slave. The masters resisted any attempt to reform slavery, let alone abolish it. But these class relations led to structural tensions and structural conflicts (so-called contradictions).

How do class relations lead to structural tensions and class conflicts

We learned in Chapter 3 and Chapter 7 that class relations may come into conflict with productive forces. Perhaps it would be more precise to say that in every class-divided society in social evolution to date, this has been a crucial relationship. In the case of capitalism, we saw that there is enormous pressure on every firm to expand production and move to more efficient technologies, a motivation that caused constant revolutions in technology. Yet we also saw in Chapter 7 that the class relations of capitalism limit demand, which eventually halts every rapid expansion of capitalism as if it met a brick wall, so the relationship between the existing class relations and the rapidly changing productive forces cause economic crises. In those recessions and depressions, production goes backward to lower levels and technology stagnates – as they did for ten years in the Great Depression. Thus, under the institutions of capitalism, the flow of new technology that could produce a wonderful life for all often produces misery for most people and, at times, even misery for the elite. But it must be emphasized that this type of scenario holds only for capitalism, so it is no universal law. We shall see below that in ancient slavery, there is also a crucial relationship between the class relations of slavery and the productive forces of Rome, but the result – while catastrophic – was entirely different. In the case of the Soviet Union, we saw in Chapter 3 that the tension between class relations and productive forces caused a fatal crisis, but it was in the form of extreme inefficiency, while the system remained at full employment. In other words, all class-divided societies examined to date have produced structural tensions (conflicts or contradictions) that have led to crises, but the nature of these crises is quite different in each society because it operates under different laws, revolving around a different form of exploitation).

How do structural tensions and conflicts lead to revolutions?

They do not always do so. It is useful to ask a question whether they will lead to a revolution, but many things have to happen just right for that to be the end result. For example, classes opposed to the status quo may have insufficient power or they may not be united against the ruling class or external circumstances may change the whole situation. Some empires just collapsed of their own weight. Some were destroyed completely by barbarian, primitive tribes. So these empires never had any further internal evolution. Many areas, such as India or almost all of Africa had their internal evolution ended by colonialism. Moreover, social tensions may lead to a counter-revolution by the elite rather than a revolution that leads to a better life for most people. That happened when the fascists captured Germany; and it happened in the Soviet Union when the elite got rid of the old system by grabbing public assets for their own private, greedy purposes. In both fascist Germany and the Soviet Union, there was a severe economic crisis, but no class with the power and the consciousness to make a revolution that would have benefited most people.

How does ideology/mythology affect class conflict?

We learned in Chapter 4 that ideology, including enabling myths such as racism or sexism or classism (each of which claims that some group is inferior and deserves their inferior status and their exploitation) play a vital role. Many of them reinforce support for the status quo. Yet there are also myths such as Liberty, Equality and Fraternity, that play a vital role in favor of a revolution, as they did in the French Revolution. He or she who looks only at economics and ignores ideology and mythology is truly blind to the actual workings of social evolution.

How does democracy contradict capitalism?

As we learned in Chapter 5, democracy means the rule of the people, including the right to run the economy. Capitalism means that the economy is run by a small elite. Furthermore, democracy itself is very much restricted by the fact that money determines the course of every political campaign. This political process affects the evolution of myths, the education system, economic institutions, and technology. For example, the political system decided to promote nuclear power rather than solar power, even though there are gestures toward solar power to appease public opinion. Thus anyone attempting to understand the process of evolution without taking into account the political process is truly blind.

To understand how evolution works – and the very different dynamics of different societies – a few examples are necessary.

The peak period of the Roman Empire

At its peak period, 90 to 95 per cent of the people in the Roman empire worked in agriculture and most were slaves on large plantations. (The best Marxist work on Roman slavery and the empire, on which the facts of this section and the following are based, is by Perry Anderson 1996.) In addition to the masters and the slaves, there were always free peasants (though their number declined over time) and a large array of craftspeople in the cities as well as merchants. The racist Roman mythology said that the slaves were not only not citizens, but were not human beings or at least not equal human beings – they were just property.

The cities were tiny islands in a sea of agriculture, yet many of the cities were glittering monuments of amazing size, beauty and complexity. The cities contained astronomers, philosophers, architects, and a whole division of labor that enormously increased productivity over the primitive period. The cities were supported by the surplus flowing from the vast countryside, as well as the labor of the slaves and the craftspeople in the cities. There was a mighty army, beautiful cities, and flowering arts. The division of labor based on the slave surplus production gave empires such as Rome many times the productivity of the primitive tribes that preceded them and surrounded them. So why did the mighty Roman empire decline and fall?

The decline of the Roman Empire and the beginnings of Feudalism

The vast wealth of Rome was all built on the wonderfully pleasant device – from the viewpoint of the masters – of slavery. "The price paid for this brutal and lucrative device was a high one. Slave relations of production determined certain insurmountable limits to ancient forces of production. Above all, they ultimately tended to paralyze productivity in both agriculture and industry" (Anderson 1996: 25). After a certain point the use of slavery as the dominant productive system caused technology to stagnate for centuries – with a stagnant capital stock and population. Why?

In the first place, slavery limited productivity because it made complex organization, such as production of many different crops on one farm, difficult to organize and supervise. It also limited productivity because any complicated machinery might be sabotaged by the slave – or broken in pieces and used as a weapon. The slave owners were always terrified by the prospect of slave revolts – which did occur frequently, sometimes on a massive scale. But this meant organizing production so as to make supervision easy, independence difficult, slave use of weapons impossible, and reliance upon heavy security forces.

While all of these direct effects were important limitations on productivity, there was also the indirect effect that slavery made all manual work and production a servile thing in the minds and mythology of the Romans.

> Once manual labor became deeply associated with the loss of liberty, there was no social rationale [for free men to do] invention.... [This formed the] ideology which enveloped the totality of manual work in the ancient world, contaminating hired and even independent labor with the stigma of debasement.
>
> (Anderson 1996: 25–27)

In such an atmosphere, nobles and gentlemen would not dream of getting their hands dirty with work, much less worry about improving productivity through inventions – though they might try to improve productivity with the lash. The slave owners often did not live on the plantations, but in Rome; they ran the empire and spent their time concerned with political and military affairs. Moreover, by reducing the pool of independent farmers, slavery undermined recruitment into the Roman army.

Thus, slave relations weakened the Roman empire. The empire was next door to large numbers of primitive, barbarian tribes in Germany. For a long time, the Romans preyed on these tribes and made slaves of them. But when the empire weakened due to the long run effect of slave institutions, the primitive tribes marched in and devastated and conquered the empire throughout western Europe. A new system arose based on the remnants of the old slave system under a conquering primitive tribal system.

There was chaotic class struggle among wandering groups of escaped slaves in revolt, Roman legions who were no longer paid, and barbarian tribes whose chiefs were acquiring property. This chaos resulted in a high priority in setting up fortified places, whether with Roman or Germanic lords, in which the peasantry were still servile, but no longer slaves, so as to give them some incentive to help defend the place. As agricultural units changed over in the midst of class conflict to the new system of serfdom, peasants gave agricultural service to the lord, while the lord and his men gave military protection to the peasantry. Unlike the slaves, the new serfs did usually help defend the feudal estate.

This new system of feudalism, however, meant an end to most trade, an end to the great cities of the Roman empire, and an actual loss of technology for some centuries. Slavery led to the decline of the Roman empire, but it did not guarantee that a new and better system would immediately appear to replace it and to increase productivity.

Lessons from the evolution of Roman slavery – the myth of inevitable progress

The distorted "Marxism" of the old Soviet Union claimed that technological growth is inevitable and that technological growth automatically leads to progress in the class relations of society. Thus it was inevitable that we would move from the primitive relations to slavery to feudalism to capitalism to the dictatorship they called "socialism" in the Soviet Union – and that each change caused the forces of production to progress much faster than before. What does the history of Rome tell us? It does show that when slavery replaced primitive relations, there was a vast increase in productivity, technology and production. But mature slavery led to stagnation. And the replacement of slavery by serfdom and feudal manors led to an actual decline for centuries. If you visit the Roman cities of Pompeii and Herculaneum that were buried by the ashes of a volcanic eruption, it is striking just how advanced was the living style of the Roman elite. They had beautiful houses, good indoor plumbing, and reasonable heating. If one visits an old feudal castle, one is struck by how uncomfortable it is, how hot water was lacking, and how cold it was with only the area around a fireplace being heated. The lesson is that a new set of class relations may lead to higher productivity, but it also may lead to stagnation or decline. And technological progress is neither automatic nor inevitable.

The US Civil War and the transition from slavery to capitalism

The many similarities and contrasts between ancient Roman slavery and slavery in the Old South of the United States before the Civil War are very revealing. As in the ancient Roman empire, the overwhelming majority of the people still worked in agriculture and slavery was the dominant institution centered on the relations between the masters and the slaves. (For very insightful and interesting Marxist analyses of the origins and operation of US slavery, see Genovese 1956 and 1992, and Blackburn 1997.) As in ancient Rome, there were also other classes in the South: free white farmers in the rural areas, as well as craftspeople, shopkeepers, and merchants in the towns.

As in ancient Rome, the South developed almost no new technology (except the cotton gin). Slavery was one major cause of stagnation. The reasons for stagnant technology were about the same in the South as in ancient Rome, the resistance of the slaves and the lack of sufficient motivation for the slave owners, as well as the myth that work was demeaning. Slavery made production of the single crop of cotton very efficient and led to the exhaustion of the land as cotton was grown year after year.

As in ancient Rome, racism was a support to slavery. Southern preachers spread the myth (which they fully believed) that slaves were inferior people, who were being done a favor by their masters, because the masters took care of the slaves as their Christian duty. This enabling myth of racism played a considerable role in legitimizing slavery in the eyes of poor white farmers in the South and of all the people of the North. Also as in ancient Rome, the combination of slavery and the myth of racism created a double standard of sex in the South, such that the slave women were exploited both economically and sexually by the men of the master race. But ruling class women were not supposed to have sex with anyone other than the master, so if a slave man was found having sex with a woman of the ruling class, he was put to death – a mythology that resulted in an excuse for lynching all the way up into the 1950s.

Also as in ancient Rome, in the political sphere, the slave owners con-trolled the political institutions of the South with an iron hand, and they used that control to support slavery, with complete resistance to any reform.

Yet there were also major differences between slavery in ancient Rome and the old South. The Roman empire had hostile barbarian tribes for neighbors, while the old South faced a hostile industrializing capitalist North. Because the Southern slave owners needed more land, while the Northern industrialists wanted to expand, both Northern industry and Southern slavery tried to expand into the West, bringing conflicts, such as the armed clashes in Missouri and Kansas. Furthermore, the Southern slave holders had a very strong influence in the US Congress, the Presidency, and the Supreme Court. They used their influence for their own interests, which frequently clashed with the needs of the Northern industrialists.

Northern interests opposed to slavery elected Abraham Lincoln. The threat to slavery represented by the election of Lincoln was resisted violently by the Southern slave owners, who launched the Civil War to protect the institution of slavery. Racism is an ideology consisting of a collection of myths, which condone and promote racist institutions. These racist myths helped to rally other Southern whites to the cause of the slave owners.

On the other side of the class conflict known as the Civil War were the slaves, the Northern industrialists, and the Northern workers. Northern workers hated and feared slavery because its products could sometimes undercut Northern prices and lower their wages down toward the level of slave subsistence by competition. As in ancient Rome, there were always numerous, violent slave revolts (see Genovese 1992). Moreover, in the US case the escaped slaves fought courageously in the Union army. Slaves also attempted to escape by the underground railroad (a secret set of refugee houses), but were often stopped by Southern military force. Many of the most dangerous missions on the underground railway were conducted by the great African American woman, Harriet Tubman, about whom there are many books and plays. The South also used its influence in the Supreme Court to gain a rule in the *Dred Scott* case that a slave was just property, so she or he should be returned from the North.

Finally, the Northern industrialists directly competed with the Southern slave owners for the control of the West, while their interests also conflicted in the battle for control of the US government, so they supported the US government in the Civil War. Replacement of slavery required the terrible class conflict of the Civil War, leading to the eventual eradication of the slave-owning class.

Through a deal with the Northern industrialists, the Southern elite continued to exercise political dominance in the South – making use of racism – for 70 or 80 years. Capitalism only slowly took root in the South, with the sharecropping system ensuring a backward agriculture, while very little industry developed in the urban areas.

Lessons of US slavery – and the myth of inevitable stages of evolution

In both ancient Rome and the United States, slavery caused technological stagnation and land exhaustion – leading eventually to a titanic class conflict. But the myth that a similar economic system must always produce the same resulting transition to a new system is just a myth. The result does not depend merely on technology, but primarily on the class relations of the whole relevant area. Thus Roman slavery weakened and was then overrun by primitive tribes, a combination that produced the western European form of feudalism. The US South, while stagnant in technology, remained militarily strong and was defeated in a war (brought on by slavery and its interests) by the slaves, free Northern workers, Northern industrialists, and free Western farmers. The result was that the South very slowly became capitalist, its national influence was greatly reduced, and capitalist industrialization could proceed without further obstacles.

These two examples provide a further basic lesson. The Marxist concept that structural tensions or conflicts (or "contradictions") lead to stronger and stronger class conflicts, which lead to evolution and revolution, is a powerful weapon of understanding. But it is not a mathematical formula nor a set of scientific laws of evolution. It is only a set of very important questions to ask of social events. There are three major reasons why this Marxist concept is a set of questions and not a set of eternal laws.

First, every major transition from one society to another witnesses a different relationship between the productive forces and the class relations. Thus, class relations may cause explosive growth of productive forces in one case, but cause successive crises in a second case, and stagnation in a third case. Second, every major transition is made different by very different ideology and myths, as well as different political and social institutions. As explained in Chapter 3, a society cannot be reduced to purely economic explanations. Rather the whole society includes relationships between myths, political institutions, class relations and productive forces. Third, every specific society has had different neighbors with different class relations, such as barbarian tribes or Northern industrialists. The process of evolution was partly external to the South, though it was internal to the whole United States (with some foreign countries considered part of the environment).

The Marxist approach allows us to understand past change and make some good guesses about the near future, but not to predict an inevitable development for the whole future. We know that structural tensions and class conflicts do sometimes produce evolutionary change, but there are many possibilities. Social tensions and class conflict may not only result in revolutionary change (such as the Civil War), but also may lead to major reforms (the New Deal), or to retrogression (fascist Germany). In struggles caused by the impasse of the old system, a new system may arise with changed institutions and higher productivity. Evolution may result in a better, more progressive economy and/or a better life for people, but it may also result in disaster for a long time (the dark ages following the Roman collapse), or complete devastation by a nuclear war or an ecological disaster. It is up to human beings to take collective action to ensure a better society rather than a disaster.

Conclusion

Institutionalists and Marxists disagree on many concepts and on how to focus their approach on these issues, but they do agree on three basic points. These three basic points are not universal laws for all societies, but are important questions to investigate. First, there has been both incremental change and fundamental structural change in evolution. Second, in stratified societies, there are often social tensions between rigid institutions and technological potential as well as conflict between the unequal strata. Third, those tensions contribute to conflict between those with an interest in the status quo and those who wish to change it. These tensions and conflicts sometimes lead to fundamental structural change.

Neither one of us believe that conflict is inevitable in social evolution. Societies can evolve without it. But both of us believe that conflict is often a significant process in evolution. The historical record cannot be denied. Nor can the fatalities. Societies frequently evolve because of conflict. We all wish that it were not so.

Part IV

DENOUEMENT

9

CONCLUSION:
RECLAIMING EVOLUTION

This chapter first presents our findings with their implications from our dialogues in previous chapters. Then it considers our separate views of the future evolution of society.

Findings and implications

Finding 1. Economic Relations. Chapter 2 found that economic institutions and economic relations play a major role in shaping industry, technology, and capital accumulation.

Implication 1. This finding contradicts those technological determinists and reductionists who believe that technology shapes society, but technology is not shaped by society. In particular, this finding shows that economic relations shape technology. But, it also illustrates that other social relations, not just economic ones, can shape technology.

Finding 2. Inequality. Chapter 2 finds that inequality is caused by institutions and that individuals are born into some group with a given place in the institutions and given relationships to other groups. If you are born a slave on a slave plantation, you can struggle against your fate and perhaps change it, but there is still a very low probability that you will get to be the king of England or the President of the United States or a millionaire. If you are born in a billionaire family, you might become a traitor to your class, forsake all your privileges, and join a militant labor union that promotes an end to capitalism, but there is a very high probability that you will not. You might be born into a privileged race, class, nation, and gender, but choose to become a radical economist and write books about capitalism, socialism, and evolution. You might choose the renegade path instead of the path of least resistance. However, there is a much higher probability that you will uncritically accept the best health care available, the best education you can utilize, with plenty

167

of recreation, food, clothing and shelter all your life. Furthermore, there is a very high probability that you will accept all these privileges as yours by right, that you will use them to your own maximum advantage, and that you will defend them against any challenges. Thus, institutions are to blame for most inequality, not the individual.

Implication 2. This finding contradicts the proposition of conservative economics that every individual can choose how to develop and every individual gets exactly the income they deserve – so women and minorities who get low incomes on the average deserve only those low incomes. Thus they blame the individual, when institutions cause inequality.

Finding 3. Technology. Chapter 3 shows that new technology can eventually undermine existing economic institutions and relations, exerting pressure for change.

Implication 3. This finding does not condone technological determinism, but it does contradict that psychological determinism (promoted by Freudian psychologists and neoclassical economists) which says that all social phenomena are explained by individual psychology.

Finding 4. Myth. Chapter 4 shows that social myths – which we call enabling myths – are used to help maintain the status quo in economic institutions and relations, political institutions, and social institutions, so they also indirectly affect technology and capital accumulation. But enabling myths do not fall from the sky; they are created by society, so they are affected by economic relations, political and social institutions, and the development of technology and capital accumulation.

Implication 4. The fact that myths affect technology is another blow against technological reductionism. The fact that myths are shaped by society is another blow against psychological reductionism.

Finding 5. Democracy. Chapter 5 shows that the democratic process in a capitalist society is shaped by economic relations, social institutions (media, education, religion and so forth), and by technology and capital accumulation. Yet the political process – with whatever degree of democracy exists – does in turn affect economic relations (for example, by laws), shape new myths, and affect the direction of technology and capital accumulation. Democracy and inequality coexist uneasily, if at all. This is true for all forms of inequality – not only class inequality, but also race, gender, religious, ethnic, national, sexual orientation, or whatever kind of inequality. And yet, people the world over place much value in democracy.

Implication 5a. Contemporary societies are in for stormy rides. People the world over value democracy but live in stratified societies with high degrees of inequality. Their democratic values do not coincide with their unequal circumstances.

Implication 5b. The fact that the political process affects technology is still another blow against technological reductionism. Furthermore, the fact that the political process is shaped by society is still another blow against psychological reductionism. Human nature is not fate. Nor is technology.

Finding 6. Structural Change. Chapter 6 finds that basic structural change really does occur in the course of evolution and that it is a result of social tensions and conflicts.

Implication 6. Our finding in Chapter 6 contradicts those who claim that nothing basic ever really changes. As we showed in Chapter 6, there really is fundamental change, but it is not necessarily "progress" nor is it inevitable. Moreover, we saw that the source of change is the internal dynamics of society, not some external force, no matter what it is called.

Finding 7. Structural Tensions. Chapter 7 finds that structural tensions between economic relations and the technical economic process of production creates the conditions and pressures for change, but does not change institutions automatically. Structural tensions also arise because of the continuing and multi-faceted resistance of the people at the bottom of the social pyramid against the powers, privileges, and wealth of those at the top of the social pyramid. Avoiding economic reductionism is just as important as avoiding technological reductionism. Economic inequality is not the only kind of inequality that creates social tension. Inequality between nations, genders, races, sexual orientations, religions, and ethnic groups are also significant.

Implication 7. The finding in Chapter 7 is completely different from the theories of inevitable progress that see new technology automatically leading inexorably to institutional change with little or no resistance.

Finding 8. Human Conflicts. Chapter 2 showed how there is usually human conflict (in the shape of religious, racial, gender, ethnic, or class conflicts) in all stratified societies, such as capitalism. Chapter 8 shows that conflict is made much worse by the structural tensions that cause some groups to resist change and some groups to fight for change.

Implication 8. Our finding in Chapter 8 flatly contradicts those theories of orthodox economics that harmony always prevails because each individual gets what they deserve. The finding of structural tensions and group conflicts leading to social change also contradicts the notions that evolution depends on human nature or on the actions of a superior race or the actions of some great men. Race is not fate. Nor is the hero.

Implication 9. Our finding also contradicts those who see social change as absolutely accidental and not understandable. Social change always begins with the existing circumstances. Change evolves out of the existing situation as the point of departure. It does not just happen, spontaneously, with no connection to anything else.

Does social evolution offer hope for the future? – an institutionalist view

The future is open-ended. That much we know. Vast structural change is possible. Given enough time, vast structural change is not just possible but highly probable. I suspect that in the future all of the particular forms of inequality we now suffer will be gone. Capitalism is doomed. European supremacy is doomed. Patriarchy is doomed. So are the other particular forms of inequality that plague us today. But, I do not know if inequality *in general* will be gone. I know that it can be eliminated. But I do not know if it will be eliminated. Capitalism will be gone, but will some other form of economic inequality replace it? White supremacy will be gone, but will some other form of racism replace it? Patriarchy will be gone, but will matriarchy replace it? And so on.

Personally, I think that we are realistic to hope for more equality in the future, but only if we work for it in the present. The following thoughts are offered toward that end.

Be careful what you hope for

Perfect inequality is impossible. You cannot have a future of perfect inequality because if you had everything and everybody except for you had nothing, they would all die and you would be left behind to wander pitifully through your world all alone till you, too, died. Do not hope for perfect inequality.

But do not hope for perfect equality either. Your critics will easily destroy your hopes for being impracticable dreams. (Read, again, the delightful poem in the appendix to Chapter 1) Instead, your hope should be simply for more equality and less inequality. The dialogue in this book should have convinced you that social evolution makes more equality possible, maybe even probable in some areas of social life.

How to measure equality so we can shape the future

Rather than endless quibbling about whether perfect equality is possible, we should construct a measure of inequality and then work toward lowering it. Economic inequality can be measured in a number of ways by looking at the distribution of income and the distribution of wealth. (For the United States, see the dramatic data in Collins, Leondar-Wright, and Sklar, 1999.) Other modes of inequality present measurement problems. But Amartya Sen provides a way to construct a simple inequality measurement in his estimate of the "missing women" (Sen 1999: 104–107). Sen's procedure for estimating how many women are "missing" in a country due to gender inequality could be used to construct a general index of inequality. Let me illustrate: First, Sen's missing women measurement could easily be adapted to measuring racial inequality. One would estimate how many African-Americans are missing in a population – say, the United States, due to the higher infant and adult mortality rates suffered by African-Americans than by European-Americans. To generalize the procedure, you would count the number of each group in the population with the inequality. Then you would estimate the number in each group, assuming the inequality was not practiced. Similar estimates could be made for other kinds of inequality – such as the number of poor people missing because of inadequate health care. Then, some kind of index of inequality could be constructed as a yardstick. The yardstick would measure the missing humans per unit of human population due to inequality. Once we had such a yardstick, we could use it to track our performance in the future. Evolution tells me that we can push the index number to zero. I hope that we do. But evolution does not tell me that we will, only that we can.

Does social evolution offer hope for the future?
– a Marxist view

Will capitalism fall and be replaced by a new society? Social evolution teaches the lesson that every set of institutions has proven to be temporary, has risen, expanded, and eventually fallen. There is no reason to think that capitalism will be any exception. Capitalism has many obvious problems: exploitation of workers, significant poverty in the richest countries, vast poverty in the less developed countries, business cycle contractions at various times, long periods of stagnant growth, a very high degree of inequality (with continuous increase in US inequality in the last three decades), demo-cratic processes controlled by the wealthy, a profitable motivation for racism and sexism and ethnic warfare, a high level of crime and drug use, a pervasive psychological alienation, and a profitable motivation for environmental

171

destruction. Given the history of social evolution, it is certainly possible that the capitalist system will some day end and be replaced – and this gives us hope. Moreover, the history of severe and continuing problems in capitalism makes it probable that a major change will occur at some point in the future – and that gives us hope.

It is surely desirable to end a system with all the problems of capitalism. Evolutionary theory shows it is possible – and perhaps even probable given the present trends. Yet it is clearly not inevitable; to be inevitable implies some outside force directing our society. But it is only all of us human beings who direct our society (starting from the existing conditions), so we can make a wonderful future or we can botch it up terribly.

Will the new society be democratic and socialist? A democratic socialist society is defined as one in which there are not only the forms of democracy in the political sphere, but also a democratic process controlling the economic sphere. The US economy is controlled by a small elite that decides in what to invest, how much to invest, and whom to hire and fire; the US economy is completely undemocratic. The old Soviet Union had a small political elite who controlled the economy and were not subject to any democratic political process; it was completely undemocratic. A democratic socialist society must have a democratic political process to control the economy in the enterprise, and/or local levels of government, and/or state and federal levels – without such a democratic process, it is not democratic socialism.

Will capitalism be replaced by democratic socialism? The history of social evolution shows that such a fundamental structural change in institutions is definitely possible – and that gives us hope. Since there are many possibilities, however, it is certainly not inevitable, only possible. Is it probable that democratic socialism will replace capitalism? That question cannot be answered positively until there is a broad international movement for democracy and socialism, involving the organization of millions of people in response to the problems of capitalism. At present one can only say that democratic socialism is desirable and possible.

Will evolution continue after a democratic socialist society is established? This is a silly question in so far as the general answer is that evolution never ends. When the old system ends, a new and different history will begin. Marx wrote:

> The bourgeois relations of production are the last antagonistic form of the social process of production – antagonistic not in the sense of individual antagonism, but of one arising from conditions surrounding the life of individuals in society; at the same time the productive forces developing in the womb of bourgeois society create the material conditions for the solution of that antagonism.

> This social formation constitutes, therefore, the closing chapter of
> the prehistoric stage of human society.
>
> (Marx 1904 [1859]: 13)

Marx sees capitalism as pre-history. So socialism is not the end of history, but the beginning of a new evolution. In fact, serious Marxists – beginning with Marx – have always viewed socialism as a process, not a static thing. Socialism can only begin – according to all the lessons of social evolution – on the basis of present, capitalist circumstances. The good thing is that capitalism has created immense possibilities for economic abundance and an end to all poverty, an end to lack of education, and an end to lack of health care. New socialist institutions can quickly end poverty and provide education and health care for all.

On the other hand, changing the enormous inequality under capitalism toward an equalitarian society – against the resistance of those who presently have wealth – will take time. Changing the present attitude, which resents all work and sees it only as a way to make money, will take more time. We shall have to begin with a society in which, even when we get rid of private ownership of the major corporations, it will still be necessary to have a system of incentives such that workers are paid according to what they produce (but with no surplus skimmed off by corporations and capitalists). We can only move slowly toward a further more equalitarian stage in which many goods and services are free. Thus it is perfectly possible in the United States – and all more developed capitalist countries – to have immediate free education at all levels and free, high quality, health care for all. Further progress must depend on the available supply of goods and services, as well as changing attitudes toward incentives. But the history of evolution says that such progress is perfectly possible – it depends only on human beings organizing to change and replace the present institutions with those of a more humane society.

Conclusion

We have defined social evolution to be endogenous change. All societies evolve. Many societies die, but none reach a stable equilibrium and live long enough for their historians to tell us much about it. Human history is characterized by evolution, not equilibrium. Social evolution incurs both incremental and cataclysmic changes that result in the rise and fall of whole social systems. Social evolution comprises a multiple of causal relationships. Far more is involved than just economic or technological change. Social evolution is also closely related to the tensions and conflicts found in societies that are divided into unequal groups.

We examined four elements of social evolution. We could have included even more, but we focused on economic relations, technology, enabling myths, and democracy. We also looked at the evolutionary processes of structural change, rising tension, and social conflict.

We have attempted to present institutionalist and Marxist alternatives to conservative denials of evolution and to conservative views of evolution. We have found differences between our views in some aspects. Critical Marxism emphasizes capital accumulation and class more than radical institutionalism and radical institutionalism emphasizes culture and vested interest more than critical Marxism. Nevertheless, we find that they complement each other overall and do give us a richly elaborated view of social evolution as a synthesis. And we both see the possibility of a hopeful future.

AFTERWORD

Technology and revolution?

The book is now complete, but this Afterword deals at greater length with some important questions in the literature on social evolution. These include what is wrong with technological reductionism, whether progress is inevitable, whether progress will be made in a smooth linear fashion, and what the role of the individual is in evolution.

Evolution or progress? – an institutionalist view

As we saw in Chapter 1, Veblen did not think that evolution meant automatic "progress" of any sort. Instead, he emphasized that continued technological change in modern times was increasing the tensions between the flow of profit for business and the production of industrial abundance for the community. Many institutionalists now refer to these tensions as the Veblenian dichotomy.

Ayres: technology versus ceremonialism

Though he drew on Veblen's work, Ayres's thought was closer to some of the cultural lag theories then current in the social sciences. (For an example of such cultural lag theory see Ogburn 1922.) Ayres cast his formulation in universalistic terms. He stated, "Two forces seem to be present in all human behavior in all ages: one progressive, dynamic, productive of cumulative change; the other counter-progressive, static, inhibitory of change" (Ayres 1978, xv). Ayres says that these two forces are "technology" (Veblen's old industrial abundance) and "ceremonialism" (Veblen's old business profit). Ayres stated,

> The history of the human race is that of a perpetual opposition of these forces, the dynamic force of technology continually making

for change, and the static force of ceremony – status, mores, and
legendary belief – opposing change

(Ayres 1978: 176)

While ceremony entails getting something for the work that is done,
technology means actually doing the work. The great liberating and forward-
looking force in social evolution is technology, defined broadly as all skills
and tools that help human beings to improve the life process. Technology,
for Ayres, was more than the activities of tinkers and the accumulation of
their gadgets. It is all demonstrable knowledge, an inherent part of culture,
an instrumental continuum that brought us not only the industrial revolution
but also the industrial way of life.

Technology developed in a cumulative process that began with the use
of the simplest tools and learning of the simplest skills. The process is cumulative because each tool and its corresponding skill can be combined with
another tool-skill pair and become a new building block. The number of
these building blocks increases in an exponential growth curve. The new
building blocks are "invented" because the combinations necessary for such
"invention" have been handed down to us as a kind of community joint
stock. The process accelerates because the number of building blocks in the
joint stock, and therefore the number of new combinations, is continually
growing (Ayres 1978: 1961).

The conflicting interests of business profit versus industrial abundance
that Veblen emphasized began to be lost in Ayres. Veblen saw the vested
interests of business as the major resistance to the progress of industrial
technology. For Ayres, mainly the forces of ignorance, superstition, and
legend gave resistance to technological change. Ayres came to call these
resistant forces "ceremonialism." These forces derive their hold upon us
from emotional conditioning to the present situation and from past-binding
myths. Ayres often acknowledged that these forces could be used in a
Veblenian manner to sanctify the upper crust's income, status and authority.
For example, in his *The Divine Right of Capital* (Ayres 1946), Ayres criticized
those who were trying to take the United States back to the gross inequality
of unregulated capitalism that existed before the New Deal. Unfortunately,
this is one of his most neglected works. In it, Ayres used his analysis of
ceremonial opposition to technological progress to criticize the reaction
against the New Deal. His students in their elaboration of his ideas almost
never cite the work.

The mature Ayres turned away from that more Veblenian line of social
criticism, in which vested interests in profit conflicted with community
interests in abundance. But the young Ayres had been a Veblenian firebrand.
At first, he had used the term "righteousness" instead of "ceremonialism."

In what was probably his first description of "ceremonialism," a much younger Ayres said,

> The temptation is very strong for any one who is making a study of the social effects of righteousness to represent it [what he would later come to refer to as "ceremonialism"] as a deliberate conspiracy of the strong against the weak, the rich against the poor, the patriot against the foreigner.
>
> (Ayres 1973: 17; parentheses added)

In his first attempt to introduce ceremonialism (righteousness) Ayres believed that the justification of inequality was the motivation behind ceremonialism. However, as Ayres continued to develop his thought, he not only replaced the word righteousness with ceremonialism, he also replaced the motivation behind it. While righteousness was motivated by the need to justify inequality, ceremonialism was motivated more by the need to defend against superstitious fears of the unknown. The inequality dimension faded out of Ayresian analysis. Also, unlike the thought of Veblen, the thought of Ayres became distinctly optimistic and perhaps even a bit teleological:

> For truth is great and will prevail. The moral confusion of our day is the counterpart of our social confusion. As we go forward, both will pass.
>
> (Ayres 1946: 189)

Nevertheless, Ayres was a careful thinker. He provided a multi-level treatment of ceremonialism. He defined it as

1 a system of social stratification;
2 a system of conventional conceptions supporting stratification;
3 an ideology that supports the system of stratification and its conventions;
4 emotional conditioning involved in enculturation and reinforced by formal education, the media, and other agencies of modern society; and
5 all of these four are "defended … and intensified in mystic rites and ceremonies" (Ayres 1978: xvi).

Unfortunately, in practice, many institutionalists who have continued working in the Ayresian branch of institutionalism have concentrated almost solely on the fifth level, which is easily interpreted simply as the effects of ignorance and superstition, and which is easily cleansed of radical Veblenian implications. In this reductionistic process, the defense of social stratification and the selfish interest in defending the status quo are de-emphasized, and the original Veblenian dimension in Ayres is lost. Although Ayres was not consistently reductionistic himself, there is much material in his work that lends itself to reductionism. For example, along with other illustrations of the power of destructive beliefs, he cites the example of early European explorers in the Arctic who, thinking that only Inuits could build igloos, lived and suffered in silken tents rather than build igloos for themselves (Ayres 1978: 159). Many such examples of ignorance, superstition, or legends holding back progress are given in his work. He emphasizes that many people oppose change merely because they hate it, and they hate it because they love "the old ways" (Ayres 1978: xvii).

What is wrong with conceptualizing the chief factor of resistance to technology as ignorance, confusion, superstition, and legend? Nothing, so far as it goes, but that is not as far as it goes. Where does the mythology come from? Ayres argued in 1961 that mythology comes from the quest for certainty and security.

> No assurance of security could be too great; and man achieved the
> most vivid sense of security when the way of life of his community
> was identified with the purposes of Higher Powers. That all systems
> of mythology have this significance and serve this purpose is now
> recognized by all students of these matters …
>
> (Ayres 1961: 207)

Writing in 1961, Ayres was not quite right. It is true that many people believe in myths because they desire security. But it is also true that many people believe in myths because those myths justify inequality. Not all students of these matters – not even all institutionalists and certainly not Veblen – recognize that mythology has precisely the origin and significance that Ayres assigned to it in 1961. Many students of these matters argue that mythology (enabling myths) originate in defense of the status quo and support inequality and injustice. (See the essays in Dugger 1996.)

Progressism: a degeneration of evolutionary theory

Theory that concentrates on "mystic rites and ceremonies" as the resistant factor to change has considerable potential for degeneration into what we call "progressism." (As noted, a classic in this genre is the cultural lag theory in Ogburn 1922 [1964].) Veblen was immune to the degeneration, and Ayres himself, particularly in his more neglected works such as *Divine Right of Capital* and *Holier than Thou*, was far more resistant to the degeneration than many who became Ayresians and conflated the work of Ayres with the Ogburn cultural lag tradition. To clarify the point, progressism posits the argument that technological change is always a form of progress and that resistance to it is always a form of regress. Progress becomes virtually a certainty and resistance to new technology becomes virtually a hopeless and irrational act of ignorance, fear, and superstition. Some of the formulations of two recent institutionalists illustrate progressism.

Progressism in John R. Munkirs

As a reader pointed out to us, the idea that the emphasis on overcoming superstition and myth comes from an over-simplified reading of John Dewey. We agree, and emphasize that the over-simplified reading of his *The Quest for Certainty* can be particularly harmful. It results in too much emphasis on resistance to change as coming from the desire to propitiate a higher power (god?) and far too little emphasis on resistance to change as coming from the desire to justify a system of institutionalized human power. To explain the Veblenian dichotomy, for example, Munkirs quotes Dewey as saying

> Man who lives in a world of hazards is compelled to seek for security. He has sought to attain it in two ways. One of them began with an attempt to propitiate the powers which environ him and determine his destiny. It expressed itself in supplication, sacrifice, ceremonial rite and magical cult. The other is to invent arts and by their means turn the powers of nature to account; man constructs a fortress out of the very conditions and forces which threaten him.
>
> (Dewey, quoted in Munkirs 1988: 1036)

In this reductionistic treatment, the first way of dealing with an uncertain world is "ceremonial;" praying to a supernatural power. The second is "instrumental," or "technological;" using demonstrable knowledge. When the ceremonial is interpreted as propitiation of (super)natural powers and not as legitimization of human powers, progressism is the logical result. After all, if superstitious belief in the supernatural is the only resistance to technological progress, then progress is assured. Furthermore, when the instrumental/technological is viewed exclusively as channeling the powers of nature to benefit humanity and never as channeling the powers of humanity to benefit particular humans, progressism is reinforced. To stand for channeling the powers of nature to benefit humanity is to stand with the angels, and no one would argue against that. So no one would resist it and progress becomes a sure thing.

Although Munkirs explains and qualifies the nuances of his position at length and in a very sophisticated manner, his formulation of ceremonial resistance has the strength of a feather, and his formulation of technology has the strength of a bull. The result of the clash between the two is not hard to determine (Munkirs 1988, Dewey 1929).

Progressism in Thomas R. De Gregori

Thomas De Gregori set off an exchange of views in a 1978 article in the *Journal of Economic Issues* by advocating technology-borrowing policies for Less Developed Countries (De Gregori 1978, 1980, 1985; Hayden 1980; Han Yu Lee and Hayden 1986; McLoughlin 1986). His position was between the go-it-alone policies of radical dependency theorists and the market-worshiping policies of the Chicago school. Peter McLoughlin, the friendly critic of De Gregori's subsequent book that expanded on his article, explains De Gregori's basic stance as follows: "Professor DeGregori's natural buoyancy and optimism overflow virtually every page of his book" (McLoughlin 1986, 789). In other words, De Gregori is a technological optimist who basically understands the problem of underdevelopment as a failure to adopt industrial technology – which will benefit all humanity – as quickly as possible. F. Gregory Hayden and Han Yu Lee criticized De Gregori for failing to put technology into its proper institutional context, a context in which specific technologies are implemented in specific ways to the advantage/disadvantage of specific interests.

When does institutionalist theory degenerate into progressism? The answer, we believe, is straightforward: when it omits the role of class interests. Neither Munkirs' formulation of the dichotomy nor De Gregori's treatment of technology includes an adequate analysis of the role of class interests. When ignorance and fear, superstition and emotional conditioning are the sole important sources of ceremonial resistance, and when technology is formulated to be inherently beneficial to all humanity, then the eventual outcome of the clash or cultural lag between them is not very doubtful. Instead, it is almost predetermined or predestined so it seems that progress will surely triumph.

Progress will surely triumph because ignorance, fear, superstition, and emotional conditioning can all be reduced through universal education and enlightenment. However, progress will not necessarily triumph when class conflict, vested interest, and other inequalities are brought into the picture – into the cumulative causation of evolution – because class conflict, vested interest, and other inequalities could be intensified rather than reduced through a reduction in ignorance, fear, superstition, and emotional conditioning. Economic interest involves the pursuit of material gain. Class interest involves the recognition of shared economic interest. Class conflict involves acting together and taking collective action in pursuit of shared economic interest in opposition to other, contending interests. The reduction of ignorance and fear does not necessarily reduce the pursuit of material gain. The well informed and the brave can be just as greedy as the ignorant and the fearful. Furthermore, the reduction of ignorance, fear, superstition, and emotional conditioning could all very readily increase the recognition of shared economic interest and increase the ability to take collective action in the pursuit thereof. The business pursuit of self-interest may become even more intense, more coordinated, and more effective with a reduction in fear (of hell for usurers) and ignorance (of new ways to get something for nothing, as Veblen would say). With inequality, economic interest, and class conflict included in the analysis, Veblenian blind drift becomes just as possible as De Gregorian technological progress. The inclusion forces evolutionary theory to become historical rather than teleological.

Veblen believed that even though class interest was important, the members of the underlying population normally encountered great difficulty in determining a class interest – which is why he frequently referred to an underlying population rather than a class. With regard to the importance of class consciousness in forming class interest, Veblen began his *Absentee Ownership* with "the effectual division of interest and sentiment is beginning visibly to run on class lines, between the absentee owners and the underlying population" (Veblen 1964: 6). However, when he proceeded to analyze the American case of absentee ownership, he pessimistically discussed class interest only as a kind of addendum to the main run of his argument. In his addendum, so to speak, he stated,

> There is also the more obscure question of what the industrial man-power and the underlying population will say to it all, if anything. Anything like reasoned conduct or articulate behavior on their part will scarcely be looked for in this connection. Yet there remains an uneasy doubt as touches the *de facto* limits of tolerance.
> (Veblen 1964: 228; emphasis in original)

Institutionalists need to go back to Veblen and pick up the importance of class. We have de-emphasized it to our own loss.

Technological reductionism – what is the role of the individual?

To oversimplify, institutionalism relies on methodological collectivism rather than on methodological individualism. Since institutionalism is a cultural science, the individual is seen as a product of culture. The individual is not a cultural marionette, because individuals can and do transform their culture through collective action and even through individual action. In fact, culture itself is continually changing through the myriad of actions, inactions, and choices of individuals separately and collectively. Nonetheless, individuals

181

do not act or choose in a vacuum. They act and choose within a particular cultural context.

To explain the individual, institutionalism begins with the context in which individuals find themselves. This is essential, for it means that economics is not merely the study of how individuals allocate scarce resources to meet alternative uses. Institutional economics asks how specific resources come into use and how science and technology affect the availability of resources. Furthermore, it asks how property rights affect the use of resources. Also of major import is how individuals come to "want" specific things. This is the point made by John Kenneth Galbraith in his theory of the revised sequence.

To defend the individual against oppression, institutionalists must not assume that the resources available to individuals are fixed by nature or that their preferences are spontaneously generated from within themselves. Instead, the myriad of property rights, civil rights, beliefs and myths, scientific knowledge and technology, and distribution of income and wealth all affect the resources available to them, the preferences they have, and the choice sets they face.

Technological reductionism – is evolution teleological and predetermined?

Radical institutionalists would answer with a resounding *no*. In the face of the bloody experience of the last century, their belief in progress has been shaken to its roots. And social "progress" generally means not just change, but movement from a lower to a higher form. Some institutionalists used to think that social evolution meant progress. Belief in progress – that society has improved and will continue to improve – may give us the strength to get up every morning, but belief in progress is not an inherent part of the evolutionary point of view.

Technological reductionism – is evolution a simple, linear process?

Evolution is never simple, never linear. It is often complex, moving in many directions at once, under the impact of many different forces. Vast increases in agricultural production have taken place, but the distribution system has broken down. Farmers cannot sell their output at prices sufficient to keep them on the farm, and millions of people at home and abroad go hungry – while grain speculators grow rich in the great trading pits of the world. The Soviet planning system developed ways of accumulating vast quantities of capital but applied it inefficiently. Advances in medical science, nutrition, and public sanitation have doubled the life span, but old people worry that they will live too long and run out of income. There is nothing linear about social change.

Furthermore, social change often leads to a dead end. The globe is littered with the ruins of dead civilizations – dead ends of evolution, societies destroyed by their own avarice, superstition, or stupidity; societies destroyed by disease and change in climate; societies destroyed by other societies. To paraphrase and update Veblen, society seldom falls back on its common sense to find ways out of precarious institutional situations such as those we now face at the beginning of the third Christian millenium (Veblen 1964: 251.) But we never stop trying, either.

Evolution or progress? – a Marxist view

Marx's evolutionary view was strongly influenced by the lessons of the French Revolution, which was not long before his birth. Therefore, it is worth beginning with a brief description of the exciting events of the French Revolution and the lessons to be gained from it.

The French revolution and the transition from feudalism to capitalism

Marxists have long discussed the transition that took place in western Europe over several centuries from feudalism to capitalism. This lengthy and controversial discussion cannot be discussed here, but the reader should start with the great pioneering work by Dobb (1946), then the excellent collection of the early debate in Hilton (1975), followed by the brilliant and definitive work of Robert Brenner. (See Brenner's article and the debate on Brenner's thesis in Ashton and Philpin, eds. 1985.) For a brief and fascinating summary of the whole debate, see Wood (1999). Wood particularly stresses the vital point that the change from feudalism to capitalism was a truly revolutionary structural change, not a mere increase in capitalist elements, because there were no capitalist elements in early feudalism. Wood writes that capitalism is not "the natural culmination of history" and that capitalism "represents a historically specific social form and a rupture with earlier social forms" (Wood 1999: 7). After an initial decline in the dark ages, the feudal system of western Europe led very, very slowly to increasing agricultural surpluses. These surpluses were produced by serfs who were forced to labor on the feudal lord's land for much of the year – though they also had their own small plots of land for their subsistence. These surpluses of food eventually supported not only the lord and his retainers, but also city craftspeople and merchants. There were also always some free peasants who did not owe direct services, but might pay certain feudal dues in money or produce.

Eventually, in England and France at least, most serfs were given their freedom, but still owed dues to the lord and tithes to the church.

England ended the remnants of the feudal system in the revolution of 1649, when the king's head was chopped off, the feudal lords crushed militarily, and the bourgeoisie took power (see the detailed and excellent Marxist analysis in Hill, 1961). One interesting point about the English revolution of 1649 was that the ideological battles were all fought out in religious terms. So each economic group and political party from right to left also had a set of myths of its own, varying from the conservative Catholic myths held by great lords to the revolutionary myths held by the sect called the Levelers. Myth thus played a central role in the class struggle in England at that time. The class struggle at the political level was fought out between the king and the parliament, each with its own political myths.

Let us examine the French Revolution of 1789 in some detail to examine both the structural tensions and the class conflicts (see the Marxist view in Hobsbawm 1996, which is the factual basis for most of this section). On the eve of the Revolution, over 80 per cent of the French people were still employed in agriculture and perhaps 85 per cent lived in rural areas. Cities were small, Paris had a population of 500,000, while only two others had over 100,000. By 1780 there were only one million serfs remaining in France, these being on the lands of the king and the church. But even after serfdom was formally ended in 1780, almost all the peasants remained in a semi-feudal system in which they were heavily exploited. Some peasants paid large rents to the landowners, who were mostly the same feudal nobility. Some peasants were sharecroppers who paid half the crop to the landowner. Most "free" peasants still had to pay feudal dues of about ten per cent, a church tithe of about ten per cent, plus taxes to localities, regions, and the king. Altogether, the average French peasant retained only about half the product of the land for themselves and their family. Since these were mostly tiny plots of land, the average peasant lived in misery on the edge of starvation. The peasants were very angry and there were uprisings even before the revolution – but no general uprising until after the revolution began in the cities.

At the same time, there were still more than 25,000 feudal lords living in luxury and accomplishing little that was constructive – though many did military service, which might be called destructive. The feudal lords were obsolete and their luxurious living turned many peasants to rage.

The rage of the peasants was greatly enhanced by the fact that stagnation prevailed in agriculture, with low productivity keeping their incomes on the border of starvation-level. Neither peasants nor lords invested much money or time or thought in technological improvements. The average peasant was at the subsistence level, so the peasant had no spare resources for new investment. Furthermore, if the peasant improved the land, then rents or the landlord's share of the crop or the feudal fees or the taxes might all rise.

The lords had large incomes from hundreds of inefficient peasant farms, so they usually had enough for their needs. If times got bad (as they did in the 1780s) or a lord wanted a higher income for some reason, they did not think of technological improvement, but of higher exploitation. They usually demanded more rents or fees or tried to take over some of the ancient common lands that belonged to everyone. Thus, when the income of the nobles declined for various reasons in the early 1780s, they "attempted to counteract the decline in their income by squeezing the utmost out of their very considerable feudal rights to exact money ... from the peasantry" (Hobsbawm 1996: 57). Moreover, the feudal lords were trained to fight, not to farm. They did military service, but they looked down on work and production activities as not gentlemanly – and they were legally prohibited from most constructive professions. So they were not usually qualified for technological innovations nor had they any interest in technological innovations (with a few exceptions).

Hence the stagnant agriculture resulted from the semi-feudal class relations. The stagnation and low standard of living – contrasted with the lord's luxury led to rebellious feelings among the peasants. They did not begin the revolution, which started in the towns and cities, but they joined it with devastating force, burning the lord's chateaux, taking over the lord's lands, and killing some of the lords.

The urban population was small in number, but the urban areas had a relatively dynamic economy. Some work was done by free artisans; some by the guilds of masters and apprentices (but they were a dying breed), and some was done by the laboring poor for merchants under the putting-out system. The putting-out system was a system in which a merchant would pay people working at home to produce some specific amount of something (such as textiles) – and it not only included people in the cities, but many peasants. There were only a few capitalist manufacturers with factories, so the bourgeoisie of that time were very different than the modern capitalist class. The urban workers were not paid even enough to feed their families for a long day's toil. So they resorted to strikes and uprisings, which were broken by the police and the army – thus the urban poor had no love for the regime.

Yet the merchants also had their grievances against the old system. The government was largely run by the aristocracy, with the king being the greatest of the aristocrats. The aristocracy used the government for easy jobs with good incomes (keeping out most of the bourgeoisie from government jobs) and to pass laws that were often inimical to the interests of the merchants. Thus the class relations of the remaining feudal relationships acted as a break to industry. This propelled the bourgeoisie to fight for political power. Since the official government offices were largely monopolized by the nobles in search of both income and power, the bourgeoisie were a long way from political power.

The fight of the bourgeoisie for power and their resentment against the obsolete remnants of feudalism were reflected in the ideology of the enlightenment philosophers, such as Voltaire and Rousseau. The enlightenment thinkers lampooned and made fun of the old system, such as the useless but luxurious living of the feudal lords, the mistresses of the king, the palaces, and all the other aristocratic privileges built on the backs of the peasants, artisans, and bourgeoisie. These enlightenment thinkers created their own revolutionary myths, such as liberty, equality, and fraternity.

The bourgeoisie at first attempted to use peaceful means to reform the system through the absolute and supposedly enlightened monarch. But the aristocracy resisted all basic reforms that took away their wealth and power. So the legal skirmishes escalated into political fights in the streets and then into revolution. The revolutionaries chopped off the heads of the king and queen and killed or imprisoned or exiled many nobles. The countryside exploded into an inferno that ended all remnants of feudalism in the rural areas. These class struggles led to the economic and political power of the bourgeoisie as a basis for capitalism in France.

Marx drew the lesson from the French Revolution that class-divided systems could run into structural tensions, actual and possible productive forces resisted by frozen class relations, and that these crises could lead to class conflict, resulting in revolution. But Marx only said this about this single revolution; he did not say that this is a general law of all social evolution. He did believe that the pattern might repeat itself in some ways in capitalism. Thus he analyzed the recurrent recessions and depressions of capitalism as reflections of the class relations sometimes holding back production – though he also pointed out that in capitalist booms there was enormous pressure on capitalists to continually revolutionize technology (a very different situation from precapitalist societies). Unlike Marx, many later Marxists did turn such possibilities into rigid and eternal laws of evolution through certain predetermined stages, all determined by the growth of technology.

Technological reductionism

Marx's historical materialism says – as we saw throughout the book – that the key relationships of society (including ideas, institutions, class relations, and the forces of production) all interact together in a complex fashion. Technological reductionism, however, has always been seductive because it appears to provide a simple, general law of evolution as technology makes steady progress and social institutions progress with it, ending up with socialism and a march to utopia. Thus official propaganda of parties calling themselves Marxist has tended toward the distorted, but pleasant, view that technological progress determines everything, that it causes progress in social institutions, that social progress is inevitable, that social progress goes through the same predetermined stages in every society, and that the stages of society are primitive, slave, feudal, capitalist, and socialist – leading to a higher stage of socialism, a utopia sometimes called communism. Each of these aspects of technological reductionism will be discussed below.

The degeneration of Marxism into technological reductionism and the rebirth of a relational approach in critical Marxism

In their popular political propaganda – and in some of their theoretical works – the strong German Social Democratic Party of the 1890s and early twentieth century made use of a technological reductionist interpretation of Marx, emphasizing that progress to socialism is the inevitable result of social evolution. The improving technology must destroy the stagnant old capitalist institutions. Then society will choose the most appropriate institutions for improvement, namely, socialism. This was powerful propaganda, creating the aura of inevitability for the socialist cause. Although this view was widespread, many Marxists, as well as many other radicals, such as Thorstein Veblen (1919), criticized and rejected such simplistic views.

For 70 years after 1917, the dominant Marxism was the Soviet type of Marxism. The Soviets claimed not to be technological reductionists. But their popular propaganda – echoed by almost every Communist party around the world until the 1960s – argued that the steady improvement of technology would make capitalist institutions obsolete. This would energize the working class to lead a socialist revolution, arriving eventually at a communist utopia. This crude propaganda constituted the official dogma called "Marxism" by the Communist parties.

Ever since the Communist monolith began to weaken and splinter in the 1950s – marked by Khrushchev's supposedly secret speech of 1956 at the Twentieth Congress of the Soviet Communist Party – there has been a vehement debate on technological reductionism and all of the related issues in Marxist literature. Even outside of the Communist ruled countries, there were many sincere, sophisticated, and eloquent defenders of technological reductionist Marxism. As late as 1978, there was a bumper crop year for such defenses of the old reductionist interpretation of Marxism, including G. A. Cohen (1978), W. H. Shaw (1978), and J. McMurtry (1978).

All such tendencies toward reductionism have been criticized – especially in the last three decades – by those who take seriously a holistic or relational view of society. To name only a few, the Marxist critics of technological reductionism have included: Michael Albert and Robin Hahnel (1978), Derek Sayer (1987), Stephen Resnick and Richard Wolff (1987), Alex

Callinicos (1988), Ellen Wood (1990), Eric Wright, Andrew Levine, and Elliott Sober (1992), and Howard Sherman (1995). Contemporary Marxism is now overwhelmingly holistic or relational and opposed to any remnant of technological reductionism.

Technological reductionism – the economic issue

Economic reductionism reduces all explanations to the economy, of which technology is just one part. Technology, however, is the most dynamic part of the economy, so economic reductionism usually amounts to the same thing as technological reductionism. The economic reductionism of scholars such as the three noted above (who published in 1978) may be summed up in two propositions:

1   The economic base of a society (emphasizing technology but including land, labor, capital, and class relations) determines its superstructure (including all political institutions, culture, and ideology).
2   The level of productive forces, of which technology is the most dynamic, determines the class relations of production. Thus, technology is primary and ultimately determines all social relationships and institutions, including class relations, economic relations, and economic institutions.

The basic problem with Marxist economic reductionism, like any reductionism, is that it is a one-way street. Technology explains society, but what explains technology? Technology is taken as a given in this theory; to explain technology means to transform the theory into something totally different.

Technological reductionism – the issue of progress

In addition to technological reductionism, there have been many Marxists who took it a step further to argue that there is always progress. Their position may be summarized in the following points:

1   A certain type of productive relations is compatible only with a certain level of productive forces. This proposition asserts that only certain types of economic institutions can operate with a given technology without running into unsolvable problems. Of course, there are limits: slavery would not work in an industrialized, computerized economy. But there is no one to one relationship, so a wide range of class relations are possible at any given level of technology and other productive forces.
2   It is a given that the forces of production, including technology, continue to develop in all societies throughout history. Actually, technology sometimes develops rapidly and sometimes stagnates. The development

of technology depends completely on the social conditions and relationships in the society.

3   At the beginning of each mode of production, the productive relations among classes are compatible with and actively encourage the development of the productive forces. But each society reaches a point where the developing forces of production are no longer compatible with the old class relationships. This has often happened, but it is not inevitable. Moreover, the forms of this disjuncture between forces and relations can be so different that they are hardly recognizable as the same process. And the results may differ from an abrupt crisis to centuries of stagnation.

4   A new class will arise that will have sufficient power and organization to overthrow the old class relations. This has happened sometimes, as when the bourgeoisie overthrew the feudal lords, but many times it has not happened – so the society just stagnates or goes downhill.

5   That new class will actually use its power to overthrow the previous economic system, including the old set of class relations. Notice that the new class, which makes the revolution, not only is assumed to have the power to overthrow the old system, but also the desire. That desire comes from the increasing frustration due to the tension between frozen class relations and rising technological potential. The new consciousness is assumed, never proven. Actually, a whole class of people may have the power to change things if they were unified and had a clear conscious view of their grievances and what to change, but this may never happen. For example, sharecroppers in the US South after slavery lived a miserable life in most cases, but they were spread out and isolated on little farms, so they were never able to unify and change the system. Not until most African Americans moved to the cities did easier organization and rapid communication make the civil rights movement possible. Chapter 5 showed that US employees have objective grievances against the capitalist system, but they are more likely to be alienated and psychologically isolated than organized with a clear vision of change.

6   It is assumed that the new economic institutions (or class relations) will allow optimal development of the productive forces. Thus, progress continues unabated. Actually, an institutional change may lead to social and technological progress, but it may also lead sideways or backwards. For example, the Mongol expansion under Gengis Khan devastated many civilizations, while fascism in the twentieth century led to genocide rather than progress. Any living society must change eventually, but change does not inevitably lead to progress. Moreover, in the modern era we tend to think of changes in short periods of time, but in ancient Egypt, for example, there were ups and downs of civilization for thousands of years with no basic structural change in institutions.

There is a more general problem with the belief of some Marxists in automatic and eternal progress. These six propositions are presented as universal laws of an inevitable, preordained development. But there is no supernatural deity directing human history, so there are no such universal laws. There are only specific laws of each social formation based on the human relationships in that society – without any predetermination and predestination.

Technological reductionism – the role of the individual

It has been shown in Chapters 4 and 5 that individual ideas (including myths that individuals believe) affect society, while society also affects individual ideas. The individual is part of society, so it is wrong to ever visualize an individual outside of society. To ask if the individual affects society is like asking if the legs of a person affect that person – both are silly questions. Every individual affects society, so "great" individuals certainly do affect society. But what an individual can accomplish certainly depends on what situation that individual has inherited. If Albert Einstein had been born into a primitive society, he could not have invented the theory of relativity. That theory was possible only when others had done a lot of previous theoretical work, when technology had reached a high enough level to make the concepts relevant, and when class relations were such as to encourage such research. Having said all that, the personality of Albert Einstein certainly affected his research and his research certainly affected society.

One type of reductionism is psychological reductionism, which holds that all social events can be explained by individual psychology. This view which reduces every explanation to individual psychology is also called individualism. Some types of psychologically oriented historians explain everything this way. For example, all the evil that happened in the Soviet Union was due to the personality of Stalin. For another example, the First World War happened because Archduke Ferdinand was assassinated by a radical student, who did it because he hated his father. For a third example, women leaders who protest gender discrimination have all been lesbians with strange paranoia. These are all real examples and many other sillier ones could be noted. Orthodox, neoclassical economists also explain everything on the basis of axioms about the psychology of individuals. Thus, if millions of Americans are unemployed in a recession, it is because they all "prefer" leisure to work! If millions of people live in poverty in the United States, it is because they "prefer" not to develop their skills. As if people were free to make any choice they wished! Actually, people do make their history, but they do under certain historical circumstances and institutions inherited from the past.

Critical Marxists do not agree that society can be explained merely by individual decisions, as if those decisions were made outside of society. For example, consumer decisions are not made from some inherent tastes we are born with – such as the taste for television or big cars – but rather are shaped by advertising and the whole social environment. Individual decisions do shape society, but individual decisions are shaped by the previous history of society – they do not just come out of nowhere. But critical Marxists also object to the extreme collectivist notion of some official Marxists that a whole class acts exactly according to its interests, regardless of individual psychology, attitudes, and prevalent myths. The views of a class are defined to be the views of all the individuals in the class – but they do have common interests that will influence their views. Critical Marxists use a relational or holistic view of the whole society that rejects any kind of reductionism. It finds that class relations are quite real, but class analysis must be supported by observations, not assumptions, about the individuals in those classes.

Technological reductionism – is evolution teleological and predetermined?

We can understand change in society in terms of social tensions and class conflict, without reducing our explanation to either technology or psychology. But that change means only a new society, not necessarily a "better" society as human beings would define it. Thus, there is no design (a teleological goal set by some outside force) that society must follow.

When Marx speaks of social evolution as the result of the conflict between class relations and the forces of production, does that mean that history is predetermined by forces external to human beings and that human beings have no free will? No, critical Marxists believe that human beings make their own history, though under given conditions. "Class relations" are human relationships, not a mere abstraction. When there is a clash between a rigid class society and the possibilities of material progress, class relations will change if, and only if, human beings become aware of the situation and are motivated to do something about it. In Chapter 6, we saw that when the US South was a slave society, industrial improvement was retarded by slave relations. The elite of every Third World country desires economic development, but holds it back when the necessary specific measures would undermine its own power – for example, they resist paying taxes necessary for governments to build roads, schools, and so forth.

The fact that the ruling class is holding back development may or may not lead to a revolutionary change. It will lead to that change only if a sufficient number of people become aware of the issues and are motivated to change it. So it is people who make changes – within given circumstances. Such changes are not predetermined by any outside force.

Technological reductionism – is social evolution a simple, linear process?

The popular propaganda of official Soviet Marxism pointed toward a simple progression from slavery to feudalism to capitalism to socialism to communism in all societies. This view was never defended by serious Marxist scholars. Society does evolve, but the path of evolution is very complex, resembling the complex tree of biological evolution with its many branches. Societies may regress in some cases (either by external invasion or internal causes such as environmental destruction). Societies may jump over any given step that others have gone through. Societies may change at very different rates.

All of this shows anything but a linear path of evolution. If one needed more evidence, the fact that Russia is regressing to capitalism from some kind of non-capitalist system should convince anyone that evolution is nonlinear. Soviet society was deep in trouble and had to change. But it could have changed in a number of directions. In its fall, its people (including a large part of the ruling class) thought that they could get the best parts of European and US capitalism while retaining the beneficial aspects of their old system (such as full employment). By hindsight, one can understand how this mistaken view became so widespread in a desperate situation. At any rate, the Soviet collapse is an example of historical evolution, but certainly not a simple linear path of "progress."

Holistic or relational Marxism

Contemporary, critical Marxism opposes any theories that reduce explanation to a single, isolated factor. Society is not determined solely by technology, and it is not determined solely by individual psychology. Society is an evolving organism, and research should start with the relationships among its integral parts. For example, to understand unemployment, one does not begin by interviewing the individual, unemployed workers to ascertain their state of mind, but begins by examining the economic institutions and class relations that produce the conditions leading to aggregate unemployment. (Of course, this is not to say that the state of mind of the unemployed individual is of no political or humanistic concern.) Moreover, one can know all about the technology of 1929 without having a clue to causes of the Great Depression. It is only by beginning with economic institutions, that is, class relations, that one can understand recessions and depressions.

The holistic or relational view of society, therefore, rules out both economic and psychological reductionism (or individualism). Starting with human relationships, as radical institutionalists and critical Marxists do, makes it impossible to entertain an individualist methodology – but it is the perfect context for institutional or class analysis. For critical Marxists, human relationships are the central focus, beginning with class relationships but including racial, ethnic, and gender relationships. To understand why an individual man or woman is depressed, before individual diagnosis, one must first understand the matrix of family, racial, ethnic, and class relationships within which he or she exists.

Finally, critical Marxists reject eternal equilibrium theories for an approach that examines how social relationships evolve over time. Marxian evolutionary theory emphasizes the reproduction of the social status quo in non-revolutionary times through its institutions and myths. It also shows that drastic change does occur at other times. How does that evolutionary change occur in the basic structure of institutions and class relations?

Marxism has emphasized two points about change. First, as shown in Chapter 7, there is, at times, an unbearable tension between the institutions (that is, the human, class relations of society) and the productive forces (including technology). Second, as shown in Chapters 2 and 8, all of recorded history is the history of class conflict, leading to revolutionary change in some cases.

If we believe the technological reductionist interpretation of Marxism, these two points are quite contradictory and cannot be reconciled. Why is that? In the reductionist view, technology inevitably progresses, and social institutions must inevitably progress as a result. This leaves no room for human actions to play a role in evolution. Class conflict – including all of human suffering and striving – is secondary, derivative, and predetermined by technology.

Critical Marxists, however, reject this technological reductionist interpretation of evolutionary change. The story must begin with the fact that there is at times a lag of institutions (that is, class relations) behind the forces of production (including technology) – within the framework of a holistic analysis of all the relationships of society. What causes the resistance to change is not primarily myth and superstition, though these play an important role, but mainly the vested interests of the ruling classes in maintaining the present class relations. The ruling class is well off and wishes to maintain the status quo, but the exploited classes – and rival elite classes in some cases – try hard to change the status quo.

The classes that fight for progress do not do so primarily because of educated enlightenment and less ignorance or myths, but because of a vital interest in changing the system. As shown above, however, critical Marxists emphasize that there is nothing inevitable about technological or social changes.

The opposite error of psychological reductionism has also been made by Marxists, a purely subjective notion of class conflict. If one has a theory of subjective class conflict but no theory of structural tensions then the notion is purely voluntary and offers no theory of evolution. To immunize Marxists against a merely subjective, voluntaristic interpretation of class conflict, they must have a theory of objective lags or tensions between institutions (class relations) and forces of production (including technology). On the other hand, only a theory of conscious class conflict can immunize Marxists from the diseases of technological reductionism and inevitable progress. For an understanding of social evolution, Marxists need theories of both class conflict and institutions versus productive forces.

Conclusion: methodological synthesis

As an afterword, we emphasize that evolutionary theory at its best is Marxist and institutionalist, in varying degrees, but omitting neither. In this Afterword, we have also emphasized that technological reductionism is wrong in all of its aspects and implications, so it must be exorcised from institutionalism and from Marxism.

With technological, psychological, economic, and any other forms of reductionism removed, a holistic, radical theory of evolution is certainly possible and can be a fruitful tool of social analysis. Such a theory should emphasize the fact that evolution causes fundamental structural change. Such a theory must include an understanding of the disruption caused in human institutions by economic change, including new technology. Furthermore, such a radical theory of evolution involves an understanding that some groups may organize to struggle against change while others may struggle to promote it. Change is not neutral and it does not just happen. Change harms some and benefits others.

Universal or eternal laws do not determine social evolution. Evolution is not necessarily progress. Evolution in some particular direction defined as progress is not inevitable. Evolution is seldom smooth and linear.

In our dialogue, we found that we easily agreed on what evolution is not. But we have also found that we agree on important aspects of what evolution is. Evolution is endogenous change. It is driven by four interrelated causes: by economic relations, technology, enabling myth, and political relations. Evolution is three interrelated processes: structural change, social tension, and social conflict. Evolution is happening, today, and will continue tomorrow. We can try to guide it. We can also try to ignore it. Even if we outlaw it, evolution is not going away.

REFERENCES

Albert, M. and Hahnel, R. (1978) *Unorthodox Marxism: An Essay on Capitalism, Socialism, and Revolution,* Boston: South End Press.

Allen, R. (1933) *The Labor of Women in the Production of Cotton,* Unpublished Ph.D. Dissertation, The University of Chicago.

Anderson, P. (1974) *Lineages of the Absolute State,* London: New Left Books.

—— (1996) *Passages from Antiquity to Feudalism,* London: Verso.

Arnold, T. (1966) *The Folklore of Capitalism,* New Haven: Yale University Press, 1937.

Ashton, T. H. and Philpin, C. H. E. (eds) (1985) *The Brenner Debate: Class Structure and Economic Development in Pre-Industrial Europe,* New York: Cambridge University Press.

Ayres, C. E. (1978) *The Theory of Economic Progress,* 3rd edn. Kalamazoo, MI: New Issues Press.

—— (1958) "Veblen's Theory of Instincts Reconsidered," in Dowd, D. F. (ed.) *Thorstein Veblen: A Critical Reappraisal,* Reprint. Westport, CT: Greenwood Press, 1977.

—— (1929) *Holier Than Thou: The Way of the Righteous,* Reprint. Clifton, NJ: Augustus M. Kelley, 1973.

—— (1946) *The Divine Right of Capital,* Boston: Houghton Mifflin.

—— (1961) *Toward a Reasonable Society: The Values of Industrial Civilization,* Austin: University of Texas Press.

Bernasek, A. and Kinnear, D. (1995) "Ruth Allen: Frontier Labor Economist," in *Economic Mavericks: The Texas Institutionalists,* Phillips, R. J. (ed.) 75–106. Greenwich, CT: JAI Press.

Bird, E. (1996) *Dressing in Feathers: The Construction of the Indian in American Popular Culture,* Boulder, CO: Westview Press.

Blackburn, R. (1997) *The Making of New World Slavery,* London: Verso.

Bourgin, F. (1990) *The Great Challenge: The Myth of Laissez-Faire in the Early Republic,* New York: Harper and Row.

Bowles, S. and Gintis, H. (1976) *Schooling in Capitalist America: Educational Reform and the Contradictions of Economic Life,* New York: Basic Books.

—— and —— (1987) *Democracy and Capitalism: Property, Community, and the Contradictions of Modern Social Thought,* New York: Basic Books.

Bowles, S., Gordon, D. M. and Weisskopf, T. E. (1990) *After the Waste Land: A Democratic Economics for the Year 2000*, Armonk, NY: M. E. Sharpe.

Bowles, S., Gintis, H. and Gustafsson, B. (1993) *Markets and Democracy: Participation, Accountability, and Efficiency*, Cambridge: Cambridge University Press.

Braverman, H. (1974) *Labor and Monopoly Capital*, New York: Monthly Review Press.

Brinkman, R. L. (1981) *Cultural Economics*, Portland, OR: Hapi Press.

Callinicos, A. (1988) *Making History*, Ithaca, NY: Cornell University Press.

Carnoy, M. and Shearer, D. (1980) *Economic Democracy: The Challenge of the 1980s*, Armonk, NY: M.E. Sharpe.

Childe, V. G. (1948) *Social Evolution*, London: Watts and Co.

—— (1951) *Social Evolution*, London: Watts and Co.

Clifford, F. (1997) "Woman's Suit Tests Law on Environmental Protection," *Los Angeles Times*, February 19, pp. 1 and 20.

Cohen, G. A. (1978) *Karl Marx's Theory of History*, Princeton, NJ: Princeton University Press.

Cohen, M. N. (1998) *Culture of Intolerance: Chauvinism, Class, and Racism in the United States*, New Haven: Yale University Press.

Collins, C., Leondar-Wright, B. and Sklar, H. (1999) *Shifting Fortunes*. Boston: United for a Fair Economy.

Commons, J. R. (1968) *Legal Foundations of Capitalism*, Madison: University of Wisconsin Press.

—— (1970) *The Economics of Collective Action*, Parsons, K. H. (ed.) Madison: University of Wisconsin Press.

—— (1934, 1961) *Institutional Economics*, Madison: University of Wisconsin Press.

Darwin, C. (1859 and 1871) *The Origin of Species and The Descent of Man* (two volumes now published as one) New York: The Modern Library, no date.

Deckard, B. S. (1983) *The Women's Movement*, 3rd edn. New York: Harper & Row.

De Gregori, T. R. (1980) "Instrumental Criteria for Assessing Technology: An Affirmation by Way of a Reply," *Journal of Economic Issues* 14 (March): 219–25.

—— (1978) "Technology and Economic Dependency: An Institutional Assessment," *Journal of Economic Issues* 12 (June): 467–76.

—— (1985) *A Theory of Technology: Continuity and Change in Human Development*, Ames: Iowa State University Press.

Dewey, J. (1961) *Democracy and Education: An Introduction to the Philosophy of Education*, New York: Macmillan.

—— (1929) *The Quest for Certainty*, Reprint. New York: Capricorn Books, 1960.

Diamond, J. (1997) *Guns, Germs, and Steel*, New York: W. W. Norton.

Dobb, M. (1946) *Studies in the Development of Capitalism*, London: George Routledge and Sons.

Dollars and Sense. (2000). *The Real Y2K Crisis: Global Economic Necessity*, No. 227 (Jan/Feb).

Dorfman, J. (1934, 1972) *Thorstein Veblen and his America*, Clifton, NJ: Augustus M. Kelley.

Dowd, D. (1997) *Blues for America*, New York: Monthly Review Press.

Dugger, R. (1974) *Our Invaded Universities: Form, Reform, and New Starts*, New York: W. W. Norton.

Dugger, W. M. (1980a) "Property Rights, Law, and John R. Commons," *Review of Social Economy*, 38 (April): 41–53.

—— (1980b) "Power: An Institutional Framework of Analysis," *Journal of Economic Issues*, 14 (December): 897–907.

—— (1981) "Sociobiology: A Critical Introduction to E. O. Wilson's Evolutionary Paradigm," *Social Science Quarterly*, 62 (June): 221–33.

—— (1984) "Veblen and Kropotkin on Human Evolution," *Journal of Economic Issues*, 18 (December): 971–85.

—— (1989a) *Corporate Hegemony*, Westport, CT: Greenwood Press.

—— (1989b) *Radical Institutionalism*, Westport, CT: Greenwood Press.

—— (1992) "The Great Retrenchment and the New Industrial State," *Review of Social Economy*, 50 (Winter): 453–71.

—— (1994) "Institutionalism and Feminism," in *The Economic Status of Women under Capitalism: Institutional Economics and Feminist Theory*, Peterson, J. and Brown, D. (eds) Brookfield, VT: Edward Elgar.

—— (1996a) "Four Modes of Inequality," in *Inequality: Radical Institutionalist Views on Race, Gender, Class, and Nation*, Dugger, W. M. (ed.) Westport, CT: Greenwood Press.

—— (ed.) (1996b) *Inequality: Radical Institutionalist Views on Race, Gender, Class, and Nation*, Westport, CT: Greenwood Press.

—— "Veblenian Institutionalism." (1995a) *Journal of Economic Issues*, 29 (December): 1013–27.

—— (1995b) "Beyond Technology to Democracy: The Tool Legacy in Institutionalism," in *Institutional Economics and the Theory of Social Value*, Clark, C. M. A. (ed.) Boston: Kluwer Academic Publishers.

—— (1988) "Radical Institutionalism: Basic Concepts," *Review of Radical Political Economics* 20 (Spring): 1–20.

—— (1992) "An Evolutionary Theory of the State and the Market," in *The Stratified State*, Dugger, W. M. and Waller, W. (eds) Armonk, New York: M.E. Sharpe.

—— and Waller, W. (eds) (1992) *The Stratified State: Radical Institutionalist Theories of Participation and Duality*, Armonk, NY: M.E. Sharpe.

—— (1992) *Underground Economics: A Decade of Institutionalist Dissent.* Armonk, NY: M.E. Sharpe.

—— (1998) "Against Inequality," *Journal of Economic Issues* 32 (June): 287–303.

—— (1994) and Sherman, H. J. "Comparison of Marxism and Institutionalism," *Journal of Economic Issues*, 28 (March): 101–27.

—— and Waller, W. (1996) "Radical Institutionalism: From Technological to Democratic Instrumentalism," *Review of Social Economy*, 54 (Summer): 169–89.

Dunbar-Ortiz, R. (1998) *Red Dirt: Growing Up Okie*, London: Verso.

Eiseley, L. (1961) *Darwin's Century*, Garden City, NY: Anchor Books.

Engels, F. (1942, 1886) *Origin of the Family, State, and Private Property*, New York: International Publishers.

—— *Ludwig Feuerbach* (N.D.) New York: International Publishers (Original published in 1888).

Fast, H. (1951) *Spartacus*, New York: Crown Publishers.

Fischer, C., Hout, M., Jankowski, M., Lucas, S., Swidler, A. and Voss, K. (1996)

Inequality By Design: Cracking the Bell Curve Myth, Princeton, NJ: Princeton University Press.

Foner, P. S. (1947, 1955, 1964, 1965) *History of the Labor Movement in the United States*, Volumes 1, 2, 3, 4. New York: International Publishers.

Foreman, G. (1934) *The Five Civilized Tribes*. Norman, OK: University of Oklahoma Press.

Friedman, M. (1962) *Capitalism and Freedom*, Chicago: University of Chicago Press.

Galbraith, J. K. (1967) *The New Industrial State*, Boston: Houghton Mifflin.

—— (1973a) "Power and the Useful Economist." *American Economic Review*, 63, No. 1 (March): 469–78.

—— (1973b) *Economics and the Public Purpose*, Boston: Houghton Mifflin.

—— (1992) *The Culture of Contentment*, Boston: Houghton Mifflin.

Genovese, E. (1956) *Roll Jordan Roll: the World the Slaves Made*, New York: Vintage.

—— (1992) *From Rebellion to Revolution: African American Slave Revolts*, Baton Rouge: Louisiana State University Press.

Gilman, C. P. (1893). "Similar Cases," in *This Our World*, Oakland, CA: McCombs and Vaughn, pp. 95–100.

Gould, S. J. (1996) *Full House: The Spread of Excellence from Plato to Darwin*, New York: Three Rivers Press.

Gramsci, A. (1971) *Selections from the Prison Notebooks of Antonio Gramsci*, Hoare, Q. and Smith, G. N. (eds and trans) New York: International Publishers.

Greenbaum, J. (1995) *Windows on the Workplace: Computers, Job, and the Organization of Office Work in the Late Twentieth Century*, New York: Monthly Review Press.

Hahnel, R. (1999) *Panic Rules: Everything You Need to Know About the Global Economy*, Cambridge, MA: South End Press.

Hall, T. W. and Elliott, J. E. (1999) "Poland and Russia One Decade after Shock Therapy," *Journal of Economic Issues*, 33 (June): 305–14.

Hayden, F. G. (1980) "An Assessment Dependent upon Technology," *Journal of Economic Issues* 14 (March): 211–19.

Henry, J. (1990) *The Making of Neoclassical Economics*. Boston: Unwin Hyman.

Herrnstein, R.J. and Murray, C. (1994) *The Bell Curve: Intelligence and Class Structure in American Life*, New York: The Free Press.

Hill, C. (1961) *The Century of Revolution 1603–1714*, New York: Norton.

Hilton, R. (ed.) (1975) *The Transition from Feudalism to Capitalism*, London: New Left Books.

Hobsbawm, E. (1996) *The Age of Revolution*, 1789–1848. New York: Vintage Books.

Hodgson, G. M. (1996). *Economics and Evolution*, Ann Arbor: University of Michigan Press.

Hofstadter, R. (1944) *Social Darwinism in American Thought, 1860–1915*, Philadelphia: University of Pennsylvania Press.

Hunt, E. K. (1979) "The Importance of Thorstein Veblen for Contemporary Marxism." *Journal of Economic Issues*, 13 (March): 113–40.

—— (1994) "Social Class in Institutional Economics," in *The Elgar Companion to Institutional and Evolutionary Economics*, Hodgson, G. M., Samuels, W. J. and Tool, M. R. (eds) Brookfield, VT: Edward Elgar, pp. 54–8.

Jahoda, G. (1995) *The Trail of Tears: The Story of the American Indian Removals 1813–1855*, New York: Wings Books.

REFERENCES

Keynes, J. M. (1936) *The General Theory of Employment , Interest, and Money*, New York: Harcourt, Brace.

Kimball, R. (1990) *Tenured Radicals: How Politics Has Corrupted our Higher Education*, New York: Harper and Row.

Krikorian, G. (1997) "Judge Slashes Life Sentence In Pizza Theft Case," *Los Angeles Times*, January 29, pp. 1 and 10.

Kuhn, T. (1962) *The Structure of Scientific Revolutions*, Chicago: University of Chicago Press.

Kuttner, R. (1998) *Everything For Sale: the Virtues and Limits of Markets*, New York: Alfred Knopf.

Landes, D. S. (1969) *The Unbound Prometheus*, Cambridge: Cambridge University Press.

Lee, H. Y. and Hayden, F. G. (1986) "DeGregori's A Theory of Technology: A Review Article." *Journal of Economic Issues*, 20 (September): 799–804.

Levinson, A. (1998) "Voice of Death Chamber Witnessed 138 Executions," *Tulsa World*, August 30, 1998, p. A5.

Marcuse, H. (1964) *One Dimensional Man*. Boston: Beacon Press.

Marx, K. (1867, 1967) *Capital*, Volume 1, New York: International Publishers.

—— (1904, 1859) *A Contribution to the Critique of Political Economy*, Chicago: Charles Kerr and Co.

Marx, K. and Engels, F. (1848, 1994) *The Communist Manifesto*. New York: International Publishers.

Mayhew, A. (1981) "Ayresian Technology, Technological Reasoning, and Doomsday," *Journal of Economic Issues* 15 (June): 513–20.

—— (1987) "Culture: Core Concept Under Attack." *Journal of Economic Issues* 21 (June): 587–603.

McLoughlin, P. F. M. (1986) "A Theory of Technology – Continuity and Change in Human Development: A Review Article," *Journal of Economic Issues*, 20 (September): 785–98.

McMurtry, J. (1978) *The Structure of Marx's World View*, Princeton: Princeton University Press.

Melman, S. (1997) "From Private to State Capitalism: How the Permanent War Economy Transformed the Institutions of American Capitalism," *Journal of Economic Issues*, 31 (June): 311–30.

Memmi, A. (1967) *The Colonizer and the Colonized*, Boston: Beacon Press.

Miliband, R. (1973) "Poulantzas and the Capitalist State," *New Left Review*, Vol. 82, pp. 83–92.

—— (1991) *Divided Societies: Class Struggle in Contemporary Capitalism*, New York: Oxford University Press.

Mills, C. W. (1959) *The Sociological Imagination*. London: Oxford University Press.

Mitchell, W. C. (1913, 1989) *Business Cycles and Their Causes*, Philadelphia: Porcupine Press.

—— (1969) *Types of Economic Theory*. New York: Augustus M. Kelley.

Munkirs, J. R. (1988) "The Dichotomy: Views of a Fifth Generation Institutionalist," *Journal of Economic Issues* 22 (December): 1035–44.

Myrdal, G. (1944) *An American Dilemma*, New York: Harper and Row.

Navarro, V. (1993) *Dangerous to Your Health*, New York: Monthly Review Press.

Nelson, R. and Winter, S. (1982) *An Evolutionary Theory of Economic Change*, Cambridge, MA: Harvard University Press.

Noble, D. F. (1979) *America By Design: Science, Technology, and the Rise of Corporate Capitalism*, New York: Oxford University Press.

—— (1984) *Forces of Production: A Social History of Industrial Automation*, New York: Knopf.

—— (1998) "Digital Diploma Mills: The Automation of Higher Education," *Monthly Review*, Vol. 49 (February): 38–52.

Ogburn, W. F. (1922) *Social Change*. Reprint. Gloucester, MA: Peter Smith, 1964.

Ollman, B. (1971) *Alienation*, New York: Cambridge University Press.

—— and Vernoff, E. (1987) *The Left Academy*. New York: McGraw-Hill.

Pappendieck, J. (1998) "Want and Plenty: From Hunger to Inequality," *Monthly Review*, Vol. 50 (July–August): 125–36.

Peterson, J. and Brown, D. (eds) (1994) *The Economic Status of Women under Capitalism*, Brookfield, VT: Edward Elgar.

Peterson, W. C. (1994) *Silent Depression*, New York: W. W. Norton.

Ransom, R. and Sutch, R. (1977) *One Kind of Freedom*, New York: Cambridge University Press.

Reich, R. (1997) *Locked In the Cabinet*, New York: Alfred Knopf.

Resnick, S. A. and Wolff, R. D. (1987) *Knowledge and Class: A Marxian Critique of Political Economy*, Chicago: University of Chicago Press.

Roemer, J. E. (1978) "Neoclassicism, Marxism, and Collective Action." *Journal of Economic Issues* 12 (March): 147–61.

—— (1982) *A General Theory of Exploitation and Class*, Cambridge, MA: Harvard University Press.

—— (ed.) (1986) *Analytical Marxism*, Cambridge: Cambridge University Press.

—— (1994) *Egalitarian Perspectives: Essays in Philosophical Economics*, Cambridge: Cambridge University Press.

Sanders, B. (1997) *Outsider in the House*, New York: Verso Publishers.

Sayer, D. (1987) *The Violence of Abstraction*, New York: Basil Blackwell.

Sen, A. (1999) *Development as Freedom*, New York: Alfred A. Knopf.

Shaw, G. B. (1971) *The Road to Equality*, Boston: Beacon Press.

Shaw, W. H. (1978) *Marx's Theory of History*, Stanford: Stanford University Press.

Sherman, H. J. (1967) "Marx and the Business Cycle," *Science and Society*, Vol. 31 (Fall): 484–504.

—— (1972) *Radical Political Economy*, New York: Basic Books.

—— (1987) *Foundations of Radical Political Economy*, Armonk, NY: M.E. Sharpe.

—— (1991) *The Business Cycle: Growth and Crisis Under Capitalism*, Princeton, NJ: Princeton University Press.

—— (1995) *Reinventing Marxism*, Baltimore: Johns Hopkins University Press.

—— (1996) "A Holistic-Evolutionary View of Racism, Sexism, and Class Inequality." in *Inequality: Radical Institutionalist Views on Race, Gender, Class, and Nation*, Dugger, W. M. (ed.): 39–52, Westport, CT: Greenwood Press.

Simon, S. (1999) "Harvest of Plenty Reaps Cashless Crops for Growers," *Los Angeles Times*, July 25, pp. 1, 10.

Sitton, J. F. (1996) *Recent Marxian Theory*, Albany, NY: SUNY Press.

Stanfield, J. R. (1995) *Economics, Power and Culture*, New York: St. Martin's Press.

Stephens, M. (1998) *A History of News*, New York: Viking Penguin.

Strobel, F. R. and Peterson, W. C. (1997) "Class Conflict, American Style: Distract and Conquer." *Journal of Economic Issues*, 31 (June): 433–43.

Sweezy, P. (1942, 1958) *The Theory of Capitalist Development*, New York: Monthly Review Press.

Symposium. (1997) "The Natural Rate of Unemployment," *Journal of Economic Perspectives*, 11 (Winter), No. 1: 1–109.

Thompson, E. P. (1966) *The Making of the English Working Class*, New York: Vintage Books.

Tool, M. R. (1979) *The Discretionary Economy*, Santa Monica, CA: Goodyear Publishing.

—— and Samuels, W. J. (eds) (1989) *State, Society, and Corporate Power*, 2nd edn. New Brunswick: Transaction Publishers.

Toruno, M. (1997) "Blind Drift and the Rightist State," *Journal of Economic Issues*, 31 (June): 585–93.

Veblen, T. (1898, 1919) "Why is Economics not an Evolutionary Science?" in *The Place of Science in Modern Civiliation and other Essays*, Veblen, T., New York: B. W. Huebsch, pp. 56–81.

—— (1899, 1975) *The Theory of the Leisure Class*, New York: Augustus M. Kelley.

—— (1904, 1975) *The Theory of Business Enterprise*, New York: Augustus M. Kelley.

—— (1906) "The Socialist Economics of Karl Marx and His Followers," *The Quarterly Journal of Economics*, 20 (April and August): page numbers unknown.

—— (1914, 1964) *The Instinct of Workmanship and the State of the Industrial Arts*, New York: Augustus M. Kelley.

—— (1918, 1965) *The Higher Learning in America: A Memorandum on the Conduct of Universities by Business Men*, New York: Augustus M. Kelley.

—— (1919) *The Place of Science in Modern Civilization*, New York: B. W. Huebsch.

—— (1919, 1964) *The Vested Interests and the Common Man*, New York: Augustus M. Kelley.

—— (1921, 1965) *The Engineers and the Price System*, New York: Augustus M. Kelley.

—— (1923, 1964) *Absentee Ownership and Business Enterprise in Recent Times*, New York: Augustus M. Kelley.

Wolff, R. and Resnick, S. (1986) "Power, Property, and Class," *Socialist Review*, Vol. 16, No. 86 (March–April): 97–124.

Wood, E. M. (1990) "Explaining Everything or Nothing?" *New Left Review* No. 184 (November/December): 116–28.

—— (1995) *Democracy Against Capitalism*, Cambridge: Cambridge University Press.

—— (1999) *The Origin of Capitalism*, New York: Monthly Review Press.

Wright, E. O., Levine, A. and Sober, E. (1992) *Reconstructing Marxism*, New York: Verso.

Wright, E. O. (1985) *Class*, New York: Verso

—— (1989) *Debate on Class*, New York: Verso.

INDEX

absentee ownership 21, 23, 181
Afghanistan 35
Africa 66, 152, 156
African Americans 28–9, 38, 55, 73, 75, 145
aggregate demand 65
agriculture 58
Air Traffic Controller's union 110
Albert, M. 187
alienation 103–4
Allen, R. 86–7
American Civil War 64, 160–2; democracy 112; social conflict 143–4, 155, 163; social tensions 138; structural change 131
American Indian Movement 99
American Railway Union workers' strike 153
American Revolution (1776) 130
ancient Egypt 24, 37, 116, 130, 189
ancient Greece 37, 75, 84, 130
ancient Rome 37, 38, 84, 88; Empire, decline of 158–9; Empire, peak period of 157–8; slavery 159–60; social conflict 153, 156, 162; social tensions 142; structural change 130
Anderson, P. 59, 157–8
anti-Semitism 75
aristocracy 185, 186; *see also* leisure class; ruling class
Aristotle 45
Arnold, T. 70
artificial selection 98
Ashton, T.H. 183
Asia 66, 99, 138, 142, 152

atomic power 78–9
Australia 138
automobile 57
Ayres, C.E. 5, 85, 114, 125–6, 147–8, 175–8; on social change 134, 142; on technology 44–5, 48–9

beliefs 55, 56, 98–9, 106, 107, 116
Bell Curves 113
Bernasek, A. 86
biology 6
Bird, E. 50
Blackburn, R. 160
bourgeoisie 39, 60, 85, 142; technology and revolution 184, 185, 186, 189
Bourgin, F. 80
Bowles, S. 49, 90
Braverman, H. 53
Brenner, R. 183
Brinkman, R.L. 55
Brown, D. 73
Burke, E. 8
Bush, G. 96
business: profit 176; system 150; values 136

Callinicos, A. 187–8
Canada 124, 138
capital 18, 36–7, 48; myths 81–2
capitalism 5, 157, 169, 171–2, 173; beginning of in United States 160–2; democracy 90, 94–7, 101, 103, 111, 112, 113, 117; economic relations 19, 24–5, 26, 27, 30–1, 32, 36, 39–42; enabling

INDEX

myth 77, 81, 82, 83, 85; French Revolution 183–6; social conflict 147, 148, 155, 156, 159, 161–2; social tensions 135, 138, 139, 140, 141, 142; structural change 128, 129, 130, 131–2, 133; technology 60–3, 64, 65–6, 67; technology and revolution 176, 186, 192
Capone, A. 119
Carnoy, M. 90
cause and effect 45
Central America 58
ceremonial learning 49–50
ceremonial resistance 180
ceremonialism 147, 175–8, 179–80
change, resistance to 179
Chicago school 180
Childe, V.G. 4, 62
Chile 61
China 58, 100, 130

Christian militancy 100
Civil Rights movement 29, 99, 131, 145, 189
class 9, 168; democracy 99, 109, 113, 115; economic relations 17, 18, 19, 22–6, 28–32, 36–8, 40, 42; enabling myth 69, 83; structural change 128, 130; technology 55–7, 63–4; technology and revolution 180
class conflict: definition 155; economic relations 18, 26, 27, 28; ideology/mythology 157; ordinary 152–4; revolutionary 154–5; social conflict 148, 152, 156, 159, 161, 162, 163; social tensions 140; technology 66, 67; technology and revolution 180, 181, 184, 186, 191, 193, 194
class consciousness 104–6, 181
class interests 180–1
class relations: democracy 94–7, 110–12, 116; enabling myth 73–7, 82–5; social conflict 154, 156, 160, 162; social tensions 137–42; structural change 127, 128, 132; technology 46, 60–1, 65, 66–7; technology and revolution 185, 186, 188, 189, 191, 192, 193

class-divided societies 58–60
classism 113, 157, 194
Clifford, F. 102
Clinton, B. 83, 95
Cohen, G.A. 187
Cohen, M.N. 72, 73
Cold War 5, 6, 7, 148
collective bargaining 147
Collins, C. 171
colonialism 139, 156
Commons, J.R. 5, 18, 34–5, 51, 110, 146–7
communism 5, 77, 99, 100, 187, 192
Communist Party 65, 75, 90–1, 112–13, 187
community interests 176
community values 136
computers 62–3; see also Internet
conflict 9, 48–50, 54–5; of interest 34–5, 42, 51, 117; see also social conflict; structural tensions and conflicts
confusion 178
conscious decisions 98
contract rights 18
contradiction 155
court decisions 110
court-ordered school desegregation 99
critical Marxism 143, 174, 187–8, 191, 193
Cuba 100, 130
culture 54–5

Darwin, C. 3, 4, 6
De Gregori, T.R. 180–1
Debs, E. 153
debt peonage process 39
Deckard, B.S. 31
Declaration of Independence (1776) 144
democractic socialism 172
democracy 89–117, 157, 168–9, 172; artificial selection and conscious decisions 98; and capitalism 94–7; class consciousness and political decisions 104–6; definition 89–91; economic institutions and class relations 94–7, 110–12; economic institutions and vested interests 91–4, 109–10; effective 90–1;